FOREWORD

CARMELO EZPELETA
DORNA SPORTS CEO

Where to begin? The 2016 MotoGP™ season has been a truly record-breaking and historic year, as nine different riders took premier-class victories – a first in the 68-year history of the Championship – and Marc Marquez took his third MotoGP™ crown in four years. It was also the 25th year of the partnership between the FIM, IRTA, MSMA and Dorna and we celebrated the 400th GP of this new era in Brno. It has been a truly incredible season.

With so many changes introduced before the lights went out in Qatar, the season ahead was a blank slate – and every chapter since written has created one of the most exciting and unpredictable Championships in history. After some incredible races showcasing the best of MotoGP, Repsol Honda's Marc Marquez emerged as the title favourite, facing down Movistar Yamaha riders Valentino Rossi and Jorge Lorenzo for the World Championship and taking his first premier-class victory at the Twin Ring Motegi to seal the crown.

Jack Miller became the first Independent Team rider to win a race since 2006 when he took victory at Assen, with Cal Crutchlow then winning an incredible two further races for an Independent Team in 2016 – and becoming the first British premier-class winner since the legendary Barry Sheene in 1981. After an incredible latter half of the season, Crutchlow was the top Independent Team rider following his comeback and collected that trophy in Valencia.

In August MotoGP™ returned to the Red Bull Ring in Austria. There, another twist was woven into the tale as Andrea Iannone took the Ducati Team's first win since 2010, becoming another first-time winner. Soon to join Iannone, Crutchlow and Miller on that illustrious list was Maverick Viñales.

Viñales took victory at Silverstone for the first Suzuki win since 2007, after having taken his maiden podium earlier in the year at Le Mans. This made Viñales the seventh different winner in a row. The story was impossible to script – and there remained lines to be written as Dani Pedrosa was then the eighth different winner of the year after an astounding victory at Misano.

When the paddock took off for the flyaway races at the end of the year, the question we were all asking was the same: could there be a ninth?

In Sepang, Ducati Team's Andrea Dovizioso gave us the answer. Taking his second premier-class victory in tough conditions, Dovizioso penned the penultimate chapter of 2016 in stunning style.

The finale in Valencia was the perfect way to say goodbye to the season, with a sell-out crowd there to witness another incredible MotoGP race, and Moto2™ and Moto3™ also showcasing the best of the World Championship.

After the year of firsts, the future of MotoGP™ has never looked brighter, and the bar is set higher than ever as I look back on 2016 and ahead to 2017. With Ducati and Suzuki both joining Honda and Yamaha on the honour roll of recent winners, and ever-increasing progress from Aprilia after their recent return to MotoGP™, 2017 will welcome another new manufacturer to the MotoGP™ grid: KTM.

The future of the MotoGP™ grid also looks bright when I look through the list of names making their way through the lower classes. Johann Zarco took his second Moto2™ title in 2016, becoming the first rider to defend that crown – as well as the first Frenchman to win more than one World Championship in Grand

Prix racing. Now he will make his way onto the MotoGP™ grid, as will some of his key rivals this year: Alex Rins, Jonas Folger and Sam Lowes. With some incredible performances in the Moto2™ field from all four, as well as the Championship runner-up Thomas Lüthi, the intermediate class gave us some incredible racing once again.

Sadly, Moto2™ was also hit by tragedy in 2016, when the grid lost young Spanish talent Luis Salom at the Catalan Grand Prix. A big presence in the paddock and on the grid, Luis was a Championship contender and race winner in Moto3™, and had begun the year with another podium in the intermediate class. I'm sure every rider in the World Championship, every team and every fan of MotoGP™ will join me in extending my condolences to his family, friends and team.

Joining Moto2™ next year will be some of the standout performers of this year in Moto3™. In the ultra-competitive lightweight class, it was Brad Binder who ran away with the title to become the first South African World Champion since Jan Ekerold in 1980, writing yet more history in this amazing season. Binder will be joined in Moto2™ by other protagonists of Moto3™ in 2016, including Jorge Navarro, Fabio Quartararo and Francesco Bagnaia – who took the first two race victories for Mahindra this year. Enea Bastianini, who played a big part in so many of the fantastic races in 2016, will remain in the class next year and will undoubtedly impress once again, alongside fellow Italian Moto3™ talent Niccoló Antonelli. The top rookie talents of this year, including Nicoló Bulega, Fabio Di Giannantonio, Joan Mir, Bo Bendsneyder and Aron Canet, also prove that the future of this Championship is amazingly bright – from Moto3™ to the top echelons of MotoGP™.

It makes me incredibly proud to see MotoGP™ emerge in 2016 with a record-breaking, historic season that will be remembered forever as the year that redefined what many thought was possible.

I hope you relive it as I do, and that you relish every twist and turn of the season through the eyes with which we first saw them written – awed by every different winner and every new chapter of one of the greatest motorsport shows on Earth: MotoGP™.

Published in November 2016

A catalogue record for this book is available from the British Library

ISBN 978-1-910505-15-1

Published by Evro Publishing, Westrow House, Holwell, Sherborne, Dorset DT9 5LF

Printed and bound in the UK by Gomer Press, Llandysul Enterprise Park, Llandysul, Ceredigion SA44 4JL

This product is officially licensed by Dorna SL, owners of the MotoGP trademark (© Dorna 2016)

Editorial Director Mark Hughes
Design Richard Parsons
Special Sales & Advertising Manager
David Dew (david@motocom.co.uk)
Photography Front cover, race action and portraits by Andrew Northcott/AJRN Sports Photography; side-on studio technical images of bikes (pp18–27) by Dorna; other technical images (pp14–27) by Neil Spalding

Author's acknowledgements
My thanks to all contributors for their hard work: Mat Oxley, Neil Spalding, Peter Clifford, Neil Morrison, Venancio Luis Nieto and photographer Andrew Northcott.
    At BT Sport: Suzi Perry, Craig Doyle, Keith Huewen, Gavin Emmett, Neil Hodgson and James Toseland.
    In the paddock: Nick Harris, Dean Adams, Dr Martin Raines, Mike and Irene Trimby and the staff of IRTA.

www.evropublishing.com

CONTENTS
MotoGP™ 2016

OCTO

The intelligence behind insurance innovation

Save up to 30% on your insurance policy

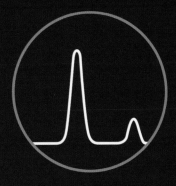

Driving assessment

Octo technology gives insurers a clear picture of your driving, so that they can design a policy around your precise needs.

Pay as you drive

Many insurance policies offer a 'pay as you drive' scheme rewarding good drivers.

Better driving

Octo lets you track your driving and get tips on how to sharpen your skills to lower your policy.

Your driving companion

Download Octo U now
Octo's free app lets you track your journeys, connect with friends and calculate your driving score. You could get up to 15% off a new policy with one of our insurance partners.

octotelematics.com

THE SEASON
MAT OXLEY

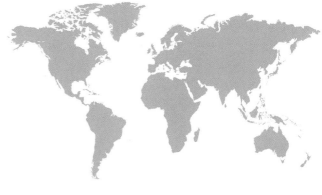

A VINTAGE SEASON

New technical regulations helped deliver a record nine different winners in a season

Racing motorcycles are mysterious contraptions. Before the 2016 MotoGP season got underway, most paddock insiders predicted that the category's new era of unified software and Michelin tyres would see the smoother riders inherit the race track.

The theory went that riders who use the throttle and tyres more gently would be the winners and that notion made a lot of sense. Reigning world champion Jorge Lorenzo certainly believed it.

'With the Michelin tyres and the new electronics it's more difficult to ride the bike,' he said in February. 'So this will be good for the more technical riders because you have to play more with the throttle and be more sensitive. So I think the more technical riders will have less problems than the more aggressive and less sensitive riders.'

The theory turned out to be 180-degrees wrong. Lorenzo and Dani Pedrosa – the neatest riders of them all – struggled horribly. Valentino Rossi – who is more physical with a motorcycle but still smoother than most – struggled less but he too was frequently lost and too often on the floor. And then there was Marc Marquez, the wildest of the bunch, whom many pundits insisted wouldn't stand a chance without Honda's high-tech electronics and Bridgestone's super-grippy front slick.

There's no doubt that 2016 was Marquez's finest season yet. He defied all predictions to deliver a jaw-dropping display of speed and consistency. Nothing is more difficult to ride than a MotoGP bike and yet Marquez was the only rider across all three classes to

score points at every race, at least until he had locked down the title.

His sheer audacity and still-flourishing talent made a mockery of all the pre-season theories. Not only did people predict a difficult season for Marquez, they also suggested that Yamaha's more neutral YZR M-1 would work better with the Michelins and unified software than Honda's harder-to-handle RC213V. Marquez turned that theory on its head, all on his own.

Yamaha spent the entire season struggling with a traction/balance problem. They adjusted chassis geometry to further load the Michelin front and generate heat, but that merely reduced rear load, which caused wheelspin on corner exits.

How did Honda react? Or rather, how did Marquez react? He crashed aplenty during the off season by overloading the front tyre, so he tried taming his wildness to distress the tyre. And still he kept crashing. Finally, he went back to being the same old Marc: charging into corners, rear wheel in the air, bike pivoting left and right around the steering head, then flicking the bike on to its side, where his knees and elbows would deal with the consequences.

And it worked. This technique asked a lot of the Michelin front during braking, plus it generated a lot of heat into the tyre, which was a good thing, except at hotter race tracks. It also minimised the time Marquez relied on front grip to get the bike into corners.

On the other hand, the Yamaha uses corner speed to win races, which requires a long, arcing corner entry that puts a lot of pressure on the front tyre for a long time. No wonder Rossi and Lorenzo lost the front so often during 2016 and no wonder Yamaha had its second-worst season since 2003.

What Marquez did was the same thing that the heroes of old did, before front tyres allowed huge corner speed.

This is Wayne Rainey, 500cc world champion in 1990, 1991 and 1992: 'What I wanted was to open the throttle to get the weight off the front. I wanted to get through that danger zone – where the throttle is off during the flick into the turn – really quick.'

That's what Marquez did: he knew the weak point was the Michelin front, so he used the tyre as little as possible.

It was inevitable that 2016 would be an R&D year for Michelin. The French company was forced out of MotoGP against its will at the end of 2008, so its engineers had a lot of catching up to do. MotoGP's crash rate rose significantly in 2016 – by almost 20 per cent – but Michelin did their best in difficult circumstances. They never stopped working, introducing better tyres throughout the season, although this brought its own problems because teams couldn't find a base set-up that lasted for more than a few races.

By the first race, in Qatar, the Michelin front's profile and construction were good enough for lap and race records to get broken. The problem for the rest of the season was the company's lack of recent experience, so they concocted ideal compounds for some races and far-from-ideal compounds for others.

Motegi, where Marquez won the title, was a case in point. Both Rossi and Lorenzo crashed out, Rossi entirely confused by his tumble. 'Sincerely, I didn't feel that I was too fast, too wide or too deep,' he said; a common sentiment last summer.

It took some riders all season to try to come to terms with the Michelin front because they had spent so long with the Bridgestone, which delivered a kind of servo effect: the deeper the rider braked into the corner, the more the tyre deflected, the more it gripped and the better the bike turned.

Marquez had his own way of dealing with this new world. Incredibly, the 23-year-old crashed more in 2016 than he did in 2015, when he finished third overall. How come? Because he focused on locating the limit in practice by pushing beyond it, then pulling back a fraction in the race.

Before he won the title he crashed in just one race, at Le Mans, where he lost the front and remounted to finish 13th. After that his mind was made up.

'I decided for the rest of the championship I would only push hard if I felt like I could push hard, but that I wouldn't push if I didn't have the right feeling with the bike.'

Marquez didn't only master the Michelins in 2016. He also had to adjust to an entirely new system of electronic rider controls. The same-for-all Magneti Marelli software was variously described as five or ten years out of date, which, of course, was half the point – to reduce riders' dependency on electronics as well to contain costs and make MotoGP more attractive to new manufacturers. KTM made it known they might never have joined the MotoGP grid but for the unified software. 'We might never have caught up with the electronics,' they said.

During pre-season testing Honda really struggled to match the RC213V to the new electronics, which was no great surprise because they were the only major factory that had no real history with Magneti Marelli. The RCV was slow and difficult to handle – too much anti-spin and then too little, or the other way around.

'The new system is less reactive, it has a time delay, so it's easy for us to overshoot the slip-ratio target and then come back too strongly,' explained Repsol Honda technical director Takeo Yokoyama. 'Wheelie control is another thing we struggle with – maybe the programme is too basic to make the bike calm down.'

All the riders – regardless of machine – realised there was only one way forward: to go backwards. Whereas veterans like Colin Edwards had previously struggled to forget years of training their right wrists and put their trust in a little black box, youngsters like Marquez had to make the opposite journey.

The Magneti Marelli kit worked, of course, but not enough to allow riders to open the throttle and let the electronics do the rest. So they had to learn how to start each race with lower-tech launch control, they had to learn to slide with less effective traction control, they had to learn how to control the bike into corners with less clever engine-braking control

and they had to learn how to use the throttle to keep the front wheel down instead of relying on anti-wheelie technology.

The unified anti-wheelie software was the biggest downgrade from the factory electronics, and this is where 2016's famous wings came in. Ducati had been experimenting with aerodynamic winglets for some years, and Suzuki also did so in the late 1970s. But it was the arrival of Gigi Dall'Igna and the unified software that turbocharged Ducati's aero R&D. The factory Desmosedicis rolled out at pre-season tests wearing multiple wings, which generated about ten kilos of downforce to do the work previously done by the factory anti-wheelie software.

Ducati's wings worked, but they were pretty unpopular. Rossi hated them aesthetically, Dani Pedrosa called them 'knives on the side of the bikes' and Bradley Smith told frightening stories of how the dirty air behind a winged GP16 threatened to have him off his Yamaha at 200mph.

Yamaha were the second factory to enthusiastically adopt the new aero aids, equipping their Movistar M-1s with large grey wings that looked like they'd been borrowed from a stingray. And when Yamaha won four races in a row – Jerez, Le Mans, Mugello and Catalunya – it seemed they were the people making the best of all the new technology.

But four race wins don't make a summer, and summer ended early in 2016. After the factory Yamahas had mostly excelled in the heat in Spain, France, Italy and Catalonia, it rained at Assen, the

BELOW Valentino Rossi, seen with Matt LeBlanc, continued to be the fans' favourite

Sachsenring and Brno, and it became apparent that the M-1 couldn't generate enough heat into the front tyre on cold, damp tracks. Rossi crashed out at Assen and Lorenzo crashed at the Sachsenring three times – as many times as he fell during the whole of 2015.

Meanwhile Marquez kept racking up the points in the most treacherous of conditions. At Assen and Brno he resisted the temptation to risk it all for victory and instead came home in steady rostrum positions.

At the Sachsenring Marquez won his finest victory of the year. As Rossi and Lorenzo floundered in eighth and 15th, Marquez switched to slicks on the drying track and rode a miracle of a race, dancing around that old racing 'Catch 22': ride too fast on cold slicks on a damp track and you'll crash because you're trying too hard; ride too slowly and you'll crash because you're not trying hard enough to generate the heat to make the tyres work. By way of proof, Pol Espargaro swapped tyres at the same time as Marquez and crashed after two corners.

The combination of ever-changing weather and ever-changing tyre specs were the main reasons for the most unpredictable premier-class season since the dawn of Grand Prix racing in 1949. For the first time ever there were eight different winners over eight consecutive races: Lorenzo at Mugello, Rossi at Catalunya, Jack Miller at Assen, Marquez at the Sachsenring, Andrea Iannone at the Red Bull Ring, Cal Crutchlow at Brno, Maverick Viñales at Silverstone and Pedrosa at Misano. Three of those races stand out for further analysis.

Viñales won at Silverstone partly because Suzuki made significant progress into their second season with the GSX-RR and partly because their Öhlins technician found the perfect suspension set-up that weekend. Suzuki's tiny racing department deserves a huge pat on the back. The GSX-RR got better and better and may just be the best-handling bike on the grid, thanks to its unique carbon-fibre engine hangers that allow engineers to precisely tune chassis flex at full lean.

Ducati's victory at the Red Bull Ring was a long time coming: one hundred races to be precise. The Bologna factory, which had caused the Japanese manufacturers all kinds of bother from 2003 to 2010, spent several years trying to build a bike that would go around corners without Casey Stoner on it. When former Aprilia engineer Dall'Igna joined Ducati Corse at the end of 2013, things finally started to happen. Dall'Igna changed the culture and organisation within the race department and completely redesigned the Desmosedici. Slowly, the results started to come.

Iannone and Andrea Dovizioso dominated in Austria, but it must be said that the track layout played a significant part in Ducati's 1–2. The circuit is dominated by three first-gear corners followed by half-kilometre straights. In other words, three drag strips – perfect Desmosedici territory.

Pedrosa's Misano win seemed to come out of nowhere. The closest he had got to winning a race previously was at Mugello, where he came home five

BELOW, LEFT Jack Miller won at Assen and introduced the world to the Aussie concept of 'the shoey'

BELOW, UPPER RIGHT Relations between the top three riders were slightly more civilised than in 2015, but still not cordial

BELOW, LOWER RIGHT Scott Redding's first year on a Ducati yielded one rostrum in Holland and a near-miss fourth place in Germany

seconds behind the victor. Often the gap was much bigger: 28 seconds in Argentina, 18 at Le Mans, 17 at the Red Bull Ring and 14 in Qatar. His problem, as usual, was his diminutive size: at just 51kg Pedrosa cannot load the tyres like his rivals, so at cooler races he struggles to get them up to temperature. He often struggled with the Bridgestones but his troubles were much magnified with the Michelins.

The former 125cc and 250cc champion – contesting an all-time record of 11 seasons with the same factory team – finally started moving forward at the post-Brno tests where his crew turned a corner on bike balance. At Misano a special-spec front slick – built to deal with the track's heavy-braking zones – gave him the winning edge because it didn't deflect so much under load, so he was able to turn his RC213V much more easily.

The randomness of the 2016 season may have had much to do with tyres and weather but another significant factor was Dorna's long-running determination to pack the grid with similarly competitive motorcycles. They did this by introducing the single ECU and by obliging the factories to lease full-spec MotoGP bikes to independent teams, instead of the Open bikes and CRT (Claiming Rule Teams) bikes of recent years.

In earlier decades the technology gap had been even greater, with full-factory four-cylinder 500s lapping ancient privateer 500s during the 1990s and four-cylinder MV Agustas lapping single-cylinder Nortons two or three times during the 1960s.

In 2016 independent team riders won three races, an achievement unheard of in many a year.

Crutchlow's performance on the independent LCR team's Honda at Phillip Island was one of the rides of the year, beating the world's best on a fully dry track, two months after he had beaten them in the wet at Brno. With his two victories Crutchlow stands alongside Leslie Graham, Geoff Duke, John Surtees, Mike Hailwood, Phil Read and Barry Sheene as the only Britons to have scored two premier-class wins in one season.

In 2017 Dorna take another step towards helping teams towards the back of the grid catch those at the front by doubling their financial support for the less well off, a policy that flies in the face of what's going on in Formula 1 and Premier League football.

The 2016 season was a great and thrilling one, even if much of it was played out beneath a dark cloud. The controversy of late 2015 hung over the year like volcanic dust following a faraway eruption. There were ugly scenes at several races, where over-zealous Rossi fans (nicknamed 'the Valeban') booed winners Lorenzo and Marquez. The brainlessness was most in evidence on social media and at Mugello, where some fans wished the worst upon the enemies of their hero. The fall-out did ebb away as the year went on, but the Neanderthals were back at Phillip Island, cheering in delight as Marquez crashed.

Hopefully, the events of 2015 will be forgotten in 2017 and fans can get back to appreciating the skill and daring of the greatest bike riders on earth.

ABOVE, UPPER LEFT
Andrea Dovizioso was the last of the nine winners of the year, in Malaysia

ABOVE, LOWER LEFT
The Tech 3 duo of Bradley Smith and Pol Espargaro will form KTM's new MotoGP team in 2017

ABOVE, RIGHT Dani Pedrosa won at Misano, maintaining his record of winning at least one race in each year of his 11-year MotoGP career

RIDERS' RIDER
OF THE YEAR 2016

Every rider who rode in more than one MotoGP race votes in our annual poll. This is what they really think of each other

As usual, the *Official MotoGP Season Review* vote among the MotoGP riders threw up some interesting results. The method is simple: the MotoGP riders list their top six of the year in order and they're not allowed to vote for themselves. The scrutineers award six points for a first place down to one for a sixth place and add up the totals to arrive at our league table.

It was no surprise that Marc Marquez was at the top of the list. Everyone who voted put him either first or second. Only three other riders got a first-place nomination: Valentino Rossi, Maverick Viñales and Cal Crutchlow. Marc's total was 25 per cent higher than Valentino's in second place and Viñales was third with 20 per cent fewer. Those numbers tell you that the top three were well ahead of the rest, which isn't surprising as a dozen voters had them as the top three, albeit in various orders.

In addition, everyone included Marquez and Rossi in their top six, and only one voter failed to mention Viñales.

No-one outside the top three enjoyed anywhere near that level of support. It's worth noting that our poll put Maverick one place higher than in the real-life championship table.

Fourth place was a much closer affair, with just a handful of votes separating Jorge Lorenzo and Cal Crutchlow – and Cal was two places higher than in the official table.

But if you're looking for someone the riders hold in particularly high regard in comparison with his championship position, then Jack Miller is your man. He was down in 18th place in the championship but his fellow riders had him 11 positions higher in seventh place. And it was a clear seventh, well clear of the three-way tie for eighth place.

As in previous years, it was very noticeable that an injury

or temporary loss of form seemed to be enough to put a rider out of the reckoning for top honours. Dani Pedrosa and Andrea Iannone suffered from this. It was also noticeable that respondents who voted late – during or even after Valencia – seemed to react to Lorenzo's late-season form, although his best placing in the poll was a solitary second place.

As usual there was very little evidence of national solidarity but this year there was more of an inclination to vote for a team-mate. This did tend to be one-sided, with the junior partner voting for the faster man, who didn't reciprocate.

The two main rules – that only MotoGP riders should receive votes and that riders aren't allowed to vote for themselves – always seem to get ignored by a few. Brad Binder will be glad to know that he has more than one major fan among Spanish factory riders. Doesn't he, Dani?

2016 TOP TEN	
1st	MARC MARQUEZ
2nd	VALENTINO ROSSI
3rd	MAVERICK VIÑALES
4th	JORGE LORENZO
5th	CAL CRUTCHLOW
6th	ANDREA DOVIZIOSO
7th	JACK MILLER
=8th	ANDREA IANNONE
=8th	DANI PEDROSA
=8th	HECTOR BARBERA

PREVIOUS WINNERS	
2004	VALENTINO ROSSI
2005	VALENTINO ROSSI
2006	LORIS CAPIROSSI
2007	CASEY STONER
2008	VALENTINO ROSSI
2009	VALENTINO ROSSI
2010	JORGE LORENZO
2012	JORGE LORENZO
2013	MARC MARQUEZ
2014	MARC MARQUEZ
2015	VALENTINO ROSSI

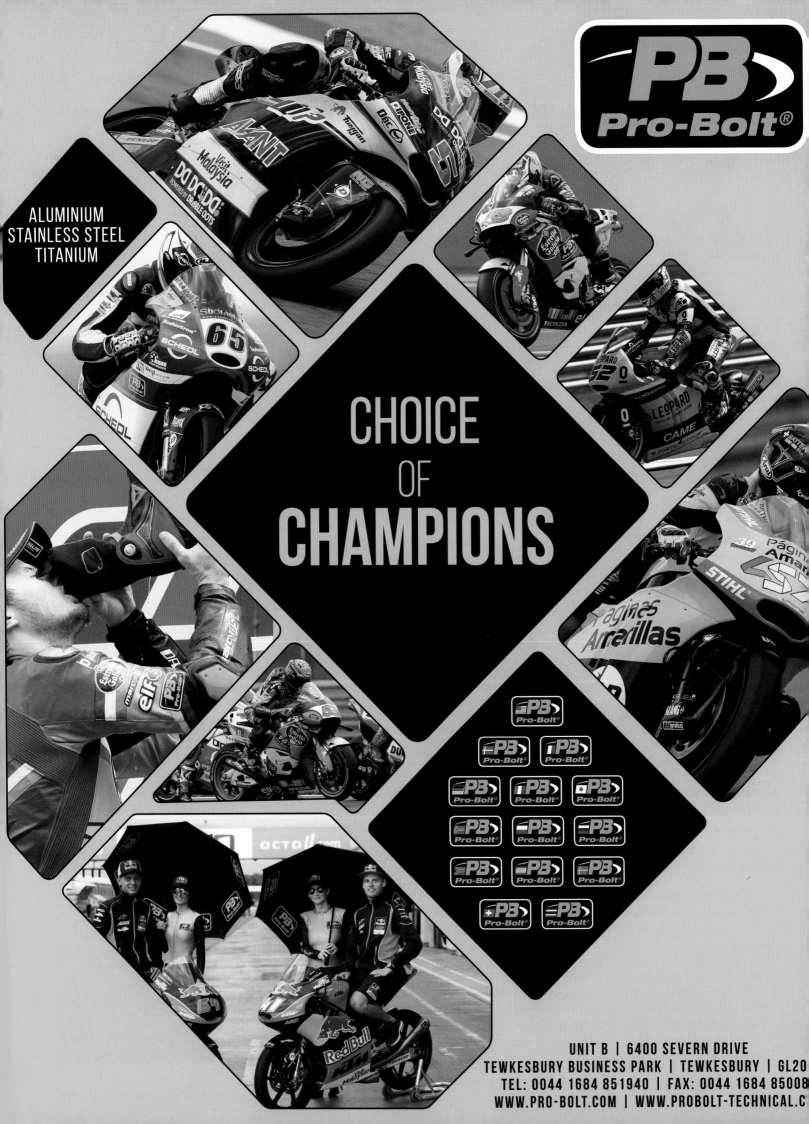

TECH REVIEW
NEIL SPALDING

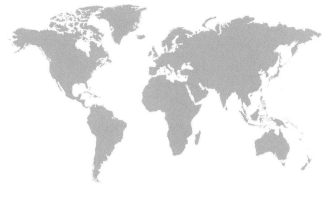

MICHELIN ARE BACK

Michelin's return to MotoGP in 2016 wasn't trouble-free and tyres played a part in nine different riders winning during the year

Michelin were for years the dominant force in MotoGP. The company had the top factories and the top riders. Dunlop occasionally spoiled their fun but the top class of MotoGP was a Michelin party from the year 2000 onwards.

Not everything was rosy. Michelin's rear tyre greatly outperformed their front. Worse for Michelin, it was quite obvious that Dunlop, who had difficulties making rear tyres last, understood front ones. On several occasions the ever-practical Team Roberts put riders out on Dunlop fronts and Michelin rears, something that would be unthinkable now.

Michelin's secret was a production process that saw several different tyre designs delivered to each circuit for Friday and Saturday practices, and data collected in those sessions would be used to produce a brief run of the 'best possible specification' tyres for their top riders on Saturday night. It was a very effective strategy as compounds and constructions would be right for that track on that day in that weather.

It didn't work so well for races that weren't within overnight driving range of the company's Clermont-Ferrand factory, and this led to several stories in the press speculating that the Michelin rubber didn't suit the type of tarmac laid outside Europe. The reality was that at non-European races Michelin, just like their competitors, had to make an educated guess as to what compounds and constructions would work on each circuit.

Then Bridgestone arrived, and to understand developments during 2016 it's necessary to study what

ABOVE Marquez at the Qatar GP, having his first race on Michelins and working them hard

UPPER RIGHT A piece of tread from the super-soft wets used at Brno – it looks like a piece of aero

LOWER RIGHT A Michelin shows the change from one compound to another; it has been eight years since we last saw this style of tyre making

Bridgestone did. The Japanese company, which has been making tyres since the 1930s and at one time also manaufactured motorcycles, entered the 125cc world championship in 1990 and achieved 30 wins before moving over to a 100 per cent MotoGP effort in 2003. It takes a lot to get a factory team to change a winning formula, and initially Bridgestone's only signings were Kawasaki and Suzuki. However, when Ducati realised that Michelin weren't going to make special tyres for them, to suit the unique weight distribution of their bikes, things took off.

Ducati were determined to break the Honda and Yamaha duopoly, and by signing with Bridgestone they were able to have tyres designed specifically for them. That generation of Ducatis had an L4 engine layout, which meant that their weight distribution was rear-biased, around 48/52 front/rear. At that time Michelin were making tyres suited to the near 51/49 weight distribution favoured by Yamaha and Honda. There was an added benefit for Ducati: Bridgestone wouldn't be at a disadvantage at MotoGP races outside Europe, and in the Far East, in fact, it would be Bridgestone who could make tyres to order during a GP.

Over the next few years Bridgestone worked hard. They developed separate 'families' of tyres to suit each of the factories they had signed. They dealt with the difficulty of having their factory in Japan by creating test teams from each of their contracted teams to evaluate new tyres on each circuit prior to each GP. There was careful development of new rubber compounds that worked well over a far greater

temperature range. By the end of the 990cc formula, in 2006, Bridgestone had become serious competitors to Michelin – but the French were still the champions.

The 2007 season was the first for the 800cc MotoGP class and this was when Bridgestone struck.

Casey Stoner signed for Ducati. During 2006 he had displayed a talent for crashing the LCR Honda, so much so that Ducati's Livio Suppo took some stick for signing him. But this time it would be different: the 800 Ducati, which had similar construction to the previous bike with a steel tube lattice chassis and an L4 engine with desmodromic valve operation, provided loads of power and had Bridgestone's finest at each end. 'Crashey' Stoner could ride it within an inch of its life.

By now the tyre war was at its height. To try to reduce costs, restrictions on the numbers of tyres were introduced in 2007. That didn't work, so for 2008 Bridgestone agreed to close down its test teams if Michelin agreed to all tyres for a race weekend being at the circuit by the Thursday afternoon. Dunlop withdrew from MotoGP competition, and, crucially, Valentino Rossi insisted on breaking from Michelin and having exactly the same family of Bridgestone tyres as Stoner. It took Rossi and Yamaha a while to realise that to make the tyres work their bike would have to be given the same weight distribution as the Ducati. Once that was done, however, Valentino could match, and beat, the Ducati. Without the ability to bring in special tyres on a Saturday evening, Michelin's fortunes took a dive – at some races at least.

By the Brno round Honda had had enough; Dani

Pedrosa finished 15th, last but one, on Michelins that were simply uncompetitive. By the end of the year Dorna decided that the only way to ensure balanced competition was to have a single tyre supplier. Michelin decided they didn't want to be the single supplier, so Bridgestone stepped in.

Bridgestone didn't have the production capacity to offer many options so they decided to provide a choice of just two types of slicks and one type of wets per race. The design chosen was their finest, as developed for Ducati and used by Yamaha to win the 2008 championship with Rossi. As a control tyre is supposed to be 'part of the problem', not 'part of the solution', Bridgestone deliberately chose to use the special heat-shedding type that they had built for high-temperature tracks such as Catalunya, ensuring that their tyres would present challenges for all of the factories, including Ducati and Yamaha.

Those tyre construction and compound decisions have shaped the bikes and riding styles we now consider to be normal. Although there were several different design upgrades over the next eight years, the underlying character of the tyres – amazing front grip, albeit without any 'feeling' for the rider, and a preference for a slightly rearwards weight bias – remained broadly the same. It took Ducati over three years to publicly concede that 'the tyre designs the bike', and it isn't unreasonable to observe that the Italian manufacturer never really understood the requirements of the tyres.

It was into this Bridgestone-centric world that Michelin stepped at the start of 2015 with a testing programme designed to push their tyre performance towards the Bridgestone norm. Michelin's testing throughout that first year was on motorcycles designed and set up for Bridgestones. The first test was a disaster as several top riders lost grip on the front and crashed, so test riders took over the task until some progress had been made. As tested, the new Michelins had massive rear grip, and, in an ominous echo from the past, limited front grip.

As 2015 went on, selected top riders had brief excursions on Michelins on the Monday after some GPs. Although the factories attempted to get Michelin to design tyres that would work on bikes built around the Bridgestone weight-distribution preferences, it began to dawn on the top engineers that in fact they were going to have to redesign their chassis to suit the new tyres.

The handover from Bridgestone to Michelin was carried out at a three-day test at Valencia at the end of 2015. This was the first time that factories were able to make big changes in the set-up of their bikes to accommodate the designed-in preferences of the Michelins. Yamaha came out with a chassis that brought the headstock back 20mm, while Honda extended their swingarm by a similar amount. Both modifications helped, but there were a lot of damaged bikes at that Valencia test and some team bosses wanted to know who was going to foot the not inconsiderable repair bill. A good example was Pol Espargaro's attempt to destroy not one but two Yamaha M-1s.

The problem seemed to be a combination of Bridgestone-nurtured rider enthusiasm coming out of corners, Bridgestone-biased chassis and a major front-to-rear traction mismatch from the Michelins. Whereas the rear tyre was shaped to give plenty of grip while exiting a corner at a considerable lean angle, the front had a squarish section, which was great for upright braking stability going into corners but meant that the tyre was on the edge of its 'square section' at the point where the rear gripped best. In addition, front rim sizes were increased, to four inches, something that doesn't help fast changes of direction.

For the next major test, at Sepang in February 2016, Suzuki and Ducati had new chassis ready. Both designs were clearly modified for the new rear bias, being stronger around the front sprocket and having beefier swingarms to make the best of the massive rear grip available. At the same time Michelin, knowing that they had to do something, offered a new design of front tyre that seemed to have a softer construction and used a lower pressure. This was a big step forwards, although it took a while for some chassis engineers to realise it. By the end of the Sepang test Yamaha were using their 2015 chassis again, and at Suzuki Maverick Viñales had also reverted to the old chassis and swingarm. Honda weren't really developing chassis at this stage, being tied up with the new electronics and trying to make their new reverse-rotating-crank engine work.

Michelin clearly wanted to go as fast on track as Bridgestone had done, but the tyres weren't really

BELOW Nicolas Goubert (left), Michelin Racing's technical director, with Tech 3's Hervé Poncharal

much for the tyre, causing it simply to overheat and destroy the glue holding it together. Most racing tyres these days are 'spun' on to the carcass and there isn't a 'join' that can separate; it's an area of development for Michelin to explore in the years to come.

Michelin knew they had faced a risk to their reputation and threw admirable resources at heading it off. New tyres were made and shipped to America for the next race one week later, using the very stiff emergency construction but with compounds suited to the Austin track. Marquez won again. For Jerez Michelin did the same thing, only here they got the compound decision wrong and the win went to Rossi, who used all his knowledge of the days before traction control to conquer a Yamaha that spun the rear tyre at the slightest excuse.

At the same time Michelin decided that its chosen approach – to make two tyres and in effect force the factories to build to their spec – was a little too challenging, at least in this first year. It was going to be easier and safer for Michelin to keep the factories on side by building a small range of tyres for each track.

Michelin kept the stiffer carcass of the emergency tyre and made that the normal fitment. That made dealing with the front easier: a harder carcass means less grip, and less grip means that the tendency of the rear tyre to push the front, sometimes into a crash, is much reduced. At last the factories had a pair of tyres that, while not the 'grippiest', were at least vaguely balanced in a way that they could understand.

Over the next few races chassis development started in earnest. Honda revised their works team swingarms for more flex while leaned over. Yamaha tried a similar modification and then also increased chassis rigidity under braking, all the better to deal with the Michelins' excellent straight-line braking characteristics (assuming the compounds were right) while also making the chassis more flexible when leaned right over. Ducati strengthened their headstock in a similar manner to Yamaha; Dovizioso adopted the modification but Iannone didn't. These modifications by the various manufacturers were intended to work the tyres harder – the bikes were becoming 'Michelin Bikes'.

The biggest changes happened at Honda. A new chassis – or 'new concept' as Honda's senior engineers described it – was tried, with side beams of significantly smaller section that took a much straighter route to the steering head. The reduced beam section allowed far more lateral flex while the straighter beams were probably intended to return some of the braking stability that was otherwise lost by the new design. Marquez and Pedrosa, however, rejected this new chassis, although Repsol team management noted that Pedrosa was faster on it – but just didn't like the 'feel'. Pedrosa was then given a revised design that retained straighter beams but with a section that was far closer to Honda's recent norm. It wasn't anywhere near as radical, but Dani did seem to like it. The chassis spurned by the works riders ended up on Cal Crutchlow's bike for the rest of the season. As an ex-Yamaha rider, Cal seemed to find the inevitable reduction in rigidity quite acceptable.

The situation for Michelin by the end of 2016, a year

ready. The first race, in Qatar, saw Jorge Lorenzo win and Andrea Dovizioso's chasing Ducati exhibit great top speed, but third-placed Marc Marquez struggled with a Honda that was reluctant to turn and teammate Dani Pedrosa finished fifth on a bike that had big chunks of rubber missing from its rear tyre when it rolled into the garage – but the first four riders did faster race laps than the best of 2015 on Bridgestones. For Michelin a great game was just beginning.

Michelin knew that it wouldn't be easy to go through this process of developing tyres while the factories simultaneously tried to work out the best chassis settings for the new tyres. Michelin's 'get out of jail' card was a 'reserve' set of stiff-carcass tyres taken to each race, to be used in the event that the more extreme race tyres were unusable for whatever reason.

In Argentina for the second round, the reserve tyres were needed. Scott Redding suffered delamination of his rear tyre in FP4, rather late in the weekend for major changes. Qualifying, with its limited number of laps, went ahead as normal, but for race day the stiff-construction 'reserve' tyres were to be used. Wet weather in warm-up prevented that (no practice on race tyres) so there was to be a compulsory bike change in the race, as when Bridgestone had similar problems in Australia in 2013.

The tyre that delaminated under Redding posed a problem. The entire tread came off, but it remained inflated and Scott was able to roll to a stop. Why had this happened? The most likely explanation is that Scott's weight and riding aggression were just too

that included many tracks where the company had previously done only a single day of testing, remained one of experimentation tempered by a desire not to repeat their Argentinian experience. Michelin were bringing up to four tyres for each end of the bike and specifying the precise track temperature range in which each compound could operate. In this way they provided a choice of durability, such that it was possible to get a 'soft' tyre that in certain circumstances lasted longer than a 'hard'. There was a return to the 'upright straight-line crash' scenario at Aragón, but on further examination the tyres that caused the crashes there were well outside their specified operating temperature ranges.

This wide range of tyres goes some way to explaining some of the results in 2016. One tyre design was a set of super-soft wets, which could only do a limited number of laps. That was fine when a rider pitted for another set at the right time, but otherwise, as many found out at Brno, different tyres could soon turn out to be a better choice. A special stiff-construction front was built for the punishing main 'straight' at Misano and it suited Pedrosa perfectly. The soft wets from Brno made a reappearance at Phillip Island with a very strict duration limit, for Michelin didn't want to take any chances on a circuit that's notorious for trashing tyre company reputations.

The factories were now realising how the Michelins work. The balance of grip and where that grip occurs shifted through the year, so that initially Yamaha had the upper hand, then Honda. At mid-season the

Hondas ruled in cooler temperatures as the Yamahas couldn't generate enough heat, but when it was hot the Yamahas were just fine. As the season came to an end, however, the top Yamaha riders were bemoaning their lost edge grip as Honda got their bike ever closer to Michelin spec.

The 2017 season will be very different. With a year under their belts, Michelin will have a far greater appreciation of what's needed. Before the end of 2016, Michelin had already started testing a front tyre of revised construction, intended to maintain braking stability while providing some additional edge grip. However, Michelin is unlikely to bring more tyres than we've been used to, and we're yet to see race tyres that have anything like the operating temperature range that Bridgestone could offer. This is a thorny issue for any tyre manufacturer: each company has a mass of suppliers that are unique to them and each supplies unique chemicals, leading to 'compounding' being a very secret and scientific process. Just because one tyre company can achieve certain performance characteristics doesn't automatically mean others can duplicate it.

Extending the acceptable working temperature range of their tyre compounds and developing similar 'continuous rubber tread' constructions to those used by other manufacturers are likely to be Michelin's new priorities. Testing of the new front will soon show whether there's enough edge grip for the high-corner-speed bikes, especially Yamaha and Suzuki. If there isn't, bigger design changes may be forced on them.

ABOVE LEFT Loris Baz walks back to his garage after a trip along the Sepang tarmac at over 200mph

ABOVE RIGHT Piero Taramasso, manager of Michelin's Two-Wheel Motorsport Group, with Ducati's Gigi Dall'Igna

HONDA
RC213V 2016

Honda's year didn't start well. The company – the paddock's biggest user of advanced electronics – were focused on the transfer to Dorna's control electronics and their first reaction bedevilled them for the whole year.

For at least the past four years, Honda have concentrated on reducing crankshaft inertia in order to make their bike – the last with a forward-rotating crank – more controllable. A forward-rotating crank makes a bike stable going into a corner and assists in holding a tight line once the bike has been forced on to its side. The design has worked well with Marc Marquez's riding style. However, the engine would have been very difficult to control without the ultra-high-speed responses provided by Honda's in-house electronics.

Honda's solution for 2016 was to build a heavier crankshaft and – like Yamaha, Suzuki and Ducati – reverse its rotation with a jackshaft. This instils different reactions into the bike: its initial roll-in is quicker, it's less stable, it understeers slightly and it has a reduced tendency to 'wheelie' on corner exit. However, it would appear that there's also a trick in not making the crankshaft too heavy, for this will cause the bike to accelerate slowly, possibly slower than its 'wheelie' limit, and at the same time will amplify understeer and tend to increase instability. We will never know the weight of this year's crankshaft, but Honda couldn't change it as engine designs are frozen by regulation.

The task taken on by Takeo Yokoyama, Honda's MotoGP technical chief, was quite complicated. He had to use his team's skills in aerodynamics, electronics and chassis design to fix all the ills caused to his project by an overly cautious engine design. They managed to perform miracles: the Honda went from the wayward and slow beast we saw in Qatar to a passable impersonation of the brilliant 2014 bike.

Chassis development was equally accomplished. First came a new swingarm, more flexible for better grip, then a really lightweight version of the basic Honda main frame design. The first version of the new frame was rejected by both Marquez and Dani Pedrosa, but passed on to Cal Crutchlow, who won at Phillip Island with it.

1 Marc Marquez used his preferred 2014 chassis with modified swingarm pivot positions from mid-season onwards

2 Cal Crutchlow inherited the 'new concept' chassis after winning at Brno and used it for the rest of the season

3 Dani Pedrosa used a modified chassis after rejecting Honda's 'new concept' solution. His chassis used side beams that weren't as curved; here the fairing follows the line of the original chassis beams

4 Chatter is a harmonic resonance that occurs at times of high load. Changing the frequency of various components can help banish the problem. Here is a tungsten plug held by silicone inside the front axle of Marquez's bike to try to damp down some of the vibrations

YAMAHA
YZR M-1 2016

Yamaha struggled in 2016. It didn't look like they would initially, but the direction in which Michelin development progressed didn't suit them. Initially it all looked good: Yamaha found that their 2015 chassis worked well with the first Michelins, but things deteriorated as the months passed.

It isn't usual for a control tyre to be developed at pace, but Michelin had no choice as this was their first year. This also meant that Yamaha didn't have a steady target to aim for. Over the past few years Yamaha have pursued a development line that rewarded really smooth inputs. That has suited Jorge Lorenzo and it has worked with the tyres most of the time. The latest Michelins, however, seemed to suit slightly more 'robust' riding styles, such as Rossi occasionally delivers – but it was clear that Lorenzo was in trouble.

Yamaha had a few problems during the year, the most spectacular bring their rev-limiter programming issues at Mugello. The software was set up so that the engine suddenly cut when it hit the rev limiter, then when the revs dropped a little the sparks were reinstated and the rev limiter came in again. That sequence of removing the entire load from the engine, especially the valve train, and then just as suddenly reinstating it, only to hit the rev limiter again, unsurprisingly caused the valve gear 'to cry enough' very quickly, leading to two very smoky engines. Lorenzo's breakdown occurred in warm-up – not really a problem – but Rossi's was in the race and cost valuable points. As any solution was going to require a broader rev range in which to operate, it's likely that the Yamahas were a few hundred rpm down thereafter.

Yamaha's foray into aerodynamics has been very effective, enough for Honda to pay them the compliment of copying their solution for Marquez. The wings aren't intended to provide downforce in the conventional sense (seemingly no suspension setting changes are required) but they do make the bike more stable, quite possibly making up for some of the Michelins' insecure feeling on corner exit acceleration. The only race where the wings didn't appear was at Phillip Island, where the crosswinds were thought to be an issue.

1 Yamaha used torque sensors at the Catalunya test to help get the best out of their new ECU and software. Note the swingarm position is as low as possible to keep load off the front tyre

2 Usually Tech 3 have to put up with year-old parts. This time the factory went back to the same 2015 chassis

3 A heavier-duty swingarm arrived at Brno and gave the team another setting option

4 From Catalunya onwards, Lorenzo used this modified design of chassis; note the weld on top of the beam to add braking stability while improving leaned-over grip

DUCATI
DESMOSEDICI GP16

Ducati brought a new chassis to the Sepang test with revised stiffness and, noticeably, no top cross-member behind the engine. The shock absorber hung off a bracket on the back of the gearbox just as Yamaha have done for years. Alone among the factories, Ducati stuck with their first shot at a Michelin chassis with some updates during the year, such as the mid-season addition of an extra brace just behind the headstock to help braking stability and simultaneously increase lateral flex.

Those original Michelin chassis were built on the premise that life with Michelins would be all about hard acceleration out of corners and braking deep at the end of the straights. Once Michelin brought their slightly revised front tyre design, everyone else went back to their 2015 chassis. Ducati noticeably didn't. They used wings (an initiative from 2015) and weight distribution to pursue their original strategy.

For 2016 Ducati decided to dedicate themselves to a downforce strategy and this was their main thrust of development. The Michelin chassis stayed because Ducati have more power than everyone else (their riders were changing gear at 18,000rpm at Mugello) and were trying to find ways to use it. The initial wing design down on the side of the bike balanced 'drag cost' with downforce. The new ones up on the front of the cowling theoretically raised the bike's centre of pressure. The higher the centre of pressure, the greater the bike's inclination to rotate backwards about the rear contact patch. That requires downforce to counteract, but these high-mounted wings have a greater effect simply because they're further away from the rear contact patch and therefore exert more leverage over the bike. As the year went on Ducati relied more and more on just these wings. The side-mounted assemblies became an additional wing to be deployed in extreme circumstances, such as at Red Bull Ring and Motegi.

In addition the bike was lowered and lengthened. Ducati's swingarm was a full 40mm longer than the Honda's, and lowering the bike also helped reduce the tendency to 'wheelie'. These changes also made it harder to change direction and hold a line in a corner.

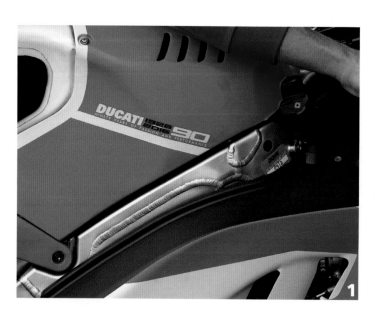

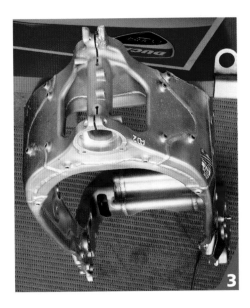

1 The small welded triangle on the top beam shows this to be a late-season chassis as preferred by Andrea Dovizioso

2 The hybrid 2015 rear/2016 front chassis tested at Phillip Island

3 A Dovizioso chassis at Catalunya clearly showing the absence of a 'top strut'. This changes the way the chassis flexes and means the crankcases carry the top mount of the shock absorber

4 Andrea Iannone's bike at Brno, with nearly the full set of wings. Note that the wings on the bike's right-hand side are set slightly higher than those on the left

SUZUKI
GSX-RR

Suzuki have been conducting a masterclass in how to create a competitive MotoGP bike. First you devise the package: everything has to work together and the entire design concept – from the engine character suiting the chassis through to the choice of riders and their styles suiting the concept – has to be in place before the bike is constructed.

It hasn't been a particularly fast process, but a series of distinct steps has led to a very complete motorcycle, one with a win under its belt already and the potential for a lot more. The Suzuki is an in-line four with a reverse-rotating cross-plane crankshaft. That's the same as the Yamaha, but choosing that design was also a major decision on how the bike should corner. Looking at the angle of the cylinders, tipped forward more aggressively than the Yamaha's, you can imagine that adequate ground clearance was a major influence. That works well with the big-radius, flowing line in a corner that the reverse-rotating crank design suits.

The chassis at first sight looks quite spindly, almost as if there isn't enough metal, but if you compare it with the Honda chassis that Cal Crutchlow likes, or the latest Yamahas, just maybe it has been right all along. The headstock area is never revealed in public and the reason is its massive structure, all the better to handle serious braking loads into corners. Usually an increase in braking rigidity affects the ability to have enough lateral flex; you have only one chassis on a motorcycle and in top-level racing it has to be able to perform three conflicting functions simultaneously. Suzuki is way ahead of the pack with the pair of carbon-fibre blades used as front engine mounts: these are bolted to the main chassis up at the beam and provide both strength for braking (because they have a wide section) and lateral flex when rolled over in a corner (because they are thin).

Suzuki is one of the factories to have gained the most from the new control electronics. It's a clear step up from what Suzuki have been used to and their position justifies both their MotoGP project and Dorna's control software.

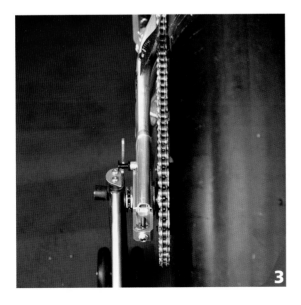

1 Suzuki were late to the wings party, and they were the only Japanese factory to increase the size of their wings by extending the width of the fairing around the handguards

2 The vertical piece of fairing with most of the 'S' on it is in fact a front engine mount made of carbon fibre

3 Suzuki turned up at Sepang with a new chassis and swingarm, but advances made by Michelin meant that it wasn't really needed

4 The older, slightly curved swingarm was reinstated by both riders most of the time

APRILIA
RS-GP

Having spent a painful 2015 learning the ropes on Bridgestones with a converted superbike, Aprilia had their all-new bike for 2016. It was a little late too, so only a few days of testing were possible before the start of the season. The first versions were somewhat underpowered as the limits of the engine design were tested, but updates kept coming.

Chassis-wise, Aprilia used at least three different designs during 2016, and all were significant steps forward. In addition to a completely new motorcycle, Aprilia also had to come to terms with the new Dorna Unified Software and the ever-changing demands of the tyres as Michelin developed their control tyres on the hoof.

The old superbike-based engine was short and to achieve this it had a 65-degree vee angle, which was too narrow to allow the throttle system to sit nicely within the vee – so the engine was also way too tall. Aprilia haven't ever released details, but it's believed that the vee angle of the MotoGP engine is 75 degrees or thereabouts, allowing the throttle bodies to be dropped down inside the vee and making the top of the engine considerably lower – which gives the chassis designers more choice for engine position. Aprilia's 2015 motor also still used the basic street-engine layout with a cam drive either side, which allowed the same cylinder head castings to be used on each bank. That too would have changed in 2016, allowing the chassis beams to be closer together, giving improved weight distribution and aerodynamics.

As with the other teams in MotoGP, Aprilia now has the gearbox separate from the engine. This allows a more gearbox-friendly oil to be used, while engine oil can be formulated to help maintain reliability. The gearbox is also released from the restriction of having to use RSV4 street-based shaft positions, so the back of the engine can be shorter to make up for the slight increase in length caused by the wider vee angle.

1 The first version of the swingarm was more flexible; the indentation added strength but wasn't welded to anything

2 The later swingarm was stronger. Although material was cut out, the welds connecting the sides added strength

3 The 2016 chassis had the longer front engine mounts added in 2015, and was a work in progress

4 By the end of the year the Aprilia were getting very close to having competitive power

Moto2-World Champions 2016

Thanks to all our riders, teams, partners, suppliers, employees and fans

THE RIDERS IN FOCUS

From the factory men to the wild cards, every MotoGP rider's season is analysed and assessed

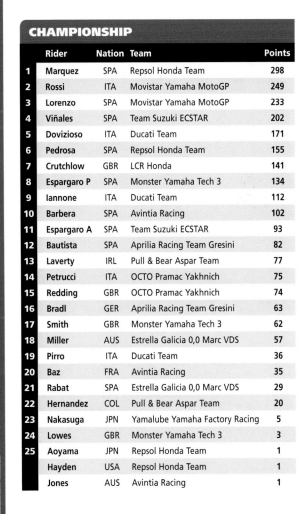

CHAMPIONSHIP

	Rider	Nation	Team	Points
1	Marquez	SPA	Repsol Honda Team	298
2	Rossi	ITA	Movistar Yamaha MotoGP	249
3	Lorenzo	SPA	Movistar Yamaha MotoGP	233
4	Viñales	SPA	Team Suzuki ECSTAR	202
5	Dovizioso	ITA	Ducati Team	171
6	Pedrosa	SPA	Repsol Honda Team	155
7	Crutchlow	GBR	LCR Honda	141
8	Espargaro P	SPA	Monster Yamaha Tech 3	134
9	Iannone	ITA	Ducati Team	112
10	Barbera	SPA	Avintia Racing	102
11	Espargaro A	SPA	Team Suzuki ECSTAR	93
12	Bautista	SPA	Aprilia Racing Team Gresini	82
13	Laverty	IRL	Pull & Bear Aspar Team	77
14	Petrucci	ITA	OCTO Pramac Yakhnich	75
15	Redding	GBR	OCTO Pramac Yakhnich	74
16	Bradl	GER	Aprilia Racing Team Gresini	63
17	Smith	GBR	Monster Yamaha Tech 3	62
18	Miller	AUS	Estrella Galicia 0,0 Marc VDS	57
19	Pirro	ITA	Ducati Team	36
20	Baz	FRA	Avintia Racing	35
21	Rabat	SPA	Estrella Galicia 0,0 Marc VDS	29
22	Hernandez	COL	Pull & Bear Aspar Team	20
23	Nakasuga	JPN	Yamalube Yamaha Factory Racing	5
24	Lowes	GBR	Monster Yamaha Tech 3	3
25	Aoyama	JPN	Repsol Honda Team	1
	Hayden	USA	Repsol Honda Team	1
	Jones	AUS	Avintia Racing	1

1 MARC MARQUEZ
REPSOL HONDA TEAM

He did what he threatened to do at the end of 2015 and accepted that he couldn't win every race. His crash at Le Mans was, he said, when realisation really set in. He went five races without a win in the middle of the year, but was on the rostrum in four of them – behaviour you just couldn't have imagined from Marc in previous seasons.

There's no doubt that the Honda was still a very difficult bike to win with, certainly early in the year before HRC got to grips with the 'spec' electronics, yet Marc still racked up the points as his opponents all made mistakes and/or suffered ill luck. His errors didn't come until after the title was secured.

It was noticeable that he saved the old aggression for occasions where he thought the risk was worthwhile, such as at Silverstone, and controlled his natural instincts when necessary, as in his decision not to chase Jack Miller at Assen. This isn't to say there weren't some astonishing exhibitions of riding: two that will live long in the memory were his slick-shod charge on an almost invisible dry line in Germany and his demolition job of the field at Aragón that ended his drought after the summer break.

Sometimes it's important to remember that Marc is still only 23 years old and has now won five world titles including the MotoGP crown three times in four years. Any weaknesses he had – and the only major one was impetuosity – have been curbed as he realised how to keep winning titles. Assuming the Honda improves again, it's difficult to see Marc being beaten in 2017.

NATIONALITY
Spanish

DATE OF BIRTH
17 February 1993

2016 SEASON
5 wins, 12 rostrums, 7 pole positions, 4 fastest laps

TOTAL POINTS
298

93

2 VALENTINO ROSSI
MOVISTAR YAMAHA MOTOGP

That tenth title is now further away than it was 12 months previously. This was despite yet another major change in Valentino's way of doing things. The return of Michelins helped him become a regular front-row qualifier as he understood them quickly and enjoyed the fact that he didn't have to make as big a leap of faith as when qualifying on Bridgestones. Similarly, his first win of the year, at Jerez, showed how he and his crew's experience could solve the problem of a tricky track more quickly than the rest.

There were some gems, like the ride from 15th on the grid to the rostrum in Australia, but there were also errors. The crash in Texas was a function of the new tyres, and most of the top men suffered a similar experience early in the race. The Assen crash, however, while due to a trivial mistake, was rider error, as was Motegi.

The incident that really rankles was the engine blow-up at Mugello – most definitely not his fault – when Vale looked odds-on for the win. Although he won next time out, that incident stalled his challenge. A consistent second half of the year was enough to see off the challenge of Lorenzo for the honour of being top Yamaha rider, but it never looked like putting Rossi on terms with Marquez.

There was also the feeling that Marc dealt better with the aftermath of the previous season's unpleasantness. Valentino's discomfort in Malaysia when questioned on the subject was clear. In 2017 he has a fresh challenge in the shape of a new team-mate who looks like he'll be just as fast as the old one.

NATIONALITY
Italian

DATE OF BIRTH
16 February 1979

2016 SEASON
2 wins, 10 rostrums, 3 pole positions, 2 fastest laps

TOTAL POINTS
249

46

3 JORGE LORENZO
MOVISTAR YAMAHA MOTOGP

Despite having misgivings about the new Michelin tyres and the implications for his high-corner-speed riding style, Jorge started the season brilliantly. In the first half of the year he eclipsed his team-mate Valentino Rossi and looked like he was capable of retaining his title.

After winning the opening round, Jorge didn't appear too affected by the change in rubber supplier. He scored a trademark lights-to-flag runaway win in France and went to the top of the points table, then he fought tooth and nail over an epic final lap at Mugello to beat Marquez by a wheel and extend his championship lead to 15 points.

However, he was in serious tyre trouble at Catalunya, where he was torpedoed by Iannone. Then things really did take a turn for the worse. A wet track at Assen awoke the ghosts of 2013 and suddenly Jorge was a shadow of his usual self; the next race, at the Sachsenring, was also wet. While everyone remembers his bravery in returning to Holland to race with a two-day-old broken collarbone, they forget that he crashed in Germany and had to have more surgery. He took only seven points from those two races and then finished outside the points in Brno, again on a wet track.

For the rest of the year Jorge was fast when the tarmac was warm, but if he couldn't get heat in the front tyre, as in a chilly Australia, he didn't trouble the leaders.

For 2017 Jorge leaves Yamaha after spending his entire nine-year MotoGP career with them and winning three titles. It will be his, and Ducati's, biggest challenge yet.

NATIONALITY
Spanish

DATE OF BIRTH
4 May 1987

2016 SEASON
4 wins, 10 rostrums, 4 pole positions, 2 fastest laps

TOTAL POINTS
233

4 MAVERICK VINALES
TEAM SUZUKI ECSTAR

It's easy to forget that when Maverick Viñales signed for Suzuki's comeback project two years ago most people thought he'd made a serious error of judgement. The idea that in just his second season as a MotoGP rider he could stand on the rostrum as early as Le Mans, win a race and then score back-to-back rostrums on tracks as diverse as Motegi and Phillip Island was, frankly, ridiculous. And yet he did all that and more. It's a measure of how far Suzuki and their rider have come in a very short time that by mid-season the paddock was thinking of anything lower than a fourth place as a disappointing result.

Right from the start of 2015 the Suzuki had fine handling and edge grip, characteristics that a gradual increase in power didn't nullify – the best phrase to describe the GSX-RR is 'user friendly'. It still had a slight acceleration deficit and distinct problems in the wet, mainly due to lack of data, but on fast, sinuous tracks like Silverstone and Phillip Island the bike was a potential winner.

Maverick himself has always been a winner. On the eve of his maiden MotoGP win, at Silverstone, he exuded an air of certainty that could be mistaken for arrogance but is actually the confidence of youth. He's still only 21 years old but has the implacable calm of a veteran, an impression amplified by his preference for one-word answers preferably delivered from behind shades.

For 2017 Maverick moves to the factory Yamaha team as the replacement for Jorge Lorenzo. That isn't a prospect that Valentino Rossi can face with equanimity.

NATIONALITY
Spanish

DATE OF BIRTH
12 January 1995

2016 SEASON
1 win, 4 rostrums, 2 fastest laps

TOTAL POINTS
202

5 ANDREA DOVIZIOSO
DUCATI TEAM

04

Apart from second place in the opening round in Qatar, a race he could and maybe should have won, the first half of Dovi's season was seriously blighted by bad luck.

If he hadn't been knocked off – by team-mate Iannone – at the last corner of the second race, in Argentina, he would have gone to Texas just one point behind Marquez. And when he got there he was felled again, this time by Pedrosa, probably the least likely man on the grid to do something reckless. This was followed by a mechanical failure in Spain and a crash of his own making in France.

All this led to the embarrassing situation, for the factory, of Hector Barbera being top Ducati rider in the championship at this stage of the season on a 14.2 Desmosedici.

Andrea's second rostrum didn't arrive until Germany, where he was third, then after the summer break he was second in Ducati's 1–2 in Austria, another race he could have won. His comments about not taking any risks for his second place in Japan and being satisfied with fourth in Australia raised some eyebrows.

In Malaysia Dovi finally got the victory his season needed. As he did it from pole position and with the fastest lap there weren't many arguments as to whether he deserved it. It was only his second win in the top class, the first having come at Donington in 2009.

Despite the relative under-achievement of his season, he's staying with the team for 2017 because he has been integral to Ducati's improvements and the factory consider that he will be a good team-mate for Jorge Lorenzo.

NATIONALITY
Italian

DATE OF BIRTH
23 March 1986

2016 SEASON
1 win, 5 rostrums, 2 pole positions, 1 fastest lap

TOTAL POINTS
171

6 DANI PEDROSA
REPSOL HONDA TEAM

26

Of all the factory riders, Dani Pedrosa had the most difficult time adjusting to the new Michelin tyres. The lightest rider on the grid, he found it difficult, not surprisingly, to get heat into the 'one size fits all' boots.

It looked as if Dani was going to go the whole season without a win for the first time in his 11-year career in the top class of racing. Then came Misano and some super-soft rubber that allowed him to get some heat into his tyres with the bonus of his light weight meaning he didn't wear them out. That handy combination enabled him to remind everybody what he can do as he ripped past Marc Marquez, Jorge Lorenzo and Valentino Rossi to win decisively.

Dani had high hopes for Japan – Motegi is one of his best tracks – but a highside on an out-lap broke his right collarbone and left leg, putting him out until the last race of the year.

Before that victory at Misano Pedrosa had only been on the rostrum twice, both times in third place. The first, in Argentina, was an extremely lucky result by his own admission, followed by a more convincing one at Catalunya.

For most of the year, though, Dani wasn't within range of the leaders, unhappy with both his bike and the tyres, but he still racked up the points for a more than respectable end-of-year position, helping Honda towards the constructors' championship to go alongside Marquez's riders' title. It's still difficult to think of someone who could do that job as well as Pedrosa does it.

NATIONALITY
Spanish

DATE OF BIRTH
29 September 1985

2016 SEASON
1 win, 3 rostrums, 1 fastest lap

TOTAL POINTS
155

7 CAL CRUTCHLOW
LCR HONDA

After the French GP, Cal Crutchlow was 20th in the championship table with just one points-scoring finish to his name, and there was speculation about him moving out of MotoGP at the end of the year.

To go from that, effectively written off, to becoming a double winner and patently one of the best racers in the world is some achievement in half a season.

In the sequence of six races book-ended by his two victories, Cal scored more points than Marquez. The man himself says it simply took a while to work out the bike, and that if he'd been able to do all the pre-season tests he would have been fast sooner. When he did work it out, Cal was never far from the rostrum.

Cal's first victory, in the Czech Republic, was the result of a brave tyre choice, the second, at Phillip Island, simply because he was the fastest man out there. The Brno win was the first in the top class by a British rider since Barry Sheene in 1981 (at the Swedish GP).

Valentino Rossi warned Cal that the first win would change things, make him a member of an exclusive club, and so it did. HRC had asked (make that 'told') him to test a chassis rejected by the Repsol riders and taken a lot of interest in his feedback. As Cal said with his usual waspishness, 'It's because I'm normal; I'm not Marc Marquez and I don't weigh 50 kilos.' There was also a visit to HRC after the Japanese GP.

Cal may ride for Lucio Cecchinello's satellite team but he was now getting factory rider treatment.

NATIONALITY
British

DATE OF BIRTH
29 October 1985

2016 SEASON
2 wins, 4 rostrums, 1 pole position, 3 fastest laps

TOTAL POINTS
141

8 POL ESPARGARO
MONSTER YAMAHA TECH 3

It wasn't an easy year for the satellite Yamaha riders of the Tech 3 team. Pol Espargaro failed to get his first rostrum in MotoGP but did start on the front row in Australia. Although that doesn't sound like much in the way of major achievement, he appeared to have got over his crashing habit and, importantly, handily won the competition with team-mate Bradley Smith, a reverse of last year's situation.

Pol no longer appears to have to get his old Moto2 self out of his system on Friday before knuckling down to work on his race pace. Eighth position in the championship rankings is no mean feat and his highlight was fourth place at the Dutch TT – doubly impressive as Pol doesn't have a history of good wet-weather results.

successful return to the Suzuka Eight Hours, which he won for the second year running. Despite this, he's having to leave Yamaha and head to the new KTM team for 2017 alongside Smith.

Pol has been with Tech 3, Yamaha's satellite team, for three seasons. He was recruited on the strength of his performances against Marc Marquez in Moto2, but despite putting together a solid 2016 season, scoring points in all but two races, he ran out of time.

Yamaha want to move new talent into the team and there was obviously no vacancy in the factory squad with Rossi staying and Viñales arriving. That left Pol out on a limb but the feeling is that he and Smith, who now get on with each other after years of animosity, will form a useful

NATIONALITY
Spanish

DATE OF BIRTH
10 June 1991

TOTAL POINTS
134

9 ANDREA IANNONE
DUCATI TEAM

NATIONALITY
Italian

DATE OF BIRTH
9 August 1989

2016 SEASON
1 win, 4 rostrums, 1 pole position, 3 fastest laps

TOTAL POINTS
112

As dramatic a year as you could imagine that will be remembered above all for the incident in Argentina where a last-corner lunge took Iannone and his team-mate out of rostrum positions. Even scoring Ducati's first win since the Stoner years, in Austria, couldn't make up for that move – it cost Andrea his job. The second half of his season was ruined by a back injury picked up at Misano that kept him out for four races. Third place at Valencia at least meant that Iannone and Ducati parted with a smile. He will be fast next year on a Suzuki.

10 HECTOR BARBERA
DUCATI TEAM / AVINTIA RACING

NATIONALITY
Spanish

DATE OF BIRTH
2 November 1986

TOTAL POINTS
102

This was the best of Hector's seven seasons in MotoGP despite him being on a two-year-old Ducati 14.2 in a customer team. His best result was fourth in Malaysia and he had a clever ride to fifth at Brno – but the highlight of the season was riding for the factory team in Japan and Australia. He grinned like a kid in a new school uniform when he first turned out in factory kit but crashed in both races while not much higher up the field than he'd been on the Avintia bike. Still, it was a combative season from Hector and his team.

11 ALEIX ESPARGARO
TEAM SUZUKI ECSTAR

NATIONALITY
Spanish

DATE OF BIRTH
30 July 1989

TOTAL POINTS
93

The older of the Espargaro brothers didn't get on with the new Suzuki and reverted to the 2015 chassis. For much of the year Aleix was overshadowed by team-mate Maverick Viñales but hit a patch of excellent form towards the end when he was regularly in contention for a rostrum only to be frustrated in the final laps. His parting with Suzuki wasn't entirely smooth: Aleix made it known that he didn't think he'd been treated very well and he will be with Aprilia for 2017 with payback on his mind.

12 ALVARO BAUTISTA
APRILIA RACING TEAM GRESINI

NATIONALITY
Spanish

DATE OF BIRTH
21 November 1984

TOTAL POINTS
82

Alvaro and the Aprilia were under the radar for much of the year, but scored points in every race after Silverstone, including seventh places in Japan and Malaysia. This was the first year for Aprilia's MotoGP bike (the 2015 bike was Superbike-based) and Alvaro and the team deserve credit for getting it to the point where it's competitive with rivals like the satellite Ducatis on handling and pace. Neither Bautista nor team-mate Bradl are being retained by the factory for 2017, so Alvaro rejoins the Aspar team, for which he won his 125cc world title, and gets a GP16 Ducati.

13 EUGENE LAVERTY
PULL & BEAR ASPAR TEAM

NATIONALITY
Irish

DATE OF BIRTH
3 June 1986

TOTAL POINTS
77

On a two-year-old Ducati, Eugene put together a solid run of points-scoring rides that was only ended by a Petrucci lunge in Austria. Eugene's best result was fourth in Argentina, but for his finest performance he's more inclined to point to his ninth place at Jerez on a tricky track in a race where nobody crashed. He leaves the Aspar team after two years to go back to World Superbike with Aprilia because he wasn't offered equal machinery with his potential team-mate Alvaro Bautista. He will be Aprilia's MotoGP test rider in 2017 and in line for wild-card entries as well as replacement rides.

14 DANILO PETRUCCI
OCTO PRAMAC YAKHNICH

NATIONALITY
Italian

DATE OF BIRTH
24 October 1990

2016 SEASON
1 fastest lap

TOTAL POINTS
75

Missed the first four races of the year after a testing accident in Australia. Did try to come back at Qatar but made things worse, turning a serious hand injury into a potential career finisher. Returned in France with a typically combative ride to seventh, his joint best result of the year. Was expected to challenge for rostrums in the wet but somehow never did thanks to crashes in the Netherlands and Germany. Attracted the attention of Race Direction after clattering Laverty in Austria and Redding at Aragón. Beat team-mate Redding for the honour of having Pramac's singleton GP17 Ducati next season.

15 SCOTT REDDING
OCTO PRAMAC YAKHNICH

NATIONALITY
British

DATE OF BIRTH
4 January 1993

2016 SEASON
1 rostrum

TOTAL POINTS
74

Scott's first season on a Ducati wasn't easy. A succession of technical problems in the first half of the year wasn't overcome until he achieved a rostrum place in the wet at Assen. That highlight was so nearly repeated at the following race in Germany but there was another low when he was knocked off by his team-mate at Aragón. Scott lost out to Petrucci in the intra-team competition for a Ducati GP17 next year, but the 2016 bike he'll get won two races and that means there's no reason for despair. Scott retains the confidence of the Ducati factory, but 2017 will be very important.

16 STEFAN BRADL
APRILIA RACING TEAM GRESINI

NATIONALITY
Germany

DATE OF BIRTH
29 November 1989

TOTAL POINTS
63

The 2011 Moto2 world champion played his part in developing the Aprilia from modified Superbike in 2015 to MotoGP contender in 2016, and it regularly raced with – and beat – satellite Ducatis. Like team-mate Bautista, Stefan had a top finish of seventh place and scored points in 13 races. Also like his team-mate, Stefan's services weren't required for 2017 so he's off to the World Superbike Championship where he will ride a Honda FireBlade for the Ten Kate team as team-mate to Nicky Hayden. He has been in MotoGP since 2012, scoring one rostrum and a pole position at Laguna Seca in 2013.

17 BRADLEY SMITH
MONSTER YAMAHA TECH 3

NATIONALITY
British

DATE OF BIRTH
28 November 1990

TOTAL POINTS
62

Bradley took a long time to adjust to the new Michelins and had to tolerate being beaten by his team-mate – a total reversal of 2015. Then he suffered a truly nasty injury while testing for a World Endurance event where he was scheduled to try to help Yamaha win the title. He needed two operations to repair ligament and soft-tissue damage to his right knee but set himself the target of returning at Motegi after missing four races. He achieved that but it hurt – a lot. He scored in all the remaining races of the year, including eighth place at Phillip Island secured by going round the outside of two riders on the final bend.

18 JACK MILLER
ESTRELLA GALICIA 0,0 MARC VDS

NATIONALITY
Australian

DATE OF BIRTH
18 January 1995

2016 SEASON
1 win, 1 rostrum

TOTAL POINTS
57

Started the season with a nasty ankle fracture from a testing accident that still hadn't healed. A heavy crash in Texas aggravated the injury but at Assen he justified Honda's faith in sending him straight from Moto3 to MotoGP with a dominant win in the wet. Another impressive ride next time out in Germany showed that Jack is one of the best wet-weather riders on the grid. Just as he became fully fit for the first time, he crashed in warm-up in Austria, hurting his back and breaking bones in his hand, putting him out for two more races. He stays with Marc VDS for 2017 and will turn 22 just before the start of the season.

19 MICHELE PIRRO
DUCATI TEAM / AVINTIA RACING

NATIONALITY
Italian

DATE OF BIRTH
5 July 1986

TOTAL POINTS
36

Ducati's test rider made eight appearances as a wild card and replacement rider for both the works and satellite teams. His best finish was seventh place at Misano, where he was supposed to be a wild card but was promoted to the factory team after Iannone's free-practice crash. As usual, it was sometimes difficult to know what his real job is – testing parts or racing – but there's no doubt that having a test rider capable of running at a very respectable race pace helped Ducati stay ahead of Suzuki in the title chases for both constructors (comfortably) and teams (by one point). The surprise is that no other factory has an equivalent.

20 LORIS BAZ
AVINTIA RACING

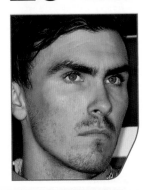

NATIONALITY French
DATE OF BIRTH 1 February 1993
TOTAL POINTS 35

The tall Frenchman suffered from injuries throughout the year and had remedial surgery over winter. The pain was eased by great wet-weather rides to fourth at Brno and fifth at Sepang, and he will be back in 2017.

21 TITO RABAT
ESTRELLA GALICIA 0,0 MARC VDS

NATIONALITY Spanish
DATE OF BIRTH 25 May 1989
TOTAL POINTS 29

The only MotoGP rookie struggled, scoring points in just nine races with a best of ninth in the crash-strewn Argentine GP. He also broke his collarbone in practice at Mugello. It's unfair to judge after one year but he will have to step up in 2017.

22 Y. HERNANDEZ
PULL & BEAR ASPAR TEAM

NATIONALITY Colombian
DATE OF BIRTH 25 July 1988
TOTAL POINTS 20

Six points-scoring rides with a best finish of 11th was a lower return than expected, so Yonny goes back to Moto2 for 2017. Assen summed up his year: crashed while leading but too early to be allowed to restart.

23 K. NAKASUGA
YAMALUBE YAMAHA FACTORY RACING

NATIONALITY Japanese
DATE OF BIRTH 9 August 1981
TOTAL POINTS 5

Yamaha'a veteran tester, and double winner of the Suzuka Eight Hour race, took his now traditional wild-card ride at Motegi and as usual scored useful points with 11th place from 16th on the grid.

24 ALEX LOWES
MONSTER YAMAHA TECH 3

NATIONALITY British
DATE OF BIRTH 14 September 1990
TOTAL POINTS 3

His win at the Suzuka Eight Hour earned Alex a MotoGP test after Brno, so when Bradley Smith was injured soon after he was able to step in for three races. A big crash at Aragón meant he only rode in two, but he scored points at Silverstone.

25 HIROSHI AOYAMA
REPSOL HONDA TEAM

NATIONALITY Japanese
DATE OF BIRTH 25 October 1981
TOTAL POINTS 1

Stood in for the injured Dani Pedrosa at short notice in Japan and again in Malaysia when Nicky Hayden was unavailable. As he is now 34 years old and hasn't raced for a couple of years, the best he could do was 15th at Motegi.

26 NICKY HAYDEN
REPSOL HONDA TEAM / MARC VDS

NATIONALITY American
DATE OF BIRTH 30 July 1981
TOTAL POINTS 1

The 2006 MotoGP world champion stood in for Jack Miller at Aragón and Dani Pedrosa at Phillip Island, where he was seriously impressive. Nicky was in the fabulous fight for seventh until he was barged out by Miller.

27 MIKE JONES
AVINTIA RACING

NATIONALITY Australian
DATE OF BIRTH 25 February 1994
TOTAL POINTS 1

The young Aussie, Troy Bayliss's protégé, stood in at Avintia when Hector Barbera rode the factory bike in Japan and Australia. Did everything right, impressed the team and was rewarded with a point from his home race.

JAVIER FORES
AVINTIA RACING

NATIONALITY Spanish
DATE OF BIRTH 16 September 1985
TOTAL POINTS 0

Rode his first MotoGP race as a stand-in for Loris Baz on the Avintia Ducati at Misano after the Frenchman's big crash at Silverstone. Retired from the race after 16 laps with arm pump.

MIKA KALLIO
RED BULL KTM FACTORY RACING

NATIONALITY Finnish
DATE OF BIRTH 8 November 1982
TOTAL POINTS 0

The 125, 250 and Moto2 runner-up débuted KTM's new MotoGP bike as a wild card at the final round. Now a test rider for the Austrian manufacturer, Kallio improved lap times through the Valencia weekend but was put out by a sensor failure.

PUT YOUR SKILLS TO THE TEST.

2-WHEEL DRIVING EXPERIENCES
AT THE RED BULL RING.

THE RACES

QATAR
ROUND 1

COMMERCIAL BANK
GRAND PRIX OF QATAR
LOSAIL INTERNATIONAL CIRCUIT

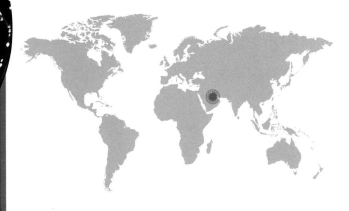

SAME OLD, SAME OLD

Lorenzo won as the new regulations failed to make any significant difference to MotoGP's plot

Anyone who has been around racing for any length of time knows one thing to be true: whatever the authorities do to the regulations, the same guys will be up front. Fast is fast.

On the surface, it looked as if 2016 would carry on where 2015 left off: world champion Jorge Lorenzo won after a struggle with the factory Ducatis and Marc Marquez; the Honda still looked recalcitrant but now it was slow as well; the top independent rider finished seventh on a Tech 3 Yamaha (although it was Pol Espargaro, not Bradley Smith, who took that honour); the Suzuki still looked to be lacking a bit of top end; and even the change to Michelin tyres didn't appear to make much difference as Lorenzo managed to break both the race and lap records.

The only surprise was that Jorge changed his mind on the grid and switched from the harder rear Michelin to the softer option – putting him well in the minority. Also, he set his best time on the 20th lap, a significant difference from previous years on Bridgestone when records were rarely set after the fourth lap. Riders didn't report significant problems with the tyres and it looked as if the narrower front tyre introduced mid-way through the pre-season tests was close enough in feel to the old Bridgestone to avoid causing any concerns.

Slightly more surprising was the early start to the silly season, kicked off by Valentino Rossi announcing that he had re-signed for Yamaha for two more years, closely followed by Bradley

'WHEN I TOUCHED THE WHITE LINE IN THE LONG RIGHT-HANDER, THE BIKE SUDDENLY WENT AWAY FROM ME AND UNFORTUNATELY I WAS UNABLE TO DO ANYTHING TO AVOID THE CRASH'
ANDREA IANNONE

Smith revealing that he would be joining the new KTM team for 2017. Rossi's decision, in fact, was precipitated by Lorenzo demanding to negotiate a new contract before the season started. Rossi was therefore treated the same way, drawing a waspish comment from Lorenzo to the effect that he – Rossi – was smart to sign because he didn't have many other options. In fact, the renewal was the precursor to Valentino cementing his links with Yamaha with commercial deals to supply bikes to his Academy and the VR-46 organisation to take over corporate merchandising.

The biennial rumours about Lorenzo going to Ducati immediately restarted, although this time with considerably more credibility than in previous years.

The other big talking point, and a story that would also have legs, was wings; specifically the double wings – biplane? – on the factory Ducatis. Clearly, Gigi Dall'Igna and the Bologna factory had been spending a lot of time at the wind tunnel. However, IRTA, Dorna and the FIM weren't so sure, forseeing an expensive arms race as well as potential safety issues. However, a change to the technical rules requires a unanimous decision from the MSMA, the manufacturers' association, and Ducati were highly unlikely to vote to waste all that work.

Ducati's place in the race didn't change either as Andrea Dovizioso repeated his second place of 12 months previously. It might have been better

ABOVE Marc Marquez seemed strangely happy with third place on the recalcitrant Honda

OPPOSITE TOP Just like the previous season, Andrea Dovizioso and Ducati started impressively

LEFT It could have been even better for Ducati had Andrea Iannone not lost the front while leading

ABOVE Maverick Viñales was by far the better of the Suzukis; Aleix Espargaro had a tough weekend

BELOW The world champion took up in 2016 where he left off in 2015

OPPOSITE The only rookie in the field, Tito Rabat, scored a point in his first MotoGP race

but Andrea Iannone crashed out while leading, from TV pictures it looked as if he'd touched a white line when on a lot of lean angle. Ducati were also missing Danilo Petrucci from their satellite team: he tried to ride but only succeeded in doing more damage to the hand he broke badly in pre-season testing at Phillip Island. The other news was the arrival of Aprilia's 'proper' MotoGP bikes in a two-man team ridden by Stefan Bradl and Alvaro Bautista. One finished, one didn't – but the only bikes Bautista beat were the Marc VDS Hondas.

If the factory Honda men were having difficulties, then the men on the satellite bikes were really suffering. In defence of the Marc VDS team, though, it should be noted that Tito Rabat was the only rookie on the grid and Jack Miller was severely handicapped by the ankle injury he suffered in the off season. However, the problems of the factory men were all too obvious. Not only was Marquez out-dragged down the front straight by the Ducatis, but he was also out-run by the factory Yamahas. This in a year, remember, when the factory bikes got two litres more fuel for each race. The problem, said every Honda rider, was acceleration – or rather lack of it from the new rearward-rotating engine. There were also problems still evident in using the 'dumbed-down' – from an HRC point of view – electronics.

Maybe we shouldn't have been surprised at Marquez's delight with third place, and he said a perfect race would only have got him second place. However, it was already becoming obvious that only Marquez could make the Honda look competitive. Dani Pedrosa spent the race disputing fifth place with Maverick Viñales on the equally underwhelming Suzuki, although it's a measure of how far Suzuki has come that a fight with a factory Honda is no longer regarded as a moral victory. With engine development frozen by regulation, it was difficult to be optimistic about any Honda rider's chances over the year – with the possible exception of Marquez.

As for Rossi, it seemed that he too was stuck in a time warp. He was fourth, right behind Marquez, but at no time looked like he had the ability to challenge for a rostrum position. In fact he was never in the top three and started the race from the second row. It all felt very familiar.

With hindsight, it is obvious that the status quo would not hold up for long. Michelin deserved all the praise they received for the performance of their tyres but they had had the advantage of a pre-season test on the Losail track. Now that testing time is such a rare commodity, it's easy to forget what can be diagnosed with just a few hours of track time.

If Losail was a known quantity with a decade of data for the teams to fall back on, that could not be said of the next two tracks on the calendar. Maybe challenges to the established order would emerge, but they didn't at the first race of 2016.

AT LAST, A MotoGP BIKE

At last. The efforts of Dorna, the FIM and IRTA came to fruition. There was only one type of motorcycle on the grid – a MotoGP bike. Gone were the confusing subsets of the Claiming Rule Teams or the Open Class and in came one set of regulations with just a few concessions on extra testing and engine development for factories that haven't won a dry race in two years. All bikes now had the same tyre choice (no softer rubber for non-factory teams) and all had the same amount of fuel in the tank, 22 litres, which meant an extra two litres for the factory machines.

The biggest hurdle to getting the factories on board was the 'specification' electronics from Magneti Marelli. Properly known as the Unified Software, this also included the most important bit of hardware – the ECU. In terms of functionality it was close to the 'spec' electronics of the previous season, meaning factories lost a good deal of their advantage, most noticeably the ability to 'learn' and adjust a setting – for instance traction control out of a certain corner – as the race progressed. Factory riders reckoned it was like stepping back the best part of ten years.

However, the system was still more complex than IRTA had envisaged at the start of the process – the price for obtaining the approval of the factories – and therefore still a major challenge for non-factory teams to deal with.

There was also the small matter of a change in 'spec' tyre supplier, from Bridgestone to Michelin. Right from the first test, there were no complaints about the rear but a few doubts about the front's ability to match it. Given the scale of the changes, the regulations emerged from their first test with credit.

COMMERCIAL BANK GRAND PRIX OF QATAR
LOSAIL INTERNATIONAL CIRCUIT
ROUND 1
MARCH 20

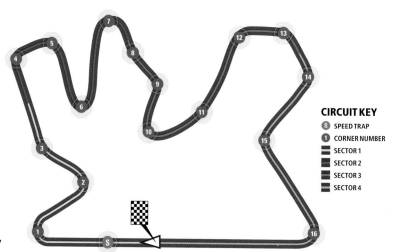

RACE RESULTS

CIRCUIT LENGTH 3.343 miles

NO. OF LAPS 22

RACE DISTANCE 73.546 miles

WEATHER Dry, 21°C

TRACK TEMPERATURE 23°C

WINNER Jorge Lorenzo

FASTEST LAP 1m 54.927s
104.7mph, Jorge Lorenzo (record)

PREVIOUS LAP RECORD 1m 55.153s,
104.5mph, Casey Stoner (2008)

CIRCUIT KEY
- **S** SPEED TRAP
- **1** CORNER NUMBER
- SECTOR 1
- SECTOR 2
- SECTOR 3
- SECTOR 4

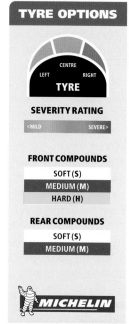

TYRE OPTIONS

LEFT — CENTRE — RIGHT

TYRE

SEVERITY RATING

<MILD — SEVERE>

FRONT COMPOUNDS
| SOFT (S) |
| MEDIUM (M) |
| HARD (H) |

REAR COMPOUNDS
| SOFT (S) |
| MEDIUM (M) |

MICHELIN

QUALIFYING

	Rider	Nation	Motorcycle	Team	Time	Gap
1	Lorenzo	SPA	Yamaha	Movistar Yamaha MotoGP	1m 54.543s	
2	Marquez	SPA	Honda	Repsol Honda Team	1m 54.643s	0.091s
3	Viñales	SPA	Suzuki	Team Suzuki ECSTAR	1m 54.638s	0.095s
4	Iannone	ITA	Ducati	Ducati Team	1m 54.693s	0.150s
5	Rossi	ITA	Yamaha	Movistar Yamaha MotoGP	1m 54.815s	0.272s
6	Dovizioso	ITA	Ducati	Ducati Team	1m 54.963s	0.420s
7	Pedrosa	SPA	Honda	Repsol Honda Team	1m 55.078s	0.535s
8	Barbera	SPA	Ducati	Avintia Racing	1m 55.165s	0.622s
9	Espargaro P	SPA	Yamaha	Monster Yamaha Tech 3	1m 55.302s	0.759s
10	Crutchlow	GBR	Honda	LCR Honda	1m 55.352s	0.809s
11	Smith	GBR	Yamaha	Monster Yamaha Tech 3	1m 55.414s	0.871s
12	Redding	GBR	Ducati	OCTO Pramac Yakhnich	1m 55.508s	0.965s
13	Hernandez	COL	Ducati	Aspar Team MotoGP	1m 56.157s	*0.866s
14	Laverty	IRL	Ducati	Aspar Team MotoGP	1m 56.186s	*0.895s
15	Espargaro A	SPA	Suzuki	Team Suzuki ECSTAR	1m 56.238s	*0.947s
16	Baz	FRA	Ducati	Avintia Racing	1m 56.375s	*1.084s
17	Bautista	SPA	Aprilia	Aprilia Racing Team Gresini	1m 56.595s	*1.304s
18	Miller	AUS	Honda	Estrella Galicia 0,0 Marc VDS	1m 56.620s	*1.329s
19	Rabat	SPA	Honda	Estrella Galicia 0,0 Marc VDS	1m 57.108s	*1.817s
20	Bradl	GER	Aprilia	Aprilia Racing Team Gresini	1m 57.216s	*1.925s
21	Petrucci	ITA	Ducati	OCTO Pramac Yakhnich	1m 55.931s	1.292s

* Gap with the fastest rider in the Q1 session

1 JORGE LORENZO
A perfect start to his title defence: pole, the win, plus the fastest lap and a new race and lap record. A late swap to the softer rear tyre helped. His only problems came from the two factory Ducatis.

2 ANDREA DOVIZIOSO
Promising, as was second place 12 months previously. Only this time it was done with no concessions. Dovi was never out of the top three and led for three laps before Lorenzo eased away.

3 MARC MARQUEZ
Difficult not to believe he made the Honda look better than it really is given the gap back to Pedrosa. Astonishing to see him being out-accelerated from slow- and medium-speed corners – maybe due to the harder rear tyre. Happy with third.

4 VALENTINO ROSSI
It felt like the 'same old same old'. Second-row start and not quite able to get on the rostrum, as the man himself admitted. Not sure if using the soft tyre would have helped.

5 DANI PEDROSA
More than ten seconds behind his team-mate despite using the softer tyre. Pushed out at the first corner, finished the lap in sixth and only gained a place when Iannone crashed. Difficult to see the positives.

6 MAVERICK VIÑALES
Equalled his best ever finish but was faster in practice and couldn't understand why race day was more difficult. However, the Suzuki's performance looked promising for a continuation of last season's progress.

7 POL ESPARGARO
An encouraging start to the season, mainly due to beating his team-mate in qualifying and the race. Then there was the small matter of being top independent (non-factory) rider.

8 BRADLEY SMITH
Not very happy with the new tyres before race day, then made a mess of the start. Recovered well and ended up in a dice with his team-mate. Made a pass on last corner but was out-dragged to the flag.

9 HECTOR BARBERA
A little disappointed with his lack of competitiveness under the new regulations. Transmitted some nerves to his team about the new situation and felt he should have fought with the Tech 3 Yamahas.

10 SCOTT REDDING
A little puzzled not to rediscover the pace he had in the test here, so happy with 10th but had expected more. Not a bad result after a hard weekend that included two crashes.

LAP CHART

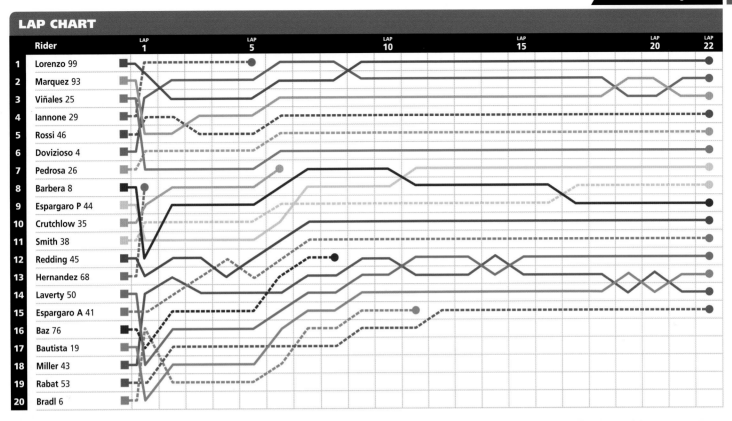

	Rider	LAP 1	LAP 5	LAP 10	LAP 15	LAP 20	LAP 22
1	Lorenzo 99						
2	Marquez 93						
3	Viñales 25						
4	Iannone 29						
5	Rossi 46						
6	Dovizioso 4						
7	Pedrosa 26						
8	Barbera 8						
9	Espargaro P 44						
10	Crutchlow 35						
11	Smith 38						
12	Redding 45						
13	Hernandez 68						
14	Laverty 50						
15	Espargaro A 41						
16	Baz 76						
17	Bautista 19						
18	Miller 43						
19	Rabat 53						
20	Bradl 6						

RACE

	Rider	Motorcycle	Race time	Time +	Fastest lap	Avg. speed	Tyres
1	Lorenzo	Yamaha	42m 28.452s		1m 54.927s	103.8mph	H/S
2	Dovizioso	Ducati	42m 30.471s	2.019s	1m 55.149s	103.8mph	S/S
3	Marquez	Honda	42m 30.739s	2.287s	1m 55.223s	103.8mph	H/M
4	Rossi	Yamaha	42m 30.839s	2.387s	1m 55.171s	103.8mph	H/M
5	Pedrosa	Honda	42m 42.535s	14.083s	1m 55.918s	103.3mph	S/S
6	Viñales	Suzuki	42m 43.875s	15.423s	1m 55.942s	103.2mph	S/S
7	Espargaro P	Yamaha	42m 47.081s	18.629s	1m 55.986s	103.1mph	S/S
8	Smith	Yamaha	42m 47.104s	18.652s	1m 55.963s	103.1mph	S/S
9	Barbera	Ducati	42m 49.612s	21.160s	1m 55.993s	103.0mph	S/S
10	Redding	Ducati	42m 52.887s	24.435s	1m 56.165s	102.9mph	S/S
11	Espargaro A	Suzuki	43m 04.299s	35.847s	1m 56.441s	102.4mph	S/S
12	Laverty	Ducati	43m 10.208s	41.756s	1m 56.841s	102.2mph	S/S
13	Bautista	Aprilia	43m 10.384s	41.932s	1m 56.739s	102.2mph	S/S
14	Miller	Honda	43m 10.434s	41.982s	1m 56.942s	102.2mph	S/S
15	Rabat	Honda	43m 23.405s	54.953s	1m 57.215s	101.7mph	S/S
NC	Bradl	Aprilia	21m 42.599s	11 laps	1m 56.961s	101.6mph	S/S
NC	Baz	Ducati	15m 44.516s	14 laps	1m 56.562s	101.9mph	S/S
NC	Crutchlow	Honda	11m 44.221s	16 laps	1m 55.780s	102.5mph	H/M
NC	Iannone	Ducati	9m 44.391s	17 laps	1m 55.632s	103.0mph	S/S
NC	Hernandez	Ducati	2m 03.498s	21 laps	–	97.4mph	H/S

CHAMPIONSHIP

	Rider	Nation	Team	Points
1	Lorenzo	SPA	Movistar Yamaha MotoGP	25
2	Dovizioso	ITA	Ducati Team	20
3	Marquez	SPA	Repsol Honda Team	16
4	Rossi	ITA	Movistar Yamaha MotoGP	13
5	Pedrosa	SPA	Repsol Honda Team	11
6	Viñales	SPA	Team Suzuki ECSTAR	10
7	Espargaro P	SPA	Monster Yamaha Tech 3	9
8	Smith	GBR	Monster Yamaha Tech 3	8
9	Barbera	SPA	Avintia Racing	7
10	Redding	GBR	OCTO Pramac Yakhnich	6
11	Espargaro A	SPA	Team Suzuki ECSTAR	5
12	Laverty	IRL	Aspar Team MotoGP	4
13	Bautista	SPA	Aprilia Racing Team Gresini	3
14	Miller	AUS	Estrella Galicia 0,0 Marc VDS	2
15	Rabat	SPA	Estrella Galicia 0,0 Marc VDS	1

11 ALEIX ESPARGARO
After a crash-strewn race weekend, including in Qualifying 1, his crew threw some major changes into the bike and Aleix was able to make up a few places on his qualifying position.

12 EUGENE LAVERTY
A new engine made all the difference and the Ulsterman recovered from a tricky first-lap encounter with Baz to win an entertaining fight with Miller and Bautista.

13 ALVARO BAUTISTA
A decent début for the new bike. Alvaro was punted to the back of the field in the first corner but was able to recover and get into the points, passing his team-mate and the Marc VDS Hondas.

14 JACK MILLER
Still severely handicapped by his ankle injury from pre-season so delighted to finish full race distance. Made a small mistake on the last lap that cost him two places.

15 TITO RABAT
Not an easy introduction to MotoGP. Happy to make the distance and collect a point but a little disconcerted by the gap to the leaders.

DID NOT FINISH

STEFAN BRADL
Faster than he'd been in qualifying and very happy until half distance when he slid out at Turn 15.

LORIS BAZ
Looking good and making up positions but started having problems front and rear. Tried to compensate but lost the front at Turn 2.

CAL CRUTCHLOW
Cut the motor late as he came to the grid which meant the software didn't know where the bike was on track. Under the circumstances, making it to the seventh lap was a minor miracle.

ANDREA IANNONE
Looked the Ducati rider most likely to win and was running at the front when he touched a white line and lost the front.

YONNY HERNANDEZ
Not a happy weekend. Had problems through practice with tyres and then crashed in warm-up. His race was ended by a sensor failing.

DID NOT RACE

DANILO PETRUCCI
The right hand damaged in pre-season testing proved not to be up to racing yet.

ARGENTINA
ROUND 2

GRAN PREMIO MOTUL DE LA REPÚBLICA
TERMAS DE RÍO HONDO

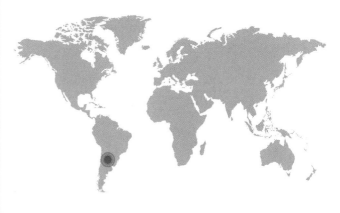

A RACE OF TWO HALVES

Marc Marquez won as Andrea Iannone handed rostrum spots to Valentino Rossi and Dani Pedrosa

It was, of course, too good to last. Having come through the first race on their 'spec' tyres with reputation not just undamaged but enhanced, Michelin suffered the sort of public humiliation that comes with the territory. As the old saying goes: when things go well they're tyres; when things go badly they're Michelins. Or, not that long ago, Bridgestones.

The crisis was precipitated in the fourth Free Practice session when the rear tyre of Scott Redding's Ducati shed its tread, which smashed through the seat unit and left the rider with severe bruising to his back. There were similarities with Loris Baz's tyre failure at the Sepang test – private Ducati, heavy rider, fast circuit – but Michelin revealed that the first failure had definitely been caused by a puncture. Once Michelin had seen Redding's tyre, however, they withdrew both types of rear tyre because they used the same carcass construction.

The plan was instead to use a tyre of stiffer construction– the so-called 'safety tyre' that is always kept in reserve for occasions such as this – after testing it in warm-up. That idea was stymied by wet weather on Sunday morning, so Race Direction had to adjust their thinking again. In a repeat of the system used at Phillip Island in 2013, the race was shortened to 20 laps with a compulsory pitstop to change bikes during a three-lap window. That enabled riders to race safely on the tyres they had tested, albeit on what

ABOVE Aleix Espargaro and Cal Crutchlow sprint for their fallen machines

OPPOSITE TOP It was a good race for the new Aprilia as both bikes finished in the points with Stefan Bradl an impressive seventh

RIGHT Valentino Rossi lost ground after the bike swap but inherited second place when Andrea Iannone torpedoed his team-mate; Maverick Viñales was also a faller

turned out to be a treacherous, drying track.

On a happier note, the meeting started with Marc Marquez finally declaring that his 2015 collision with Valentino Rossi had been a racing incident stemming from a mistake of his own. By any sensible analysis, Marquez's crash was self-inflicted but the people around him were happy to let him carry on believing it was Rossi's fault. His public retraction was both gracious and welcome. This welcome return to reality coincided with the appointment of Carlo Fiorani as Honda's Motorcycle Racing Director of Communications, and the two events are probably linked. Valentino wasn't in such a conciliatory mood. Invited to condemn or at least comment on the booing of Marquez and Lorenzo in Qatar, he declined. It was this race 12 months previously that started the real bad blood between the two.

Marquez did all right in the race too, overhauling quick starters Jorge Lorenzo and Andrea Dovizioso and then dicing for the lead with Rossi. The Yamaha was clearly faster on to the straight but Marc again demonstrated that he alone can make the Honda competitive. He managed to lead into the pits and, thanks to his usual acrobatic bike change, took a few bike lengths out of Rossi and put Tito Rabat into the gap. Marc immediately opened up an advantage, one that Valentino couldn't recover after he got past Rabat. It was obvious that Rossi was nowhere near as happy with his second bike as with the one

'WITH THE SECOND
BIKE I HAD BIG
PROBLEMS WITH
THE REAR TYRE.
I DIDN'T HAVE
ANY FEELING AND
COULDN'T STOP
UNDER-BRAKING'

VALENTINO ROSSI

on which he'd started the race, and he was closed down by Dovizioso and Iannone on the factory Ducatis and an inspired Maverick Viñales, who was racing with a fully seamless gearbox for the first time on the Suzuki.

When the bike changes shook out, Viñales was third and looking set for his first rostrum until he fell victim to the track, running slightly wide and hitting a damp patch just three laps from the flag. Those patches had already taken a heavy toll, starting with Aleix Espargaro and Cal Crutchlow, who essayed synchronised get-offs and sprints to their bikes. The most significant victim was Lorenzo, who was running sixth, again unhappy in mixed conditions.

The factory Ducati riders, who had followed Viñales up to Rossi, were able to get past the Yamaha where the Suzuki hadn't and pull away. It looked over and done with: Marquez's first win of the year, two Ducatis on the rostrum, and Rossi fourth, just as he'd been in Qatar. In fact it looked that way right up to the final left/right corners. Then Iannone, who the previous year had lost third place here to a beautiful move from Crutchlow, tried to go inside Dovizioso in the right-hander but lost the front and scooped up his team-mate. It was a truly bone-headed move.

How crazy was this race? Eugene Laverty started the last lap in eighth place and ended it in fourth thanks not just to Iannone but also to Pol Espargaro and Hector Barbera, who looked

ABOVE Eugene Laverty survived the chaos of the last lap to finish a career-best fourth

BELOW Marc Marquez and team celebrate his first win of the year

WHY THE PANIC OVER TYRES?

The failure of the rear tyre on Scott Redding's Ducati during practice was severely embarrassing for Michelin.

Tyres are supposed to fail gradually, giving some warning to the rider, not suddenly. It isn't uncommon to see tyres looking very secondhand at the end of a race, even to the point of having small chunks of tread missing, but what happened to Redding's tyre was a catastrophic failure in which the

tread rubber peeled off in one piece.

To understand what happened, a few words about tyre construction may be helpful. A tyre has a carcass, often common to several 'different' tyres, and this acts as the container for the pressurised air that keeps the tyre inflated. Tread rubber is then fixed to the carcass with adhesive. The enemy of tyres is heat, specifically overheating of the carcass due to internal friction – which isn't the same as spinning a rear tyre, melting the surface of the tread and leaving a black line on the tarmac. When a carcass starts to overheat, the adhesive holding it and the tread rubber together starts to fail. Think of it as a safety fuse: it is designed to fail gradually so that the tread starts to lose small chunks of rubber.

The sudden failure is what would have really worried the Michelin men. It meant that the tyre had been operating outside the parameters they used in the design process. The most powerful motor in the field being used hard by one of the heaviest riders on

the grid may have been a factor, but clearly the energy those loads pumped into the tyre exceeded design limits. As soon as they realised that, Michelin had no option but to withdraw the tyres constructed on that carcass.

It is worth noting that Michelin hadn't been able to do any serious testing at the Termas de Río Hondo circuit. Colin Edwards did try, but didn't get any dry track time. This contrasts with Losail, the first race of the year, which hosted a full-scale test. Essentially, Michelin had no data with which to select tyres for this event.

like they were trying to ram each other but were, according to Eugene, 'like drunks trying to fight outside a pub at closing time' and never made contact. Another almost unbelievable result was that Dani Pedrosa, unnoticed, came home third, nearly 30 seconds behind the winner. A trip to the rostrum did not cheer him up at all, for his race was compromised at the start by another wild Iannone move in the first corner – Dani said it was 'the luckiest rostrum of my life'.

But to find real anger and despair, you needed to look no further than the Ducati pit, where the fixtures and fittings had been randomly rearranged. Dovizioso should have been second in the championship, just one point behind Marquez, but instead he found himself fifth, 18 points down. If Dovi was angry, Ducati management were incandescent. The contract that Iannone was due to sign the following week in Texas was torn up and his manager was told that talks would resume at Mugello. That was as good as a public sacking.

Who would have thought the sight of two Ducatis sliding to earth would be the enduring image of the Argentine Grand Prix rather than Scott Redding's self-destructing rear tyre?

RIGHT Andrea Dovizioso pushes his bike to the line for 13th place after being knocked off by his team-mate on the final corner

GRAN PREMIO MOTUL DE LA REPÚBLICA

TERMAS DE RÍO HONDO

ROUND 2
APRIL 3

RACE RESULTS

CIRCUIT LENGTH 2.986 miles

NO. OF LAPS 20

RACE DISTANCE 59.720 miles

WEATHER Dry, 25°C

TRACK TEMPERATURE 30°C

WINNER Marc Marquez

FASTEST LAP 1m 40.243s
107.2mph, Marc Marquez

LAP RECORD 1m 39.019s,
108.6mph, Valentino Rossi (2015)

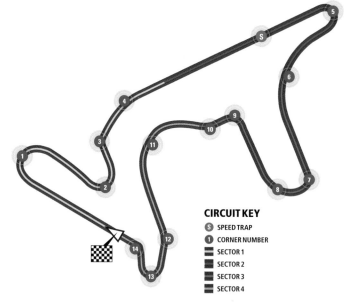

TYRE OPTIONS

SEVERITY RATING
<MILD   SEVERE>

FRONT COMPOUNDS
MEDIUM (M)
HARD (H)

REAR COMPOUNDS
MEDIUM (M)
HARD (H)

MICHELIN

CIRCUIT KEY
- (S) SPEED TRAP
- (1) CORNER NUMBER
- SECTOR 1
- SECTOR 2
- SECTOR 3
- SECTOR 4

QUALIFYING

	Rider	Nation	Motorcycle	Team	Time	Pole +
1	Marquez	SPA	Honda	Repsol Honda Team	1m 39.411s	
2	Rossi	ITA	Yamaha	Movistar Yamaha MotoGP	1m 39.786s	0.375s
3	Lorenzo	SPA	Yamaha	Movistar Yamaha MotoGP	1m 39.944s	0.533s
4	Pedrosa	SPA	Honda	Repsol Honda Team	1m 40.011s	0.600s
5	Dovizioso	ITA	Ducati	Ducati Team	1m 40.198s	0.787s
6	Iannone	ITA	Ducati	Ducati Team	1m 40.272s	0.861s
7	Viñales	SPA	Suzuki	Team Suzuki ECSTAR	1m 40.375s	0.964s
8	Barbera	SPA	Ducati	Avintia Racing	1m 40.524s	1.113s
9	Crutchlow	GBR	Honda	LCR Honda	1m 40.528s	1.117s
10	Espargaro P	SPA	Yamaha	Monster Yamaha Tech 3	1m 40.654s	1.243s
11	Espargaro A	SPA	Suzuki	Team Suzuki ECSTAR	1m 40.708s	1.297s
12	Smith	GBR	Yamaha	Monster Yamaha Tech 3	1m 40.893s	1.482s
13	Baz	FRA	Ducati	Avintia Racing	1m 40.744s	*0.192s
14	Redding	GBR	Ducati	OCTO Pramac Yakhnich	1m 40.750s	*0.198s
15	Miller	AUS	Honda	Estrella Galicia 0,0 Marc VDS	1m 40.881s	*0.329s
16	Bradl	GER	Aprilia	Aprilia Racing Team Gresini	1m 40.897s	*0.345s
17	Laverty	IRL	Ducati	Aspar Team MotoGP	1m 40.990s	*0.438s
18	Pirro	ITA	Ducati	OCTO Pramac Yakhnich	1m 41.116s	*0.564s
19	Rabat	SPA	Honda	Estrella Galicia 0,0 Marc VDS	1m 41.157s	*0.605s
20	Bautista	SPA	Aprilia	Aprilia Racing Team Gresini	1m 41.611s	*1.059s
21	Hernandez	COL	Ducati	Aspar Team MotoGP	1m 41.692s	*1.140s

* Gap with the fastest rider in the Q1 session

1 MARC MARQUEZ
Neck and neck with Rossi until the bike change, after which Marc pushed for five laps and opened up an advantage that couldn't be challenged. Revenge for Australia 2013. Outgunned onto the back straight by Yamaha and Ducati.

2 VALENTINO ROSSI
Indulged in a thrilling dice with Marquez until the bike change, after which he was held up by Rabat then never rediscovered the feeling he had with the first bike. Passed by the Ducatis on the penultimate lap but gifted second.

3 DANI PEDROSA
Looked less happy than anyone has ever done on a GP podium. Punted wide by Iannone on the very first corner then spent the race in the second group only to benefit from the Ducatis' last-corner coming together.

4 EUGENE LAVERTY
Career-best finish – and top Ducati. Started the last lap eighth and ended it in fourth, underlining the promise shown at the first race of the year with a great ride from distinctly average qualifying.

5 HECTOR BARBERA
Top independent after a barging match with Pol Espargaro on the last lap. Not a bad finish to a weekend that started with many set-up problems and a nasty dose of the flu.

6 POL ESPARGARO
Didn't enjoy losing out on top independent to Barbera but did beat his team-mate. Came off worse in the last-lap bout of handbags with Barbera and crossed the line doing a lot of arm waving.

7 STEFAN BRADL
After a tough first race, this was a real turn-around for rider and team. Changed bikes early, a good decision, and fast straight away with the second bike, but did not have same feeling with the rear tyre.

8 BRADLEY SMITH
Went to the back on the opening lap avoiding another rider then made six overtakes before the bike change. Made a guess at the setting, which didn't work on either bike.

9 TITO RABAT
The reigning Moto2 champion's first points in MotoGP in his first flag-to-flag race. Learned from a lap behind Marquez thanks to a late pit stop then from fighting with Crutchlow and Smith.

10 ALVARO BAUTISTA
Up with Laverty before crashing on his in-lap, remounting and then crashing again in pit lane. Pleasantly surprised to finish at all, let alone in the top ten.

11 ALEIX ESPARGARO
Crashed on the second lap but got the damaged bike to the changeover. Not as happy with the front of the second machine, and also starting to feel some pain from the crash. Another surprised points scorer.

LAP CHART

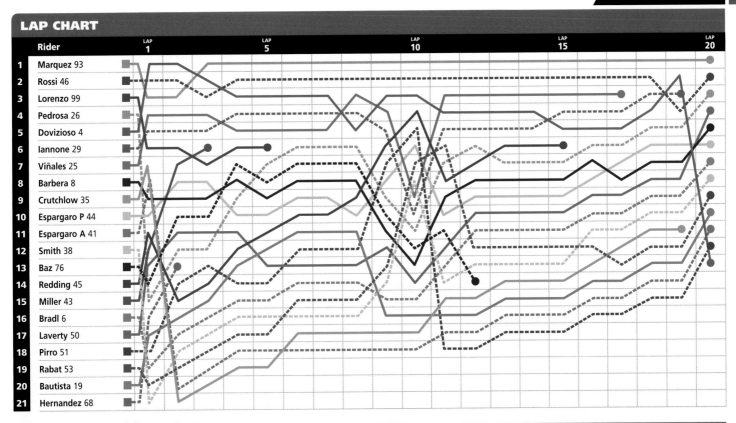

	Rider	LAP 1	LAP 5	LAP 10	LAP 15	LAP 20
1	Marquez 93					
2	Rossi 46					
3	Lorenzo 99					
4	Pedrosa 26					
5	Dovizioso 4					
6	Iannone 29					
7	Viñales 25					
8	Barbera 8					
9	Crutchlow 35					
10	Espargaro P 44					
11	Espargaro A 41					
12	Smith 38					
13	Baz 76					
14	Redding 45					
15	Miller 43					
16	Bradl 6					
17	Laverty 50					
18	Pirro 51					
19	Rabat 53					
20	Bautista 19					
21	Hernandez 68					

RACE

	Rider	Motorcycle	Race time	Time +	Fastest lap	Avg. speed	Tyres
1	Marquez	Honda	34m 13.628s		1m 40.243s	104.6mph	H/M
2	Rossi	Yamaha	34m 21.307s	7.679s	1m 40.635s	104.3mph	H/M
3	Pedrosa	Honda	34m 41.728s	28.100s	1m 41.609s	103.3mph	H/M
4	Laverty	Ducati	34m 50.170s	36.542s	1m 41.988s	102.8mph	H/M
5	Barbera	Ducati	34m 50.399s	36.711s	1m 41.535s	102.8mph	H/M
6	Espargaro P	Yamaha	34m 50.873s	37.245s	1m 41.822s	102.7mph	H/M
7	Bradl	Aprilia	34m 54.981s	41.353s	1m 41.951s	102.6mph	H/M
8	Smith	Yamaha	35m 04.337s	50.709s	1m 42.191s	102.2mph	M/M
9	Rabat	Honda	35m 04.611s	50.983s	1m 42.747s	102.2mph	H/M
10	Bautista	Aprilia	35m 15.016s	1m 01.388s	1m 42.313s	101.7mph	H/M
11	Espargaro A	Suzuki	35m 22.496s	1m 08.868s	1m 42.087s	101.3mph	M/H
12	Pirro	Ducati	35m 32.615s	1m 18.987s	1m 41.103s	100.8mph	H/M
13	Dovizioso	Ducati	35m 47.047s	1m 33.419s	1m 40.433s	100.1mph	H/M
NC	Iannone	Ducati	32m 38.879s	1 lap	1m 40.342s	104.3mph	H/M
NC	Crutchlow	Honda	33m 21.160s	1 lap	1m 41.167s	102.0mph	H/M
NC	Viñales	Suzuki	29m 15.756s	3 laps	1m 40.695s	104.1mph	M/M
NC	Redding	Ducati	26m 10.378s	5 laps	1m 41.414s	102.7mph	H/M
NC	Baz	Ducati	21m 23.722s	8 laps	1m 42.543s	100.5mph	H/M
NC	Lorenzo	Yamaha	8m 35.054s	15 laps	1m 41.695s	104.3mph	H/M
NC	Miller	Honda	5m 11.057s	17 laps	1m 41.898s	103.6mph	H/M
NC	Hernandez	Ducati	3m 30.785s	18 laps	1m 43.297s	102.0mph	H/M

CHAMPIONSHIP

	Rider	Nation	Team	Points
1	Marquez	SPA	Repsol Honda Team	41
2	Rossi	ITA	Movistar Yamaha MotoGP	33
3	Pedrosa	SPA	Repsol Honda Team	27
4	Lorenzo	SPA	Movistar Yamaha MotoGP	25
5	Dovizioso	ITA	Ducati Team	23
6	Espargaro P	SPA	Monster Yamaha Tech 3	19
7	Barbera	SPA	Avintia Racing	18
8	Laverty	IRL	Aspar Team MotoGP	17
9	Smith	GBR	Monster Yamaha Tech 3	16
10	Viñales	SPA	Team Suzuki ECSTAR	10
	Espargaro A	SPA	Team Suzuki ECSTAR	10
12	Bautista	SPA	Aprilia Racing Team Gresini	9
	Bradl	GER	Aprilia Racing Team Gresini	9
14	Rabat	SPA	Estrella Galicia 0,0 Marc VDS	8
15	Redding	GBR	OCTO Pramac Yakhnich	6
16	Pirro	ITA	OCTO Pramac Yakhnich	4
17	Miller	AUS	Estrella Galicia 0,0 Marc VDS	2

12 MICHELE PIRRO

Replaced the injured Petrucci and was running with his team-mate until the bike swap. In seventh but made a mistake and ran on at Turn 2, which put him to the back of the field.

13 ANDREA DOVIZIOSO

Pushed across the line after being torpedoed by his team-mate at the penultimate corner. Did everything right and should have been second again and gone to Texas one point behind Marquez.

DID NOT FINISH

ANDREA IANNONE

Tried to pass his team-mate at the final right, lost the front and scooped up Dovi. Probably a move that cost him his job.

CAL CRUTCHLOW

Crashed twice, first when unsighted by Lorenzo's spray on lap two and then, after a superb comeback, out of eighth place on the last lap.

MAVERICK VIÑALES

Looked set for his first podium in MotoGP when he fell out of third only a few laps

SCOTT REDDING

Still not comfortable with qualifying but much better than in Qatar, had just passed Pedrosa with only five laps to go when his engine lost power. Will be remembered for the tyre incident in practice.

LORIS BAZ

Started well and was ahead of his team-mate when they swapped bikes. Nothing worked on the second bike and he retired

from the flag. Another victim of the patchy tarmac at Turn 1.

JORGE LORENZO

Did not look happy all weekend. A brilliant start followed by fading to seventh, then caught out by a damp patch at Turn 1.

JACK MILLER

Looking good and passed Lorenzo before crashing out at Turn 3 on lap four.

YONNY HERNANDEZ

The first victim of Turn 1's damp patches. Yonny crashed third time round.

– for only the second time in his life.

DID NOT RACE

DANILO PETRUCCI

Recovering from second operation on the hand broken in pre-season testing. Replaced by Pirro.

RED BULL GRAND PRIX OF THE AMERICAS
CIRCUIT OF THE AMERICAS

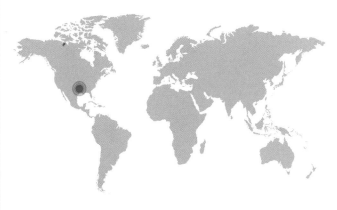

BACK TO EARTH

Marc Marquez continued his winning streak on American tracks as most of his championship rivals fell

If you ever need evidence of just what a remarkable rider Marc Marquez is, watch him in Texas. He has now won all four races he has contested at the Circuit of the Americas by margins of three seconds, twenty-one seconds, two-and-a-third seconds and now six seconds. He also started from pole position every time.

This may have been the most impressive victory of the lot. It was scored on brand new tyres flown in for the event and on a bike that, contrary to everything you expect of HRC, was still very difficult to ride and well down on acceleration. That doesn't sound like a recipe for success on a very technical circuit with three first-gear corners and the longest straight of the year. The second Honda on the grid was Cal Crutchlow's satellite bike in sixth spot, the small matter of one second slower. Crutchlow was clear that he had put the Honda where it deserved to be, so the one second was down to Marquez and nothing else.

Marc himself said all the right things about expecting the Yamahas and Ducatis to be closer than in previous years, and the fact that the factory Yamahas were beside him on the front row seemed to support that assumption. But we should have known that in this year of shocks and surprises the assumption would be short-lived.

Jorge Lorenzo did manage to get the holeshot but couldn't get his bike stopped for the first corner and then had the same problem in the slow corner on to the back straight. Apart from

ABOVE The fight for second place before Dani Pedrosa took out Andrea Dovizioso

OPPOSITE Marc Marquez marches on to yet another win on an American circuit

RIGHT Suzuki had their best result since returning to MotoGP; fourth and fifth places

those couple of moments when Jorge got to the front, Marc was never headed. It took Lorenzo five laps to fight his way up to second place and when he got there Marquez was already over two seconds up the road. That gap never came down and it looked as if Jorge's problems were instead in his wake, in the shape of Andrea Dovizioso and surprise package Dani Pedrosa.

Valentino Rossi was already out. He had a bad start because, he later said, he overheated the clutch, which explained why he looked distinctly short of top speed. He was back in fifth place on the third lap when he lost the front at Turn 2. It was his fault, he said, but showed that you could not afford to make even the smallest mistake with Michelin's front tyres.

Valentino was far from the only rider to make such a mistake but it was Turn 1 that claimed most victims, probably with a contribution from a ridge just where you get on the brakes. Cal Crutchlow and Bradley Smith fell there at almost the same time, and Cal was involved in his second competitive sprint to a fallen bike in two races. Smith thought there was something on the track – and indeed there had been an engine blow-up in a support race – but Crutchlow wasn't so sure. Both men got back on track but didn't score any points, Smith going so far as to prove his theory by falling a second time at the same corner.

Andrea Dovizioso was even more unlucky, and given what happened to him in Argentina

'I LOST CONTROL AND TRIED TO SAVE THE CRASH, BUT I ENDED UP GOING DOWN AND TAKING DOVIZIOSO WITH ME. IT'S A SHAME TO HAVE FINISHED THE RACE IN THAT WAY AND I FEEL ESPECIALLY BAD FOR ANDREA'

DANI PEDROSA

LEFT Andrea Dovizioso's luck didn't improve; he was taken out by a crashing bike for the second race in succession

ABOVE Cal Crutchlow's season had still to yield a point. He fell and remounted to finish 16th

unbelievably so. He ran a little wide into Turn 1 while in close contact with Lorenzo only to be skittled by Pedrosa. It looked as if Dani was sucked in by Dovi's small mistake and was also going a little wide when he locked the front brake as he crossed the ridge. The Honda slammed into the left side of the Ducati frighteningly hard and Dovi was lucky to escape without a nasty injury.

Pedrosa's first move was to run not to his bike but to Andrea to check on his welfare. Later, still in his leathers, Dani walked down pitlane – without his crash helmet – to the Ducati pit to offer his apologies. The discreet handshakes and pats on the back from Ducati personnel told their own story. 'He isn't a kamikaze who tries to overtake every corner,' said a forgiving Dovi. At some point he also dropped the phrase 'unlike last week' into the conversation in a less than forgiving manner. The subject of this acerbic comment, Andrea Iannone, also came up with a pertinent remark. He rode a sensible, controlled race and was rewarded with third place. 'It was,' he said, 'the minimum required.' Quite.

Behind Iannone came the Suzukis, with Maverick Viñales fourth in front of his more experienced team-mate Aleix Espargaro. It was the team's best result since the return to MotoGP, and especially impressive since Viñales suffered tyre troubles in the second half of the race. With rumours about Lorenzo moving to Ducati for 2017 hardening into accepted fact, Maverick's stock was rising. Next, in sixth and first independent, came Scott Redding, gaining some recompense for his recent traumas.

Marquez's tenth win (in all classes) on American soil gave him a 21-point championship lead thanks in part to both factory Yamaha riders already having donated him a zero-score race. The question now, given the nature of the Honda, was when rather than if Marc would have a similarly unpleasant experience. At the end of 2015, he'd said that he'd learned the need to accept third or fourth places if he couldn't win. He did that in the first race of 2016 but now he appeared to have forgotten.

It was well understood before the start of the year that the new regulations and tyres would conjure up some surprises. There'd already been a few, and there was no reason to expect them to stop once back in Europe.

BELOW Everything is bigger in Texas, especially the hats

TYRES – AGAIN

The fall-out from Michelin's problems in Argentina continued. There was the distraction of some sniping from Valentino Rossi and Jorge Lorenzo, who didn't appreciate having to use tyres of stiffer contruction because of a problem that they saw as a Ducati one.

However, the tyre failure that befell Scott Redding at the Termas de Río Hondo circuit inevitably meant that Michelin had to act. Given the trans-Atlantic distances involved, the company did so with amazing speed. In the week between the races, new tyres were designed and manufactured in sufficient quantity to ensure that the Texan race went ahead on schedule, although it was a close-run thing. Enough soft rear tyres arrived in time for the first day of free practice and then the mediums turned up on Saturday morning, more than a few of them brought as hand luggage.

The new tyres had softer tread rubber built on a stiffer carcass – the safety-first response to Redding's incident. As work had to get going before Redding's failed tyre could be shipped back to France for analysis at Michelin's headquarters in Clermont-Ferrand, the new design was based on the extra tyre – the so-called safety tyre – that is taken to every track as a contingency in case of dire emergencies. Michelin tailored their new tyres for the Circuit of The Americas, another track where the weather had prevented any serious testing, so a race time just over ten seconds slower than the previous year's and a best lap time just over a second slower can hardly be regarded as a disaster.

Ironically, it was the front tyre that got all the attention on race day, with Marquez crediting his Michelin engineer's insistence on using the soft front as vital to his win.

RED BULL GRAND PRIX OF THE AMERICAS
CIRCUIT OF THE AMERICAS
ROUND **3**
APRIL 10

RACE RESULTS

CIRCUIT LENGTH 3.426 miles

NO. OF LAPS 21

RACE DISTANCE 71.938 miles

WEATHER Dry, 26°C

TRACK TEMPERATURE 34°C

WINNER Marc Marquez

FASTEST LAP 2m 04.682s, 98.9mph, Marc Marquez

LAP RECORD 2m 03.575s, 99.8mph, Marc Marquez (2014)

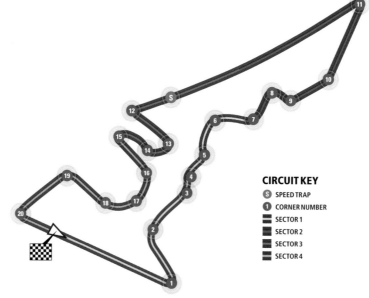

CIRCUIT KEY
- Ⓢ SPEED TRAP
- ① CORNER NUMBER
- ▬ SECTOR 1
- ▬ SECTOR 2
- ▬ SECTOR 3
- ▬ SECTOR 4

TYRE OPTIONS

CENTRE / LEFT / RIGHT
TYRE

SEVERITY RATING
< MILD — SEVERE >

FRONT COMPOUNDS
SOFT (S)
MEDIUM (M)
HARD (H)

REAR COMPOUNDS
SOFT (S)
MEDIUM (M)

MICHELIN

QUALIFYING

	Rider	Nation	Motorcycle	Team	Time	Pole +
1	Marquez	SPA	Honda	Repsol Honda Team	2m 03.188s	
2	Lorenzo	SPA	Yamaha	Movistar Yamaha MotoGP	2m 03.257s	0.069s
3	Rossi	ITA	Yamaha	Movistar Yamaha MotoGP	2m 03.644s	0.456s
4	Iannone	ITA	Ducati	Ducati Team	2m 03.913s	0.725s
5	Viñales	SPA	Suzuki	Team Suzuki ECSTAR	2m 04.247s	1.059s
6	Crutchlow	GBR	Honda	LCR Honda	2m 04.265s	1.077s
7	Dovizioso	ITA	Ducati	Ducati Team	2m 04.339s	1.151s
8	Pedrosa	SPA	Honda	Repsol Honda Team	2m 04.379s	1.191s
9	Espargaro A	SPA	Suzuki	Team Suzuki ECSTAR	2m 04.408s	1.220s
10	Redding	GBR	Ducati	OCTO Pramac Yakhnich	2m 04.485s	1.297s
11	Smith	GBR	Yamaha	Monster Yamaha Tech 3	2m 04.988s	1.800s
12	Baz	FRA	Ducati	Avintia Racing	2m 05.159s	1.971s
13	Espargaro P	SPA	Yamaha	Monster Yamaha Tech 3	2m 04.867s	*0.127s
14	Barbera	SPA	Ducati	Avintia Racing	2m 04.944s	*0.204s
15	Laverty	IRL	Ducati	Aspar Team MotoGP	2m 05.425s	*0.685s
16	Bradl	GER	Aprilia	Aprilia Racing Team Gresini	2m 05.625s	*0.885s
17	Pirro	ITA	Ducati	OCTO Pramac Yakhnich	2m 05.702s	*0.962s
18	Hernandez	COL	Ducati	Aspar Team MotoGP	2m 06.029s	*1.289s
19	Bautista	SPA	Aprilia	Aprilia Racing Team Gresini	2m 06.049s	*1.309s
20	Rabat	SPA	Honda	Estrella Galicia 0,0 Marc VDS	2m 06.562s	*1.822s
21	Miller	AUS	Honda	Estrella Galicia 0,0 Marc VDS	2m 05.684s	1.943s

* Gap with the fastest rider in the Q1 session

1 MARC MARQUEZ
Yet another victory on American soil, his tenth, and his fourth from pole at COTA. Needless to say, another lights-to-flag win with the fastest lap for good measure. And he wasn't pressed at any time in practice or the race.

2 JORGE LORENZO
Got over a big crash in warm-up to take the holeshot but immediately ran wide and dropped to fourth. Understood that the job was not to crash again, as opposed to catching Marquez.

3 ANDREA IANONNE
Penalised by a row of the grid after Argentina but rode a sensible race after a bad start. Stayed calm as others crashed, overtook Aleix Espargaro's Suzuki and lapped very close to Lorenzo's pace.

4 MAVERICK VIÑALES
Recovered from a bad start to duel with his team-mate despite rear tyre performance dropping off steeply and preventing him fighting for the rostrum.

5 ALEIX ESPARGARO
Back on the 2015 chassis and a lot happier. Knew he had to take advantage of the softer rear tyre at the start of the race, so charged early and then tried to defend his position.

6 SCOTT REDDING
Happy to finish as top independent despite losing a second a lap when the front tyre dropped off. Kept his focus, changed his riding style and made up for the disappointment of the previous race.

7 POL ESPARGARO
Not his best weekend but still consolidated fourth place in the championship table – far and away the best independent. Found it impossible to follow the others with a soft front tyre and a full fuel load but fast and consistent later.

8 MICHELE PIRRO
Improved throughout the weekend after a difficult start. Passed Barbera at three-quarters distance, then closed on Pol Espargaro but couldn't pass.

9 HECTOR BARBERA
Thought he may have been over-confident after Argentina, and then suffered from arm pump after just five laps.

10 STEFAN BRADL
Very happy with progress with the electronics, surprisingly fast mid-race, then defended his position cleverly for a second consecutive 10th place.

11 ALVARO BAUTISTA
In the points again despite getting a knock from Baz on the first lap, which meant Alvaro had to use up his tyres early in the race to get back to a respectable position.

12 EUGENE LAVERTY
Happy to finish in the points on a day when many didn't. His main problem in a difficult race was the right side of the front tyre.

LAP CHART

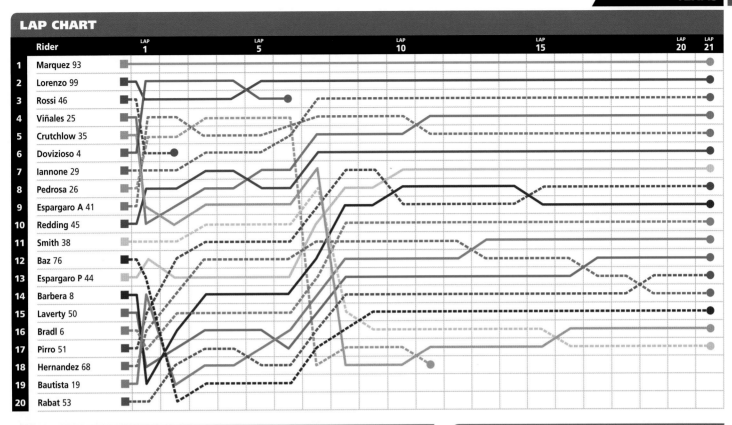

	Rider						
1	Marquez 93						
2	Lorenzo 99						
3	Rossi 46						
4	Viñales 25						
5	Crutchlow 35						
6	Dovizioso 4						
7	Iannone 29						
8	Pedrosa 26						
9	Espargaro A 41						
10	Redding 45						
11	Smith 38						
12	Baz 76						
13	Espargaro P 44						
14	Barbera 8						
15	Laverty 50						
16	Bradl 6						
17	Pirro 51						
18	Hernandez 68						
19	Bautista 19						
20	Rabat 53						

RACE

	Rider	Motorcycle	Race time	Time +	Fastest lap	Avg. speed	Tyres
1	Marquez	Honda	43m 57.945s		2m 04.682s	98.1mph	S/M
2	Lorenzo	Yamaha	44m 04.052s	6.107s	2m 04.908s	97.9mph	M/M
3	Iannone	Ducati	44m 08.892s	10.947s	2m 05.275s	97.7mph	M/M
4	Viñales	Suzuki	44m 16.367s	18.422s	2m 05.479s	97.4mph	M/S
5	Espargaro A	Suzuki	44m 18.656s	20.711s	2m 05.734s	97.4mph	S/S
6	Redding	Ducati	44m 26.906s	28.961s	2m 06.004s	97.1mph	S/M
7	Espargaro P	Yamaha	44m 30.057s	32.112s	2m 06.254s	96.9mph	S/S
8	Pirro	Ducati	44m 30.702s	32.757s	2m 06.494s	96.9mph	M/S
9	Barbera	Ducati	44m 32.537s	34.592s	2m 06.199s	96.9mph	S/S
10	Bradl	Aprilia	44m 38.156s	40.211s	2m 06.471s	96.7mph	S/S
11	Bautista	Aprilia	44m 43.368s	45.423s	2m 06.866s	96.5mph	S/S
12	Laverty	Ducati	44m 45.072s	47.127s	2m 07.208s	96.4mph	M/M
13	Rabat	Honda	44m 45.371s	47.426s	2m 06.988s	96.4mph	S/S
14	Hernandez	Ducati	44m 49.135s	51.190s	2m 06.494s	96.3mph	S/M
15	Baz	Ducati	45m 10.874s	1m 12.929s	2m 06.582s	95.5mph	M/M
16	Crutchlow	Honda	45m 17.197s	1m 19.252s	2m 05.910s	95.3mph	M/M
17	Smith	Yamaha	45m 25.981s	1m 28.036s	2m 06.042s	94.9mph	M/S
NC	Pedrosa	Honda	24m 34.568s	10 laps	2m 04.950s	92.0mph	M/S
NC	Dovizioso	Ducati	12m 34.320s	15 laps	2m 05.181s	98.1mph	M/M
NC	Rossi	Yamaha	4m 14.030s	19 laps	2m 05.801s	97.1mph	M/M

CHAMPIONSHIP

	Rider	Nation	Team	Points
1	Marquez	SPA	Repsol Honda Team	66
2	Lorenzo	SPA	Movistar Yamaha MotoGP	45
3	Rossi	ITA	Movistar Yamaha MotoGP	33
4	Espargaro P	SPA	Monster Yamaha Tech 3	28
5	Pedrosa	SPA	Repsol Honda Team	27
6	Barbera	SPA	Avintia Racing	25
7	Dovizioso	ITA	Ducati Team	23
8	Viñales	SPA	Team Suzuki ECSTAR	23
9	Laverty	IRL	Aspar Team MotoGP	21
10	Espargaro A	SPA	Team Suzuki ECSTAR	21
11	Iannone	ITA	Ducati Team	16
	Redding	GBR	OCTO Pramac Yakhnich	16
	Smith	GBR	Monster Yamaha Tech 3	16
14	Bradl	GER	Aprilia Racing Team Gresini	15
15	Bautista	SPA	Aprilia Racing Team Gresini	14
16	Pirro	ITA	OCTO Pramac Yakhnich	12
17	Rabat	SPA	Estrella Galicia 0,0 Marc VDS	11
18	Miller	AUS	Estrella Galicia 0,0 Marc VDS	2
19	Hernandez	COL	Aspar Team MotoGP	2
20	Baz	FRA	Avintia Racing	1

13 TITO RABAT
Again managed to fight for places rather than ride round on his own, but still disconcerted by the way the front was moving in the early laps.

14 YONNY HERNANDEZ
Fighting with Pol Espargaro and Hector Barbera for the first third of the race but slowed when he suffered tyre degradation. Nevertheless, relieved to score his first finish – and points – of the year.

15 LORIS BAZ
His first point of the season thanks to remounting following a crash at the first corner of the second lap. Not bad with a bent swing arm and a stub of a gear pedal.

16 CAL CRUTCHLOW
Fell and remounted in sync with Smith after running wide at Turn 1 while lying seventh; blamed having to push to make up for his Honda's lack of acceleration.

17 BRADLEY SMITH
Lying eighth when he fell at Turn 1, he thought because of something on track. Remounted and finished with no gear lever and no anti-wheelie.

DID NOT FINISH

DANI PEDROSA
Looking much better than in practice and closing fast on the dice for second place when he lost the front in Turn 1 and his bike scooped up Dovizioso.

ANDREA DOVIZIOSO
Shadowing Lorenzo in third as Pedrosa closed, only to yet again have somebody else's accident, this time Dani's. Lucky not to be injured by the sliding Honda.

VALENTINO ROSSI
Consecutive front-row grid positions for the first time since the end of 2013 followed by a bad start – Vale said he over-heated the clutch. He crashed on lap three when he lost the front at Turn 2.

DID NOT RACE

JACK MILLER
Forced to withdraw after a big crash in the first free practice cracked bones in his right foot and aggravated his already damaged ankle.

DANILO PETRUCCI
Still recovering from the operation on his right hand after Qatar. Again replaced by Pirro.

GRAN PREMIO RED BULL DE ESPAÑA
CIRCUITO DE JEREZ

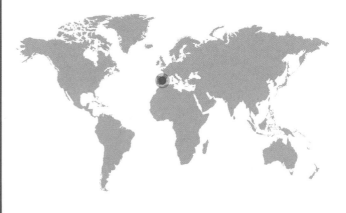

OLD DOG, OLD TRICKS

Valentino Rossi added another chapter to his legend with a weekend that made it clear he was still a championship contender

A new MotoGP control tyre means everyone has to cope with new circumstances at nearly every race. Not surprisingly, those who've been around longest – in the saddle or in the garage – tend to solve those problems more quickly. Valentino Rossi and his crew have been around longer than most.

Jerez's puzzle was set by worn-out tarmac that changes characteristics radically for small variations in temperature and gets extremely slick at 40 degrees surface temperature. It was at least five degrees above that threshold on race day, much hotter than at any other time in the weekend, so many people had to make a lot of set-up decisions without any experience in these conditions of the new stiffer-construction Michelin rear tyre introduced at the previous race.

The men who coped best were in the garage of number 46. Their rider put on a magnificent demonstration, rolling back the years with pole position, a lights-to-flag win plus fastest lap. Others complained about the stiffness of the rear tyre, the mismatch with the front, and especially wheelspin – even in a straight line in top gear. Rossi and his crew had a handle on things right from the first free practice session. The evidence was a smiling, exuberant Valentino who appeared to know right from the start that he was on to a good thing. Pole position appeared to be a by-product of preparing a race set-up to cope with the conditions he knew were coming on race day.

ABOVE Pol Espargaro was top independent team rider for the second time in four races

RIGHT Valentino Rossi leads into the first corner on his way to a dominant victory

It was quite astonishing to go to the record books and discover that the last time Rossi was on pole here was in 2005 and this was only his fourth pole since the start of the 2010 season.

How difficult was the track? Rossi's fastest lap of the race was one-and-a-quarter seconds slower than Lorenzo's lap record, set 12 months previously, and the race was over 30 seconds slower than the previous year's. The good news was that there wasn't one crash in the race.

Frankly, Valentino made it look easy. Jorge Lorenzo gave chase but was reduced to leading the complaints about the rear tyre spinning, saying he thought he could have won by a distance without it. Marc Marquez, now the only one of the championship contenders to have scored in every race, stopped pressing at about half distance and settled for third place. He did have the decency to admit that he had an inner struggle before making that decision but it was another indication that the new-model Marc was indeed willing to take the long view when winning wasn't possible.

Ducati had a terrible time, although Andrea Iannone did well to ride through to seventh from bad qualifying and a terrible start that put him back in 14th place at the end of the first lap. Yet again Andrea Dovizioso's luck was out, to put it mildly. This time a failure in the cooling circuit resulted in water being sprayed directly on his back tyre. 'If he had a duck,' said one paddock wit, 'it would sink.'

At Suzuki Aleix Espargaro again beat his team-mate, although Maverick Viñales also reverted to the 2015 chassis. It didn't look as if the old order would be challenged any time soon.

Valentino was cautious about his immediate prospects. Just because he won at Jerez, it didn't mean that he could win at Le Mans or Mugello. There were, he pointed out, so many new variables this season that every weekend was different. He was willing to admit, though, that he had 'grown up' on Michelins and understood them. All that experience helps, of course, but it isn't of any use without the motivation to apply it. Yet again Rossi has adapted his riding style to suit the new tyres, this time with the help of his training ranch, and there was the sight of ex-250 champ and 500 GP winner Luca Cadalora as his new spotter. Complete with incongruous baseball hat with 'COACH' on the front, Cadalora spends his time watching what Valentino and, maybe more importantly, his competition are doing in critical areas of the track and feeding back information and suggestion to the rider. Cadalora was never a member of Valentino's circle of close

LEFT Michele Pirro stood in for the injured Danilo Petrucci for the third race in a row

BELOW Jerez wasn't an easy proposition for Honda; both Marc VDS riders finished out of the points

LORENZO TO DUCATI FOR 2017

The rumour about Jorge Lorenzo going to Ducati has been a regular biennial story. This time round the whispers evolved into certainty, and before the Spanish GP weekend it was confirmed that Jorge would indeed be leaving Yamaha after nine years.

With all major players at the end of their contracts in 2016, some rapid decisions had to be made. Yamaha gave both of their riders an early deadline, hence Rossi's announcement that he was staying for two more years and Lorenzo having to go public with his decision. Why did he decide to jump off the bike on which he has won titles and is regarded as the best on the grid?

The Yamaha factory have always made great play of the fact that they treat their riders equally, although there's no denying that the VR46 organisation is now inextricably linked to the company. Lin Jarvis, MD of Yamaha Racing, implied that one reason Lorenzo was off to Ducati was to have number-one status. He said Yamaha had made the best offer they could, but it wasn't enough.

There's no doubt that Lorenzo's new contract is worth an awful lot of money – probably more than £10 million. Undoubtedly he will be the number one and the Ducati factory will do anything they can to keep him happy. The presence of Gigi Dall'Igna, who worked with Jorge when he won his 250cc titles for Aprilia, would also have been a factor, as would the bike's competitive performance. In addition there's the small matter of Casey Stoner's role as test rider. He and Jorge have always got on, and the Aussie's lap times offer further confirmation of the Desmosedici's potential. Then there's the unquantifiable matter of the need for a new challenge. Winning on a bike that Rossi couldn't master, maybe?

friends – he's from Modena and of a different generation – but his presence was just another indicator of how Rossi uses every means at his disposal to gain even the slightest advantage over his competition. Valentino still trains hard, both on and off the bike, and still delights in winning. It's a drug that he cannot wean himself off. That was abundantly clear on Friday when he pulled an enormous wheelie down the back straight and arrived back at his pit garage with an enormous grin on his face to talk animatedly with his crew. He knew victory was possible and it excited him just as much as it had done when he first raced.

Impossible as it seems, Valentino set a few new personal records and marks at Jerez, even though he is now 37 years old. He became the oldest man to start from pole since Jeremy McWilliams gave two-strokes their last hurrah at Phillip Island in 2002, and his win was the first time he has ever led every lap of a race off pole position. Yeah, I know. That doesn't seem possible after 334 GP starts and 113 victories, but it's a fact.

As for Ago's all-time record of 122 wins, nobody seemed willing to talk about that. Not yet.

RIGHT The combination of new Michelin tyres and worn-out tarmac posed questions to which only Valentino Rossi had the answers

GRAN PREMIO RED BULL DE ESPAÑA
CIRCUITO DE JEREZ
ROUND 4
APRIL 24

OFFICIAL TIMEKEEPER

TYRE OPTIONS

CENTRE
LEFT   RIGHT
TYRE

SEVERITY RATING
<MILD   SEVERE>

FRONT COMPOUNDS
SOFT (S)
MEDIUM (M)
HARD (H)

REAR COMPOUNDS
SOFT (S)
MEDIUM (M)

MICHELIN

RACE RESULTS

CIRCUIT LENGTH 2.748 miles

NO. OF LAPS 27

RACE DISTANCE 74.205 miles

WEATHER Dry, 25°C

TRACK TEMPERATURE 40°C

WINNER Valentino Rossi

FASTEST LAP 1m 40.090s, 98.8mph, Valentino Rossi

LAP RECORD 1m 38.735s, 100.2mph, Jorge Lorenzo (2015)

CIRCUIT KEY
- **S** SPEED TRAP
- **1** CORNER NUMBER
- SECTOR 1
- SECTOR 2
- SECTOR 3
- SECTOR 4

Circuit labels: Expo-92, Michelin, Álex Crivillé, Ferrari, Jorge Martinez Aspar, Peluqui, Ángel Nieto, Ducados, Sito Pons, Dry Sack

QUALIFYING

	Rider	Nation	Motorcycle	Team	Time	Pole +
1	Rossi	ITA	Yamaha	Movistar Yamaha MotoGP	1m 38.736s	
2	Lorenzo	SPA	Yamaha	Movistar Yamaha MotoGP	1m 38.858s	0.122s
3	Marquez	SPA	Honda	Repsol Honda Team	1m 38.891s	0.155s
4	Dovizioso	ITA	Ducati	Ducati Team	1m 39.580s	0.844s
5	Viñales	SPA	Suzuki	Team Suzuki ECSTAR	1m 39.581s	0.845s
6	Espargaro A	SPA	Suzuki	Team Suzuki ECSTAR	1m 39.588s	0.852s
7	Pedrosa	SPA	Honda	Repsol Honda Team	1m 39.678s	0.942s
8	Espargaro P	SPA	Yamaha	Monster Yamaha Tech 3	1m 39.720s	0.984s
9	Barbera	SPA	Ducati	Avintia Racing	1m 39.742s	1.006s
10	Crutchlow	GBR	Honda	LCR Honda	1m 39.881s	1.145s
11	Iannone	ITA	Ducati	Ducati Team	1m 40.054s	1.318s
12	Baz	FRA	Ducati	Avintia Racing	1m 40.184s	1.448s
13	Bautista	SPA	Aprilia	Aprilia Racing Team Gresini	1m 40.239s	*0.332s
14	Smith	GBR	Yamaha	Monster Yamaha Tech 3	1m 40.242s	*0.335s
15	Laverty	IRL	Ducati	Aspar Team MotoGP	1m 40.292s	*0.385s
16	Hernandez	COL	Ducati	Aspar Team MotoGP	1m 40.335s	*0.428s
17	Redding	GBR	Ducati	OCTO Pramac Yakhnich	1m 40.595s	*0.688s
18	Bradl	GER	Aprilia	Aprilia Racing Team Gresini	1m 40.835s	*0.928s
19	Miller	AUS	Honda	Estrella Galicia 0,0 Marc VDS	1m 40.968s	*1.061s
20	Pirro	ITA	Ducati	OCTO Pramac Yakhnich	1m 40.985s	*1.078s
21	Rabat	SPA	Honda	Estrella Galicia 0,0 Marc VDS	1m 41.039s	*1.132s

* Gap with the fastest rider in the Q1 session

1 VALENTINO ROSSI
Started from pole for the first time at Jerez since 2005. Only lost the lead for a few corners then pulled out a gap of nearly three seconds before slowing and protecting his advantage. Uncharacteristic wheelies on Friday suggested Valentino knew early on that he had the answers.

2 JORGE LORENZO
Felt he had been prevented from fighting for the lead by wheelspin on the back straight in the closing stages. Nevertheless, happier with the bike than he'd been in Texas and with his 100th premier-class podium.

3 MARC MARQUEZ
The elevated race-day temperature reduced front-tyre performance on the Honda, so after a few big moments Marc settled for 16 points. A perfect race, he said, would have got him second place.

4 DANI PEDROSA
Qualified badly but found his old ability to start well. Third early on until passed by Marquez, after which Dani conserved his tyre and finished exactly where he expected to after a lonely race.

5 ALEIX ESPARGARO
A distinct improvement on the first races of the year. Worked on race pace but still frustrated by lack of grip when track temperature goes up and tyre wears.

6 MAVERICK VIÑALES
Like his team-mate, frustrated by lack of rear grip. The team was convinced it was a mechanical problem, not electronics, so the Monday test was vital.

7 ANDREA IANNONE
A terrible start saw him 14th at the end of the first lap, after which he rode well and without error – important to him – to salvage something from a weekend on which Ducatis weren't competitive.

8 POL ESPARGARO
Top independent in qualifying and the race thanks mainly to a cautious start to ensure he had some rear-tyre grip in the final laps. The strategy worked but Pol couldn't hold off Iannone in the closing stages.

9 EUGENE LAVERTY
Benefited from a new clutch and for once got a superb start. Rated his second top-ten finish of the year as better than his fourth in Argentina. Was closing on Pol Espargaro when the new clutch started slipping six laps from the flag.

10 HECTOR BARBERA
Handicapped by the traction control cutting in too early on every corner exit from the second lap onwards. Still top Ducati in the points standings.

11 CAL CRUTCHLOW
Points at last! Uncharacteristically happy with 11th place, especially as Cal thought he had the pace to fight with Pedrosa. Particularly puzzled by the lack of pace in the last ten laps. Used sixth, not fifth, on straight to avoid wheelspin.

LAP CHART

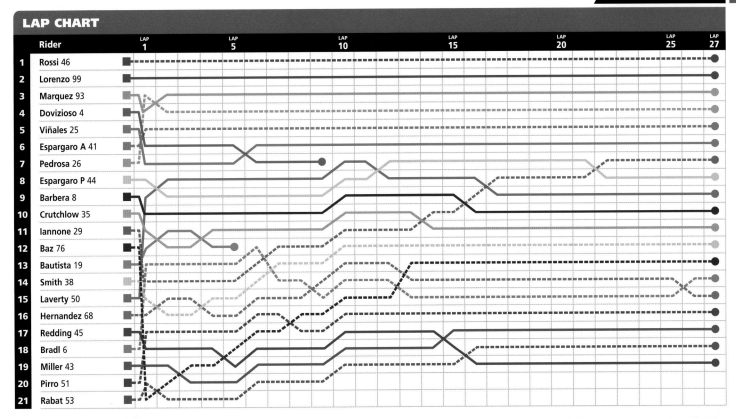

	Rider	LAP 1	LAP 5	LAP 10	LAP 15	LAP 20	LAP 25	LAP 27
1	Rossi 46							
2	Lorenzo 99							
3	Marquez 93							
4	Dovizioso 4							
5	Viñales 25							
6	Espargaro A 41							
7	Pedrosa 26							
8	Espargaro P 44							
9	Barbera 8							
10	Crutchlow 35							
11	Iannone 29							
12	Baz 76							
13	Bautista 19							
14	Smith 38							
15	Laverty 50							
16	Hernandez 68							
17	Redding 45							
18	Bradl 6							
19	Miller 43							
20	Pirro 51							
21	Rabat 53							

RACE

	Rider	Motorcycle	Race time	Time +	Fastest lap	Avg. speed	Tyres
1	Rossi	Yamaha	45m 28.834s		1m 40.090s	97.9mph	H/M
2	Lorenzo	Yamaha	45m 31.220s	2.386s	1m 40.317s	97.8mph	H/M
3	Marquez	Honda	45m 35.921s	7.087s	1m 40.317s	97.6mph	H/M
4	Pedrosa	Honda	45m 39.185s	10.351s	1m 40.688s	97.5mph	H/M
5	Espargaro A	Suzuki	45m 42.977s	14.143s	1m 40.704s	97.4mph	H/M
6	Viñales	Suzuki	45m 45.606s	16.772s	1m 40.996s	97.2mph	M/M
7	Iannone	Ducati	45m 55.111s	26.277s	1m 41.079s	96.9mph	H/M
8	Espargaro P	Yamaha	45m 59.584s	30.750s	1m 41.395s	96.7mph	S/S
9	Laverty	Ducati	46m 01.159s	32.325s	1m 41.162s	96.7mph	S/M
10	Barbera	Ducati	46m 01.458s	32.624s	1m 41.355s	96.7mph	S/S
11	Crutchlow	Honda	46m 07.331s	38.497s	1m 41.348s	96.5mph	H/M
12	Smith	Yamaha	46m 08.503s	39.669s	1m 41.676s	96.4mph	M/S
13	Baz	Ducati	46m 14.061s	45.227s	1m 41.789s	96.3mph	S/M
14	Bradl	Aprilia	46m 16.720s	47.886s	1m 41.796s	96.2mph	H/M
15	Hernandez	Ducati	46m 16.822s	47.988s	1m 41.646s	96.2mph	H/M
16	Pirro	Ducati	46m 18.248s	49.414s	1m 42.107s	96.1mph	S/M
17	Miller	Honda	46m 18.347s	49.513s	1m 42.234s	96.1mph	H/M
18	Rabat	Honda	46m 22.168s	53.334s	1m 42.231s	96.0mph	M/M
19	Redding	Ducati	46m 34.389s	1m 05.555s	1m 42.187s	95.6mph	M/S
NC	Dovizioso	Ducati	15m 20.050s	18 laps	1m 41.025s	96.7mph	S/M
NC	Bautista	Aprilia	8m 37.003s	22 laps	1m 41.648s	95.6mph	M/M

CHAMPIONSHIP

	Rider	Nation	Team	Points
1	Marquez	SPA	Repsol Honda Team	82
2	Lorenzo	SPA	Movistar Yamaha MotoGP	65
3	Rossi	ITA	Movistar Yamaha MotoGP	58
4	Pedrosa	SPA	Repsol Honda Team	40
5	Espargaro P	SPA	Monster Yamaha Tech 3	36
6	Viñales	SPA	Team Suzuki ECSTAR	33
7	Espargaro A	SPA	Team Suzuki ECSTAR	32
8	Barbera	SPA	Avintia Racing	31
9	Laverty	IRL	Aspar Team MotoGP	28
10	Iannone	ITA	Ducati Team	25
11	Dovizioso	ITA	Ducati Team	23
12	Smith	GBR	Monster Yamaha Tech 3	20
13	Bradl	GER	Aprilia Racing Team Gresini	17
14	Redding	GBR	OCTO Pramac Yakhnich	16
15	Bautista	SPA	Aprilia Racing Team Gresini	14
16	Pirro	ITA	OCTO Pramac Yakhnich	12
17	Rabat	SPA	Estrella Galicia 0,0 Marc VDS	11
18	Crutchlow	GBR	LCR Honda	5
19	Baz	FRA	Avintia Racing	4
20	Hernandez	COL	Aspar Team MotoGP	3
21	Miller	AUS	Estrella Galicia 0,0 Marc VDS	2

12 BRADLEY SMITH
Another disappointing weekend. Happier with the front tyre than in early races but another rider handicapped by rear grip problems.

13 LORIS BAZ
Knocked off track by Redding on the first lap, then ran off by himself next time round. After that, he made a good recovery from last place.

14 STEFAN BRADL
A cautious race, certainly compared with his team-mate. A good move on the final lap nabbed an extra point.

15 YONNY HERNANDEZ
Puzzled by the lack of feeling and grip, front and rear, on race day. Couldn't get the bike to turn.

16 MICHELE PIRRO
Another Ducati rider who never found any grip, leaving him confused and unable to work out what to do.

17 JACK MILLER
Happy to finish after the injury sustained in Texas but couldn't find the confidence to push at all in slower corners.

18 TITO RABAT
Like his team-mate, posted good lap times towards the closing stages. Happy to be able to stay with other riders and not be tailed off.

19 SCOTT REDDING
Spent three days trying to find grip and didn't succeed. The first time in his life that Scott has finished a race in last place. Yes, it was that bad.

DID NOT FINISH

ANDREA DOVIZIOSO
Eliminated by coolant spraying on the rear tyre thanks to a water-pump connector failing.

ALVARO BAUTISTA
In the group fighting for eighth when he crashed after losing the front.

DID NOT RACE

DANILO PETRUCCI
Still convalescing from the operation to repair his hand. Replaced by Michele Pirro.

MONSTER ENERGY
GRAND PRIX DE FRANCE
LE MANS

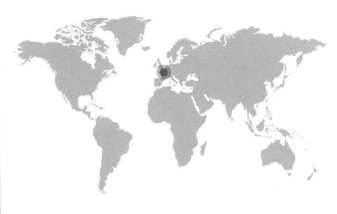

ALL FALL DOWN

Jorge Lorenzo was back to his imperious best in a Yamaha 1–2 and Maverick Viñales took his first MotoGP rostrum

Anyone who thought that Jorge Lorenzo was going to roll over and give up his championship easily was forcibly disabused of that notion by a lights-to-flag win from pole position. The winning margin was well into double figures from a not-too-disappointed Valentino Rossi.

Rossi had started from the third row of the grid and was seventh at the end of the first lap. He had to fight past both Espargaros and then put in a sublime pass on Marc Marquez on the brakes going down to Garage Vert, one of the trickiest corners on the track, to make progress. It wasn't until the 14th lap that Rossi passed Andrea Dovizioso to take second place, only to find that he had 5.3 seconds of empty tarmac in front of him. A couple of laps pushing hard convinced him that settling for second was no bad thing.

It was a wise decision. A combination of worn-out tarmac, bumps, new softer-construction rear tyres, and lack of testing with all the new Michelins saw a lot of riders crash. Eight hit the deck, two more than in 2015: Yonny Hernandez, Andrea Iannone, Cal Crutchlow, Tito Rabat, Marc Marquez, Andrea Dovizioso, Jack Miller and Bradley Smith – that's every Honda rider except Dani Pedrosa. Another indication of the RCV's front-end problems was that they fell at downhill corners – Chapelle, Musée and Garage Vert.

Michelin had said that the tyre construction introduced in Texas would be used for the rest of the year. Jerez, where wheelspin was endemic,

'IT IS SUCH A
SPECIAL FEELING TO
BE ON THE PODIUM.
MARC AND DOVI
HAD BAD LUCK BUT
I WAS RIDING WELL
AND AT ABOUT
THE SAME PACE
AS VALENTINO'
MAVERICK VIÑALES

convinced them to rush through a new design. So both rear tyres were built on a softer carcass that appeared to have the desired effect of controlling wheelspin. It was certainly good enough for Lorenzo to set a new absolute lap record in qualifying. Rossi's best race lap was just over 0.4 second slower than his own lap record from 2015, and his race time only seven seconds slower.

The only crasher to get back on and finish was Marquez. He and Dovizioso fell simultaneously, but not together, at Musée two laps after Rossi had gone past them. First reaction was that there must have been something on the track; second reaction, after viewing TV replays, was that a patch of new tarmac may have been responsible. The truth was more prosaic. Dovi's data showed he had two degrees more lean angle than on previous laps, while Marc said it was the sort of thing that happens when you're at the limit trying to regain on braking what you've just lost on acceleration.

Marquez managed to get back on his bike, minus some bodywork, and collect three points. It wasn't enough to prevent Lorenzo from taking the championship lead for the first time since the opening round, but as Jorge himself pointed out the main title contenders had now all had one race with a return of zero, or very few, points. It felt like the season had been reset.

There was one other crash that bears examination. Andrea Iannone followed team-mate Dovizioso off the start, pushing past to

ABOVE Hector Barbera getting a little aggressive with Stefan Bradl early doors

OPPOSITE TOP Marc Marquez, his Honda minus a little bodywork, continues after his crash

LEFT Maverick Viñales on the way to his first MotoGP podium – the first dry-weather top-three finish by a Suzuki rider since 2001

take second on lap six and immediately closing on leader Lorenzo. Next time round Iannone fell, a front-end crash like the rest. After the mistake of Qatar and the calamity of Argentina, this crash was closely examined, not least by Ducati management. Should he have been warned by the speed with which he was closing down on the World Champion, or was he no more culpable than any of the other high-profile crashers? The consensus came down on the side of the latter option.

No-one predicted after practice that Maverick Viñales would give Suzuki their first rostrum in MotoGP since Loris Capirossi at the 2008 Czech GP. In Argentina the young Spaniard had looked set for a top-three finish until bad luck intervened, but here in France his result felt like a reward for the Suzuki team's good work rather than an epic ride. Maverick started from the third row, worked his way past his team-mate and was around three seconds adrift of Marquez and Dovizioso when they fell. That put him in third place and for the second half of the race it was a matter of concentrating and not making a mistake.

When the Suzuki factory returned to MotoGP at the start of the 2015 season, the paddock expected to be underwhelmed. In fact Suzuki surprised everybody by fielding a very capable, user-friendly motorcycle that only needed a few extra horsepower to be truly competitive. Despite a false start with this year's chassis, prompting both riders to revert to the 2015 frame, double

ABOVE Dani Pedrosa in fourth place was the first Honda finisher and the only Honda man not to crash

BELOW The Tech 3 Yamahas of Pol Espargaro and Bradley Smith chase the Suzuki of Pol's brother Aleix in the fight for fifth place

WELCOME BACK

It would have been great to talk to Danilo Petrucci after the French GP, but he couldn't be found. He was in the Clinica Mobile hooked up to a drip after fighting to a remarkable seventh place. This, remember, was his first race of the season following a high-speed crash in testing at Phillip Island that disassembled most of his right hand. He tried to race in Qatar and made things worse. It took 20 screws and a couple of plates to sort it out.

At Le Mans he didn't know whether he could complete a free practice session let alone race. In the end, he did all that and more. Petrucci was in seventh place going into the last lap but in severe trouble. The hand, the lack of training, the lack of bike time – all this was torturing him. His whole body was shouting at him to stop, lack of race fitness magnified by having to compensate for his injury. And Hector Barbera was right behind him.

Hector observed Danilo patently struggling to brake or hit an apex. At Garage Vert, under heavy braking from

speed, Danilo left a big gap and Hector accepted the invitation. It looked like a done deal. Until the second apex. Petrucci slammed back under the Spaniard, punting Hector out of the way with enough force to ensure there was no comeback. Danilo is a big bloke and knows how to use his weight. Andrea Dovizioso, who raced with legendary motocrosser Tony Cairoli as a youngster and therefore knows what he's talking about, says Petrucci isn't a man you want to tangle with when training on

the dirt. Hector is also now well aware of that.

Danilo arrived back in pitlane and slumped over his tank to be instantaneously submerged by his deliriously tearful team.

The thing about Danilo is that he isn't just brave, he's immensely likeable and funny. Well aware that it wasn't that long ago that he was watching GPs from his sofa, he does a nice line in self-deprecating humour. I recommend his Twitter feed – follow @Petrux9.

top-ten finishes in Texas and Spain meant that the rostrum at Le Mans wasn't a complete surprise. Given the volatility in the rider market, with all the top riders' contracts running out at the end of the season, the result also underlined just what a valuable property Viñales is. The general view was that it would be difficult for Suzuki to retain him.

Lorenzo's assertion that it felt like the season was starting again may have been true for him, but it also felt like we'd travelled back to the end of the previous season, when the Yamaha was the best bike and the Honda the most difficult. Pol Espargaro was top independent in fifth place, the third time in five races that he'd won that fight, underlining the Yamaha's usability. And yet again, Ducati wasn't figuring in anyone's calculations: a double retirement for the factory riders put Ducati a distant third in the constructors' standings and the factory team fifth in their championship, just one point in front of Avintia. That felt like an echo of 2015, when Dovi started the year with three rostrums before fading rapidly from view.

If normality in 2015 was Lorenzo stringing together a race's worth of perfect laps every weekend, 2016 felt much the same after Le Mans.

RIGHT Jorge Lorenzo celebrates his second win of the season, this time a lights-to-flag victory

MONSTER ENERGY
GRAND PRIX DE FRANCE
LE MANS

ROUND 5
MAY 8

CIRCUIT KEY
- **S** SPEED TRAP
- **1** CORNER NUMBER
- SECTOR 1
- SECTOR 2
- SECTOR 3
- SECTOR 4

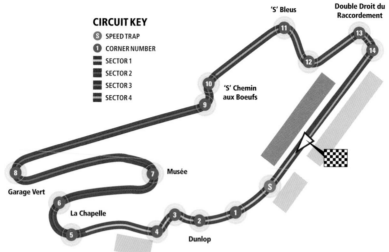

RACE RESULTS

CIRCUIT LENGTH 2.600 miles

NO. OF LAPS 28

RACE DISTANCE 72.812 miles

WEATHER Dry, 22°C

TRACK TEMPERATURE 35°C

WINNER Jorge Lorenzo

FASTEST LAP 1m 33.293s, 100.2mph, Valentino Rossi

LAP RECORD 1m 32.879s, 100.8mph, Valentino Rossi (2015)

TYRE OPTIONS

TYRE

CENTRE
LEFT   RIGHT

SEVERITY RATING

<MILD   SEVERE>

FRONT COMPOUNDS

SOFT (S)
MEDIUM (M)
HARD (H)

REAR COMPOUNDS

SOFT (S)
MEDIUM (M)

MICHELIN

QUALIFYING

	Rider	Nation	Motorcycle	Team	Time	Pole +
1	Lorenzo	SPA	Yamaha	Movistar Yamaha MotoGP	1m 31.975s	
2	Marquez	SPA	Honda	Repsol Honda Team	1m 32.416s	0.441s
3	Iannone	ITA	Ducati	Ducati Team	1m 32.469s	0.494s
4	Espargaro P	SPA	Yamaha	Monster Yamaha Tech 3	1m 32.502s	0.527s
5	Dovizioso	ITA	Ducati	Ducati Team	1m 32.587s	0.612s
6	Smith	GBR	Yamaha	Monster Yamaha Tech 3	1m 32.820s	0.845s
7	Rossi	ITA	Yamaha	Movistar Yamaha MotoGP	1m 32.829s	0.854s
8	Viñales	SPA	Suzuki	Team Suzuki ECSTAR	1m 32.933s	0.958s
9	Crutchlow	GBR	Honda	LCR Honda	1m 32.963s	0.988s
10	Petrucci	ITA	Ducati	OCTO Pramac Yakhnich	1m 33.102s	1.127s
11	Pedrosa	SPA	Honda	Repsol Honda Team	1m 33.109s	1.134s
12	Espargaro A	SPA	Suzuki	Team Suzuki ECSTAR	1m 33.115s	1.140s
13	Barbera	SPA	Ducati	Avintia Racing	1m 33.291s	*0.152s
14	Redding	GBR	Ducati	OCTO Pramac Yakhnich	1m 33.310s	*0.171s
15	Hernandez	COL	Ducati	Aspar Team MotoGP	1m 33.360s	*0.221s
16	Laverty	IRL	Ducati	Aspar Team MotoGP	1m 33.452s	*0.313s
17	Bradl	GER	Aprilia	Aprilia Racing Team Gresini	1m 34.003s	*0.864s
18	Miller	AUS	Honda	Estrella Galicia 0,0 Marc VDS	1m 34.049s	*0.910s
19	Bautista	SPA	Aprilia	Aprilia Racing Team Gresini	1m 34.333s	*1.194s
20	Rabat	SPA	Honda	Estrella Galicia 0,0 Marc VDS	1m 34.348s	*1.209s
21	Baz	FRA	Ducati	Avintia Racing	1m 34.455s	*1.316s

* Gap with the fastest rider in the Q1 session

1 JORGE LORENZO
The champion at his best: started from pole position and led every lap to return to the top of the points table. Only dropped out of the 33s for the last three laps and won by well over 10 seconds.

2 VALENTINO ROSSI
Started from seventh and had to fight hard with the Tech 3 Yamahas before closing on Marquez and Iannone with the fastest lap. Tempting to wonder what would have happened if he'd qualified well.

3 MAVERICK VIÑALES
His first rostrum in MotoGP and Suzuki's first in eight years. The only reason it was a surprise was that Mack had troubles through practice and qualified eighth. In the race, he stayed on where others fell and got his reward.

4 DANI PEDROSA
The usual pattern: bad qualifying and early laps followed by good pace in the final laps. Felt the end result was probably better than his race deserved.

5 POL ESPARGARO
Top independent for the third time this season. Very fast in warm-up and at the start, although a little erratic and was pushed back to eighth. Fought back past his brother and settled in fifth.

6 ALEIX ESPARGARO
Realised very early in the race that, like many others, he had front-tyre issues, so adopted a cautious strategy to bring the bike home for useful points.

7 DANILO PETRUCCI
Back from his career-threatening hand injury to finish top Ducati rider. A great display of bravery topped off by a last-lap bout of fairing-bashing with Barbera.

8 HECTOR BARBERA
Happy with his position on a track neither Hector nor the bike likes very much, especially as first-corner, first-lap barging put him to the back of the field. Passed Petrucci on the last lap but was retaken.

9 ALVARO BAUTISTA
Put in a great race after a crash in

warm-up and having warning lights on his dash at the start. Benefited from others crashing, but still an impressive effort.

10 STEFAN BRADL
Took a whack from Barbera early on after which he took two laps to straighten his front brake lever. Nevertheless, his fourth points-scoring ride in a row.

11 EUGENE LAVERTY
Running with Petrucci and Barbera before feeling a fault with the bike. After that, it was a case of bringing it home to extend the run of points-scoring races to five.

LAP CHART

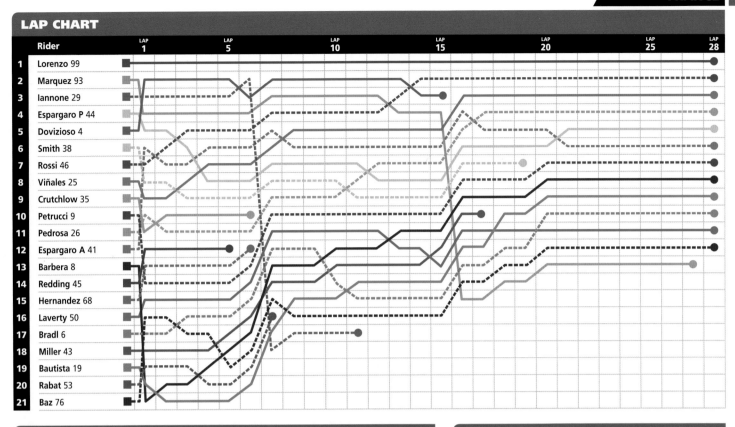

	Rider		LAP 1	LAP 5	LAP 10	LAP 15	LAP 20	LAP 25	LAP 28
1	Lorenzo	99							
2	Marquez	93							
3	Iannone	29							
4	Espargaro P	44							
5	Dovizioso	4							
6	Smith	38							
7	Rossi	46							
8	Viñales	25							
9	Crutchlow	35							
10	Petrucci	9							
11	Pedrosa	26							
12	Espargaro A	41							
13	Barbera	8							
14	Redding	45							
15	Hernandez	68							
16	Laverty	50							
17	Bradl	6							
18	Miller	43							
19	Bautista	19							
20	Rabat	53							
21	Baz	76							

RACE

	Rider	Motorcycle	Race time	Time +	Fastest lap	Avg. speed	Tyres
1	Lorenzo	Yamaha	43m 51.290s		1m 33.432s	99.6mph	M/S
2	Rossi	Yamaha	44m 01.944s	10.654s	1m 33.293s	99.2mph	M/S
3	Viñales	Suzuki	44m 05.467s	14.177s	1m 33.803s	99.0mph	M/S
4	Pedrosa	Honda	44m 10.009s	18.719s	1m 33.941s	98.9mph	M/S
5	Espargaro P	Yamaha	44m 16.221s	24.931s	1m 33.917s	98.7mph	M/S
6	Espargaro A	Suzuki	44m 24.211s	32.921s	1m 34.054s	98.4mph	M/S
7	Petrucci	Ducati	44m 29.541s	38.251s	1m 34.720s	98.2mph	M/S
8	Barbera	Ducati	44m 29.794s	38.504s	1m 34.561s	98.2mph	M/S
9	Bautista	Aprilia	44m 39.826s	48.536s	1m 34.903s	97.8mph	M/S
10	Bradl	Aprilia	44m 45.792s	54.502s	1m 34.770s	97.6mph	M/S
11	Laverty	Ducati	44m 53.967s	1m 02.677s	1m 34.971s	97.2mph	M/S
12	Baz	Ducati	44m 58.948s	1m 07.658s	1m 35.359s	97.1mph	H/S
13	Marquez	Honda	44m 27.515s	1 lap	1m 33.576s	94.7mph	H/S
NC	Smith	Yamaha	30m 02.401s	9 laps	1m 34.040s	98.7mph	M/S
NC	Miller	Honda	27m 07.407s	11 laps	1m 34.824s	97.8mph	M/S
NC	Dovizioso	Ducati	23m 34.694s	13 laps	1m 33.520s	99.2mph	M/S
NC	Iannone	Ducati	17m 56.425s	17 laps	1m 33.374s	95.6mph	M/S
NC	Rabat	Honda	11m 17.332s	21 laps	1m 35.283s	96.7mph	H/S
NC	Crutchlow	Honda	9m 33.909s	22 laps	1m 34.135s	97.9mph	H/S
NC	Hernandez	Ducati	9m 37.441s	22 laps	1m 34.833s	97.2mph	M/S
NC	Redding	Ducati	8m 00.164s	23 laps	1m 34.175s	97.4mph	M/S

CHAMPIONSHIP

	Rider	Nation	Team	Points
1	Lorenzo	SPA	Movistar Yamaha MotoGP	90
2	Marquez	SPA	Repsol Honda Team	85
3	Rossi	ITA	Movistar Yamaha MotoGP	78
4	Pedrosa	SPA	Repsol Honda Team	53
5	Viñales	SPA	Team Suzuki ECSTAR	49
6	Espargaro P	SPA	Monster Yamaha Tech 3	47
7	Espargaro A	SPA	Team Suzuki ECSTAR	42
8	Barbera	SPA	Avintia Racing	39
9	Laverty	IRL	Aspar Team MotoGP	33
10	Iannone	ITA	Ducati Team	25
11	Dovizioso	ITA	Ducati Team	23
12	Bradl	GER	Aprilia Racing Team Gresini	23
13	Bautista	SPA	Aprilia Racing Team Gresini	21
14	Smith	GBR	Monster Yamaha Tech 3	20
15	Redding	GBR	OCTO Pramac Yakhnich	16
16	Pirro	ITA	OCTO Pramac Yakhnich	12
17	Rabat	SPA	Estrella Galicia 0,0 Marc VDS	11
18	Petrucci	ITA	OCTO Pramac Yakhnich	9
19	Baz	FRA	Avintia Racing	8
20	Crutchlow	GBR	LCR Honda	5
21	Hernandez	COL	Aspar Team MotoGP	3
22	Miller	AUS	Estrella Galicia 0,0 Marc VDS	2

12 LORIS BAZ
The worst weekend of his career and the first time Loris has never been able to find a solution to set-up problems. Managed to avoid crashing and score points but a very unhappy home GP.

13 MARC MARQUEZ
Crashed and remounted just after half-distance to get three points that could be invaluable come the end of the year. Took risks and paid the price for trying to regain on the brakes what he lost on acceleration.

DID NOT FINISH

BRADLEY SMITH
Was looking at his best weekend of the year until he pushed too hard chasing the Espargaros following a coming-together with Pedrosa.

JACK MILLER
Lost the front at Musée while making progress and looking good in an impressive tenth place.

ANDREA DOVIZIOSO
Crashed in tandem with Marquez, although the incidents were unrelated. Was third and pressing to keep a rostrum place when he lost the front because, the data suggested, he had two degrees more lean than previous laps.

ANDREA IANNONE
Closing down the leader Lorenzo when he lost the front. As it was the lap after he had pushed past his team-mate to go second, some eyebrows were raised.

TITO RABAT
Very upset to crash going down into Chapelle just after upping his pace and passing Baz.

CAL CRUTCHLOW
Crashed when he lost the front going into Chapelle – a similar fate to the other Honda riders who chose the hard front tyre.

YONNY HERNANDEZ
Crashed early on when one of the circuit's many bumps caused him to lose the front.

SCOTT REDDING
Looking good when forced to stop by a technical problem.

GRAN PREMIO D'ITALIA TIM
AUTODROMO DEL MUGELLO

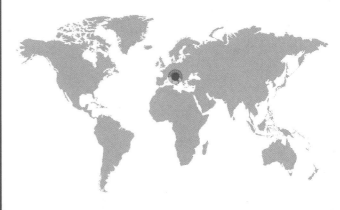

BLOW-UP

Lorenzo won the best last-lap shoot-out for years but all of Italy was more concerned with Rossi's engine failure

It looked like the script was written. A whole country rejoiced as Valentino Rossi took his first pole position at Mugello since 2008, making it two poles in a season for the first time since 2009. MotoGP timing sponsor Tissot hands out watches on Saturday evening to the pole men from each class, usually employing a local celebrity or sports person to do the necessary. And so it came to pass that Rossi was handed his new timepiece by ex-Miss Italy and TV personality Eleonora Pedron, better known until the previous October as the wife of Max Biaggi, Valentino's implacable long-time enemy. There was a lot of giggling, not least from Andrea Iannone who photo-bombed the official pictures, forming a heart shape with his fingers over the heads of the happy couple.

There was no deviation from the script first thing on Sunday morning when Rossi followed Jorge Lorenzo off the start to lead the opening laps with Marc Marquez struggling to stay with them in third. Lorenzo's record at Mugello is nearly on a par with Rossi's seven in a row from 2002; Jorge won in 2011, '12, '13 and '15, and finished second in '14. Until the ninth lap it looked as if Valentino was going to win again and send Italy into orbit. He never led but the gap to Lorenzo never climbed much above a tenth of a second – in other words he was right there waiting. He looked in control. Until there was a plume of white smoke from the exhaust

of Valentino's Yamaha M-1. Lorenzo's bike had suffered an identical failure, but his was at the end of warm-up.

This wasn't just a home-race disaster for Rossi and the yellow hordes on the hillsides, it was also his second retirement of the year. It's very difficult to envisage anyone winning a championship in this era if opposition like Marquez and Lorenzo are given such an advantage.

Italy's hopes now rested with Andrea Iannone, who had been expected to take pole and wasn't at all happy to be pushed back to third on the grid not just by Rossi but also by the ever-more-impressive Maverick Viñales. Iannone's race was compromised by what looked like a very 'grabby' carbon clutch off the start. The Ducati snatched the front wheel up in a very jerky movement and it was bad enough to put Andrea back in

ABOVE Valentino Rossi's Yamaha comes to a smoky halt and 25 points vaporise. How useful would they have been later in the season?

LEFT Jorge Lorenzo and Marc Marquez fought out the best last lap we've seen since Barcelona 2009. This time Jorge won

'IT'S A GREAT SHAME, BECAUSE IT'S ALWAYS A PITY WHEN YOU HAVE A PROBLEM WITH THE BIKE IN THE RACE, BUT HERE EVEN MORE SO'
VALENTINO ROSSI

ABOVE Cal Crutchlow scored points for only the second time in the season at his team's home race

BELOW Bradley Smith's season had its first bright spot with seventh place – and top independent

OPPOSITE Andrea Iannone enjoyed the rostrum appearance at his home race

eighth place at the end of the first lap. Under those circumstances, his ride to third place, which included setting the fastest lap of the race (on the last lap) and a new top-speed record, was more than praiseworthy. Not that Iannone or the Ducati factory were happy. They knew another chance of that longed-for victory had escaped.

Iannone needed that last lap to hold off Pedrosa. Dani had again been unhappy early on with a full tank and new tyres but had the speed to follow the Ducati when it came past just after half distance. What he didn't have was enough speed to make a pass.

It was much the same at the front, where Marquez was forcing the Honda to do things it didn't want to do to keep up with Lorenzo's Yamaha. It was again obvious that the Yamaha was quicker out of corners and down the straight. It was always going to come down to a last-lap shoot-out, and what we saw was certainly the best for years.

It started with Marquez's elbow slider being ripped off as he outbraked Jorge into Turn 1 and tried to open a gap. As they plunged down Casanova-Savelli it looked as if he had succeeded but by Correntaio Jorge had closed the gap and, recalling a move he'd made on Hector Barbera during their 250cc days, Jorge made a completely unexpected pass in the final chicane only to be repassed on the exit. Marc then shut the door so firmly on Jorge going into the final long left-hander that Jorge had to run up the kerb. The Honda came on to the straight just ahead but Jorge took a wider exit and, as the Honda pulled a small wheelie, used the slipstream to get alongside and win by 0.019 second.

Marquez said afterwards that he knew he would be beaten to the line, but that he had never been beaten in the last few metres of a race. He also said that his attitude to winning changed when he saw that Rossi was out. He didn't want it to, but it did. From trackside, it certainly didn't look as if Marc had held anything back. In fact it looked like he'd risked everything – as usual. A little later in the season he did explain that he hadn't risked too much once he knew Rossi wasn't going to score points, but he did give it all on the final lap. Our eyes weren't deceiving us.

It's true that Marc gave up five points to Jorge, allowing the lead to extend to ten points. More importantly, in Marc's mind at least, was the fact that Rossi now found himself 37 points adrift of the leader thanks to two points-free races. As Marquez said at the start of the year, he considered the races at Mugello and Catalunya to be those where his Honda would put him at the greatest disadvantage compared with the Yamahas, so he could be forgiven for thinking that way. What he didn't mention was the fact that Lorenzo had just won back-to-back GPs to become the first man to take three victories in 2016. It's safe to assume Marc was thinking about it though.

WHAT HAPPENED TO THE YAMAHAS?

Lorenzo's Yamaha blew its engine at the end of morning warm-up and Rossi's followed suit in the race.

The guilty engines were both the third of each rider's seven for the year. Jorge's had done 14 sessions including all of the Saturday and Sunday running at the last two races. Rossi's had fewer miles on it having done only nine sessions, including warm-up and the race at the last two GPs.

The failures looked identical: loads of smoke out of the exhaust but no oil visible on the exterior of the engine.

Two similar, if not identical, failures to factory Yamahas on one day – unheard of. Jorge's rear wheel also locked when he released the clutch.

Yamaha's investigation did indeed conclude that the failures had the same cause – over-revving at full throttle over the crest in the main straight. The blame was laid on the 'spec' software, not a design failure with the hardware, so no remedial action was needed on the remaining motors for the season. Specifically, according to Yamaha, the rev limiter worked differently from the in-house software of previous years.

The surprising aspect is that the team didn't pick up on the problem early in the weekend and adjust the setting accordingly. However, there certainly wasn't time to reach a diagnosis from Lorenzo's motor before the race and in any case Rossi's was much fresher.

The only after-effect was that the other engines used by the team at Mugello were only fitted for practice at subsequent rounds.

GRAN PREMIO D'ITALIA TIM
AUTODROMO DEL MUGELLO
ROUND 6
MAY 22

RACE RESULTS

CIRCUIT LENGTH 3.259 miles

NO. OF LAPS 23

RACE DISTANCE 74.959 miles

WEATHER Dry, 26°C

TRACK TEMPERATURE 48°C

WINNER Jorge Lorenzo

FASTEST LAP 1m 47.687s, 108.9mph, Andrea Iannone

LAP RECORD 1m 47.639s, 109.0mph, Marc Marquez (2013)

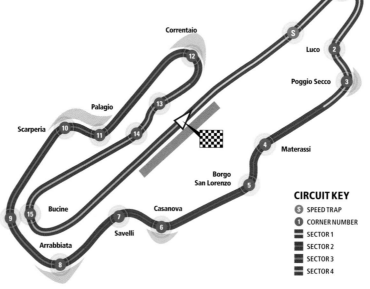

CIRCUIT KEY
- **S** SPEED TRAP
- **1** CORNER NUMBER
- SECTOR 1
- SECTOR 2
- SECTOR 3
- SECTOR 4

MotoGP · TISSOT SWISS WATCHES SINCE 1853 · OFFICIAL TIMEKEEPER

TYRE OPTIONS

TYRE — LEFT / CENTRE / RIGHT

SEVERITY RATING
<MILD   SEVERE>

FRONT COMPOUNDS
SOFT (S)
MEDIUM (M)
HARD (H)

REAR COMPOUNDS
SOFT (S)
MEDIUM (M)

MICHELIN

QUALIFYING

	Rider	Nation	Motorcycle	Team	Time	Pole +
1	Rossi	ITA	Yamaha	Movistar Yamaha MotoGP	1m 46.504s	
2	Viñales	SPA	Suzuki	Team Suzuki ECSTAR	1m 46.598s	0.094s
3	Iannone	ITA	Ducati	Ducati Team	1m 46.607s	0.103s
4	Marquez	SPA	Honda	Repsol Honda Team	1m 46.759s	0.255s
5	Lorenzo	SPA	Yamaha	Movistar Yamaha MotoGP	1m 46.882s	0.378s
6	Espargaro A	SPA	Suzuki	Team Suzuki ECSTAR	1m 47.186s	0.682s
7	Pedrosa	SPA	Honda	Repsol Honda Team	1m 47.218s	0.714s
8	Smith	GBR	Yamaha	Monster Yamaha Tech 3	1m 47.247s	0.743s
9	Petrucci	ITA	Ducati	OCTO Pramac Yakhnich	1m 47.261s	0.757s
10	Redding	GBR	Ducati	OCTO Pramac Yakhnich	1m 47.359s	0.855s
11	Pirro	ITA	Ducati	Ducati Team	1m 47.361s	0.857s
12	Hernandez	COL	Ducati	Aspar Team MotoGP	1m 47.436s	0.932s
13	Dovizioso	ITA	Ducati	Ducati Team	1m 47.089s	*0.203s
14	Espargaro P	SPA	Yamaha	Monster Yamaha Tech 3	1m 47.159s	*0.273s
15	Barbera	SPA	Ducati	Avintia Racing	1m 47.555s	*0.669s
16	Crutchlow	GBR	Honda	LCR Honda	1m 47.659s	*0.773s
17	Miller	AUS	Honda	Estrella Galicia 0,0 Marc VDS	1m 47.830s	*0.944s
18	Laverty	IRL	Ducati	Aspar Team MotoGP	1m 48.111s	*1.225s
19	Bautista	SPA	Aprilia	Aprilia Racing Team Gresini	1m 48.372s	*1.486s
20	Bradl	GER	Aprilia	Aprilia Racing Team Gresini	1m 48.646s	*1.760s
21	Baz	FRA	Ducati	Avintia Racing	1m 48.991s	*2.105s
22	Rabat	SPA	Honda	Estrella Galicia 0,0 Marc VDS	1m 49.648s	1.952s

* Gap with the fastest rider in the Q1 session

1 JORGE LORENZO
Looked lost until the lights went out and he got the holeshot from the second row. Led Rossi round until he dropped out then had to fight off Marquez over the closing laps. The lead changed four times on the last lap, the last time as Jorge slipstreamed past right on the line.

2 MARC MARQUEZ
Risked everything trying to win but couldn't overcome the Honda's lack of top-end speed. Shut the door very hard on the final corner but Lorenzo was still able to drive past with the help of the slipstream.

3 ANDREA IANNONE
A rostrum, the fastest lap, and a new top-speed record – but also a feeling of under-achievement. Andrea's race was compromised by a 'grabby' clutch that ruined his start, but his comeback was impressive.

4 DANI PEDROSA
Fast enough at the end to follow Iannone to the front of the field, but unable to pass due to speed differential. Again lost ground at the start with a full tank but happier than after last few races.

5 ANDREA DOVIZIOSO
Looked like a rostrum contender despite problems in qualifying until he slowed dramatically with arm pump. Glad to finish a race for a change.

6 MAVERICK VIÑALES
Lost nine places off his front-row start as his electronics malfunctioned. After they reset, Mack's pace was good enough for the rostrum but he used his tyres up regaining places.

7 BRADLEY SMITH
Top independent in qualifying and the race for the first time this season. Third

into the first corner but aware he couldn't abuse the tyres early on. Able to fight off Petrucci in the closing stages to finish only 13 seconds behind the winner.

8 DANILO PETRUCCI
Another solid race despite not being fully fit. Struggled for the first four or five laps but then pursued Smith and was disappointed to be be beaten by him, as he was in qualifying.

9 ALEIX ESPARGARO
Started well but the bike had been hastily rebuilt after a big crash in morning warm-up and didn't give Aleix the same

confidence. Not the way he wanted to finish his 100th GP.

10 MICHELE PIRRO
Wild card riding full factory bike. Nearly made his objective of finishing within 20 seconds of the leader but felt a vibration from the rear tyre late on.

11 CAL CRUTCHLOW
Happy to finish for only the second time this season, but not thrilled about the position. Got boxed out at the first corner and had problems with the brakes – which meant managing the situation to bring the bike home.

LAP CHART

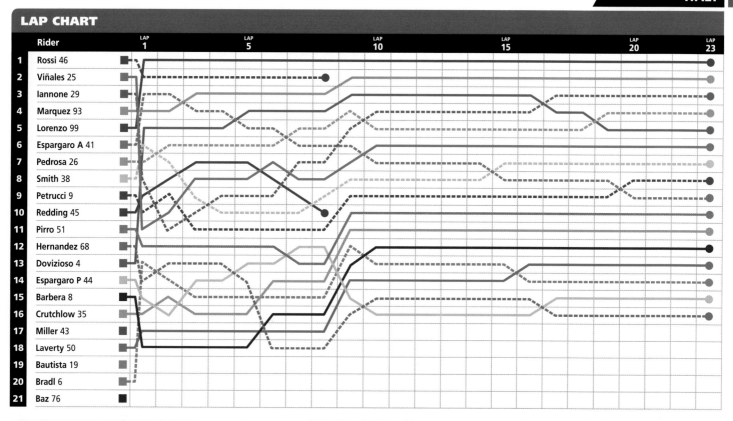

	Rider	LAP 1	LAP 5	LAP 10	LAP 15	LAP 20	LAP 23
1	Rossi 46						
2	Viñales 25						
3	Iannone 29						
4	Marquez 93						
5	Lorenzo 99						
6	Espargaro A 41						
7	Pedrosa 26						
8	Smith 38						
9	Petrucci 9						
10	Redding 45						
11	Pirro 51						
12	Hernandez 68						
13	Dovizioso 4						
14	Espargaro P 44						
15	Barbera 8						
16	Crutchlow 35						
17	Miller 43						
18	Laverty 50						
19	Bautista 19						
20	Bradl 6						
21	Baz 76						

RACE

	Rider	Motorcycle	Race time	Time +	Fastest lap	Avg. speed	Tyres
1	Lorenzo	Yamaha	41m 36.535s		1m 47.961s	108.1mph	H/S
2	Marquez	Honda	41m 36.554s	0.019s	1m 47.871s	108.1mph	M/S
3	Iannone	Ducati	41m 41.277s	4.742s	1m 47.687s	107.9mph	H/S
4	Pedrosa	Honda	41m 41.445s	4.910s	1m 47.734s	107.9mph	H/S
5	Dovizioso	Ducati	41m 42.791s	6.256s	1m 47.997s	107.8mph	H/S
6	Viñales	Suzuki	41m 45.205s	8.670s	1m 48.147s	107.7mph	H/S
7	Smith	Yamaha	41m 49.875s	13.340s	1m 48.371s	107.5mph	H/S
8	Petrucci	Ducati	41m 51.133s	14.598s	1m 48.428s	107.4mph	H/S
9	Espargaro A	Suzuki	41m 55.178s	18.643s	1m 48.571s	107.2mph	H/S
10	Pirro	Ducati	41m 58.833s	22.298s	1m 48.746s	107.1mph	H/S
11	Crutchlow	Honda	42m 04.471s	27.936s	1m 48.623s	106.9mph	M/S
12	Barbera	Ducati	42m 12.247s	35.712s	1m 48.873s	106.6mph	H/S
13	Laverty	Ducati	42m 14.567s	38.032s	1m 49.260s	106.4mph	H/S
14	Bradl	Aprilia	42m 16.629s	40.094s	1m 49.248s	106.4mph	H/S
15	Espargaro P	Yamaha	42m 36.346s	59.811s	1m 48.357s	105.5mph	H/S
16	Hernandez	Ducati	42m 40.932s	1m 04.397s	1m 49.159s	105.3mph	M/S
NC	Rossi	Yamaha	14m 31.924s	15 laps	1m 48.092s	107.6mph	H/S
NC	Redding	Ducati	14m 39.026s	15 laps	1m 48.581s	106.7mph	H/S
NC	Miller	Honda	–	–	–	–	H/S
NC	Bautista	Aprilia	–	–	–	–	H/S
NC	Baz	Ducati	–	–	–	–	H/S

CHAMPIONSHIP

	Rider	Nation	Team	Points
1	Lorenzo	SPA	Movistar Yamaha MotoGP	115
2	Marquez	SPA	Repsol Honda Team	105
3	Rossi	ITA	Movistar Yamaha MotoGP	78
4	Pedrosa	SPA	Repsol Honda Team	66
5	Viñales	SPA	Team Suzuki ECSTAR	59
6	Espargaro A	SPA	Team Suzuki ECSTAR	49
7	Espargaro P	SPA	Monster Yamaha Tech 3	48
8	Barbera	SPA	Avintia Racing	43
9	Iannone	ITA	Ducati Team	41
10	Laverty	IRL	Aspar Team MotoGP	36
11	Dovizioso	ITA	Ducati Team	34
12	Smith	GBR	Monster Yamaha Tech 3	29
13	Bradl	GER	Aprilia Racing Team Gresini	25
14	Bautista	SPA	Aprilia Racing Team Gresini	21
15	Pirro	ITA	OCTO Pramac Yakhnich	18
16	Petrucci	ITA	OCTO Pramac Yakhnich	17
17	Redding	GBR	OCTO Pramac Yakhnich	16
18	Rabat	SPA	Estrella Galicia 0,0 Marc VDS	11
19	Crutchlow	GBR	LCR Honda	10
20	Baz	FRA	Avintia Racing	8
21	Hernandez	COL	Aspar Team MotoGP	3
22	Miller	AUS	Estrella Galicia 0,0 Marc VDS	2

12 HECTOR BARBERA

Unhappy all weekend, despite his crew chief pointing out he's doing the same times the factory riders were doing on his bike two years ago. Still top Ducati rider in the standings.

13 EUGENE LAVERTY

Had to play catch-up after a crash on Friday and only qualified 18th. Got faster through the race to make it six points-scoring finishes out of six this season – keeping him in the championship top ten.

14 STEFAN BRADL

Never found a set-up he was comfortable with. Then in the race lost his stomp pad (sticky surface to help brace leg against tank), so relieved to get some points.

15 POL ESPARGARO

Crashed in qualifying so started from 14th, which meant some desperate moves early on, resulting in another crash when he was trying to pass Pirro. Got back on to salvage a point.

16 YONNY HERNANDEZ

Having a great weekend right up to the moment he pulled the clutch in for the start and the bike moved forward, earning him a ride-through penalty.

DID NOT FINISH

JACK MILLER

Scooped up at the first corner by Bautista's sliding Aprilia, luckily without injury.

ALVARO BAUTISTA

Started on his second bike after crashing in warm-up. Had to adjust the brake before the start and locked the front at Turn 1, collecting Baz and Miller.

LORIS BAZ

Caught up in Bautista's first-corner crash. Suffered four broken metatarsals, including a dislocation, a complicated injury that required surgery and lengthy recuperation.

VALENTINO ROSSI

Lying second and comfortably shadowing Lorenzo when his engine failed, as the Spaniard's had done in warm-up.

SCOTT REDDING

Started well and was up to seventh place before another technical problem forced him to stop.

DID NOT RACE

TITO RABAT

Broke his left collarbone in Saturday afternoon free practice and returned to Barcelona for surgery.

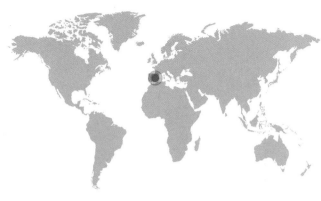

GRAN PREMI MONSTER ENERGY DE CATALUNYA
CIRCUIT DE CATALUNYA

CONFLICT RESOLUTION

Tragedy, acrimony and finally rapprochement of a sort as Valentino Rossi won from Marc Marquez

In the middle of Friday afternoon practice Cal Crutchlow forced his recalcitrant Honda around the Circuit de Catalunya to the third fastest time of the day. The TV director cut to the LCR Honda pit and caught Lucy Crutchlow cuddling her pregnancy bump and smiling. Then he cut back to Cal's on-board camera. Mr Crutchlow had obviously seen his wife on one of the giant screens around the circuit and was delightedly miming the dimensions of said bump over his own tummy. It was a truly lovely moment. One that might even have brought a tear to the eye of some observers.

Half an hour later, Luis Salom fell entering Turn 12 and followed his bike into the barriers. It was time for more tears.

It was immediately obvious that Salom's fatal fall came early in the corner, a fact later substantiated by the MotoGP Technical Director's investigation, and that he and his bike slid over tarmac run-off rather than the gravel trap, which was further round the corner, so hardly any speed was scrubbed off.

The issue of what to do was handed over to the Safety Commission. They came up with track modifications, essentially adopting the F1 layout for the fourth sector, which includes a tight chicane. Against expectations, this seemed to favour the Hondas. Marc Marquez took pole and Dani Pedrosa started from the front row for the first time this year.

Jorge Lorenzo and Valentino Rossi both had a bit of a moan: Rossi said he didn't understand why Turn 10 was modified and Lorenzo wondered why he wasn't consulted about it. As neither of them went to the Safety Commission meeting that convened at its usual time on Friday (after Salom's death was officially announced), there wasn't a lot of sympathy from those who did attend.

Marquez took a long time to explain, in a sombre and measured tone, how the Safety Commission met as usual and then went to the corner where the accident happened. The riders weren't prepared to carry on unless the corner was altered. With the adoption of the F1 chicane, Turn 10 had to be moved back or there would have been a situation like that at Suzuka, where the run-off can't be extended at the right after the hairpin without going on track at R120. Lorenzo, always able to say the wrong thing at the wrong time, harrumphed and 'stood on his dignity' as champion and championship leader. Pedrosa issued a curt remark along the lines of 'Cry or don't cry.' Marquez looked furious.

Valentino said he'd been asking for changes to the corner for six years, especially two years ago when one of his Acadamy riders, Nicco Antonelli, hit the fence hard crashing his Moto3 there, but his comments were disputed.

Meanwhile, the riders who had been at the Safety Commission meeting were certainly

ABOVE Tito Rabat was back from injury for his home race and scored points

RIGHT Andrea Iannone pulled away from the pack and closed on Lorenzo only to ram him and then, as seen in the inset photo, walk away from his victim

'I AM VERY SORRY FOR WHAT HAPPENED WITH LORENZO BECAUSE I WAS DOING A GOOD RACE WITH THE LIMITED GRIP I HAD. I WAS RIDING WELL AND PUSHING HARD'

ANDREA IANNONE

not happy with the factory Yamaha boys. Pol Espargaro's Twitter feed was Not Suitable For Work and Bradley Smith got irritated and turned his guns on Rossi, whom he said hadn't been to a Safety Commission meeting since Sepang in 2015.

Thankfully, dignity was restored on race day, which went ahead at the express request of the Salom family. Luis's memory was honoured with some fine racing.

'It's not much but it's all a rider can do,' said Valentino afterwards. He'd won, turning the form from qualifying on the revised layout on its head. Marquez had pursued him doggedly but when he saw on his pit board that Lorenzo was out his attitude changed markedly, much more so than at Mugello. From then on, second place was fine. As Marc reasoned, 40 points wasn't a bad return from the two tracks he thought would be the most difficult for him.

Lorenzo was soon in trouble with his front tyre and was dropping back from the leaders when he was inexplicably rammed by Andrea Iannone while braking for Turn 10. The Italian protested that he had braked as usual and that Lorenzo must have had a problem. Well, indeed he did and Andrea failed to notice. Jorge was livid. He was lucky to avoid injury and he lost his championship lead to Marquez. Race Direction sided with Lorenzo and decided that Iannone would start from the back of the grid at the next race.

ABOVE Michele Pirro was again on replacement duty, this time for Loris Baz on the Avintia Ducati

BELOW It was Aprilia's best weekend so far. Both bikes were in the points and Bautista was particularly impressive

OPPOSITE After the flag, Marc Marquez's Honda wore number 39 in tribute to Luis Salom

LUIS JAIME SALOM HORRACH

Despite his moniker of 'El Mexicano', Luis Salom was born into a Mallorcan motorcycle dynasty. Grandfather Toni owns the biggest dealership on the island, and from a young age Luis and his endurance racing cousins David and Toni were riding around the workshop. Salom's untimely death at 24 was felt heavily in the Balearic community.

It came during his third season of Moto2, and although he had enjoyed a relative amount of success with three podium finishes in the class, including at 2016's opening round in Qatar, he will undoubtedly be best remembered for his performances in the nascent Moto3 World Championship.

Having graduated from both the CEV Spanish Nationals and Red Bull Rookies Cup as runner-up in 2008, he took his first GP podium finishes as a 125cc rider in 2011. Staying with the Dutch RW Racing Team, he then finished runner-up to Sandro Cortese in the inaugural Moto3 series in 2012.

The following year was his stand-out one. He won seven times and developed a useful habit of stealing victory from under his rivals' noses in the final corner. That the title was taken from him by MotoGP's new superstar Maverick Viñales in the final corner of the final race is a cruel irony.

Salom was an effervescent character of wild contrasts. He made the sign of the cross every time he headed out on the bike, with his doe-eyes peering skywards through his visor, but they belied his fiery temperament on track. His beaming smile could be quickly forgotten in one of his many entertainingly flamboyant tantrums following a crash. His heavily tattooed body was softened by a forearm bearing a portrait of his mother María.

The unique bond between son and mother was clear to see. While father Toni would stay in Palma with his younger brother Jaume, who has cerebral palsy, María was like Luis's shadow. As they travelled the world for his racing career, he would enjoy playing with his mother's curly hair for luck, as he had as a child. At his funeral his mother appeared with a shaved head, having placed her distinctive curly black locks in her son's hands for eternity.

Luis had been affectionately dubbed 'El Mexicano' by his manager's brother, who had owned a racehorse by the same name. Said horse once refused to leave the starting gate, and the brother had suggested that Salom might go much the same way. Nine victories, 25 podiums, four pole positions and a world championship runners-up medal suggest he couldn't have been more wrong. *Gavin Emmett*

After that incident, Pedrosa and Maverick Viñales were able to follow unchallenged at a respectable distance from the top two, with the Suzuki man setting the fastest lap of the race for the first time. Pol Espargaro was next, top independent yet again, with Cal Crutchlow having his best ride of the season so far in sixth place.

There was one final piece of drama to be played out in *parc fermé*. Rossi and Marquez made eye contact and a handshake followed. It was spontaneous, it was genuine, and it was a welcome moment for many reasons. First and foremost, it was a gesture the day required. Secondly, it hopefully marked an end to the open hostility that had existed between the two champions since Sepang, although Valentino was far from comfortable in the post-race press conference. When Marc put a hand on his shoulder after answering a question about their relationship with a smile, it was all Valentino could do to blurt out a one-word answer: 'Errr... Yes.' There were also clear indications that both Rossi and Lorenzo would start attending the Safety Commission again.

One aspect of the tragic accident that befell Luis Salom that would have repercussions was the extent of tarmac run-off on some other circuits, not only specifically on that corner of the Circuit de Catalunya, where it's extremely unlikely that the old layout will be used again for motorcycle racing.

GRAN PREMI MONSTER ENERGY DE CATALUNYA
CIRCUIT DE CATALUNYA
ROUND 7
JUNE 5

RACE RESULTS

CIRCUIT LENGTH 2.892 miles
NO. OF LAPS 25
RACE DISTANCE 73.312 miles
WEATHER Dry, 27°C
TRACK TEMPERATURE 48°C
WINNER Valentino Rossi
FASTEST LAP 1m 45.971s, 98.2mph, Maverick Viñales (record)
PREVIOUS LAP RECORD New circuit layout

CIRCUIT KEY
- **S** SPEED TRAP
- **1** CORNER NUMBER
- SECTOR 1
- SECTOR 2
- SECTOR 3
- SECTOR 4

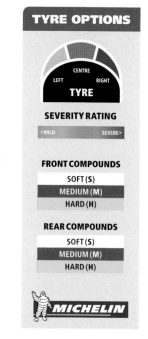

TYRE OPTIONS

LEFT | CENTRE | RIGHT
TYRE

SEVERITY RATING
<MILD   SEVERE>

FRONT COMPOUNDS
| SOFT (S) |
| MEDIUM (M) |
| HARD (H) |

REAR COMPOUNDS
| SOFT (S) |
| MEDIUM (M) |
| HARD (H) |

MICHELIN

QUALIFYING

	Rider	Nation	Motorcycle	Team	Time	Pole +
1	Marquez	SPA	Honda	Repsol Honda Team	1m 43.589s	
2	Lorenzo	SPA	Yamaha	Movistar Yamaha MotoGP	1m 44.056s	0.047s
3	Pedrosa	SPA	Honda	Repsol Honda Team	1m 44.307s	0.718s
4	Barbera	SPA	Ducati	Avintia Racing	1m 44.322s	0.733s
5	Rossi	ITA	Yamaha	Movistar Yamaha MotoGP	1m 44.324s	0.735s
6	Viñales	SPA	Suzuki	Team Suzuki ECSTAR	1m 44.329s	0.740s
7	Crutchlow	GBR	Honda	LCR Honda	1m 44.366s	0.777s
8	Iannone	ITA	Ducati	Ducati Team	1m 44.458s	0.869s
9	Petrucci	ITA	Ducati	OCTO Pramac Yakhnich	1m 44.911s	1.322s
10	Dovizioso	ITA	Ducati	Ducati Team	1m 45.029s	1.440s
11	Redding	GBR	Ducati	OCTO Pramac Yakhnich	1m 45.030s	1.441s
12	Espargaro P	SPA	Yamaha	Monster Yamaha Tech 3	1m 45.218s	1.629s
13	Espargaro A	SPA	Suzuki	Team Suzuki ECSTAR	1m 44.914s	*0.420s
14	Smith	GBR	Yamaha	Monster Yamaha Tech 3	1m 45.197s	*0.703s
15	Pirro	ITA	Ducati	Avintia Racing	1m 45.538s	*1.044s
16	Hernandez	COL	Ducati	Aspar Team MotoGP	1m 45.690s	*1.196s
17	Laverty	IRL	Ducati	Aspar Team MotoGP	1m 45.885s	*1.391s
18	Bradl	GER	Aprilia	Aprilia Racing Team Gresini	1m 45.892s	*1.398s
19	Miller	AUS	Honda	Estrella Galicia 0,0 Marc VDS	1m 45.942s	*1.448s
20	Rabat	SPA	Honda	Estrella Galicia 0,0 Marc VDS	1m 46.205s	*1.711s
21	Bautista	SPA	Aprilia	Aprilia Racing Team Gresini	1m 46.463s	*1.969s

Gap with the fastest rider in the Q1 session

1 VALENTINO ROSSI
His first win here for seven years, which Rossi himself put on a par with the 2009 classic with Lorenzo. Started from the second row, badly, then had to pass all of the championship contenders and finally fight off Marquez. Brilliant.

2 MARC MARQUEZ
Not as happy in the higher temperatures of race day as in practice. Had a couple of major moments chasing Rossi and when he saw that Lorenzo was out was happy to settle for a rostrum finish.

3 DANI PEDROSA
Started from the front row for the first time this year, and unlike the other factory men used the softer rear tyre. It was good decision, although he used it up fighting Viñales after which he had a lonely race.

4 MAVERICK VIÑALES
Started the race with frenzied attacks on Pedrosa, set the fastest lap fifth time round, then suffered from the Suzuki's usual problem with rear grip when tyre performance dropped.

5 POL ESPARGARO
Went with the softer tyres front and rear and made them work. Used the extra grip at the start and held on to fifth place as they dropped off. Top independent for the fourth time this season.

6 CAL CRUTCHLOW
Managed tyre wear cleverly for his best result of the season so far. Started badly, worked his way up to fight with and pass Dovizioso, then had a lonely ride to the flag. Not happy with gap to the leaders but otherwise satisfied.

7 ANDREA DOVIZIOSO
Noticed a problem with his rear tyre on the warm-up lap. Never happy on a track that doesn't suit the Ducati.

8 ALVARO BAUTISTA
The best finish so for the Aprilia. Understood the need to conserve the tyre and was as quick as the leaders in the closing stages. If he hadn't crashed in FP4 and had to use his second bike in qualifying it could have been even better.

9 DANILO PETRUCCI
Saved his rear tyre to fight with Dovi for top Ducati on the final laps. Got to seventh then felt the tyre drop off instantly.

10 JACK MILLER
The first top-ten finish in his MotoGP career and just what the Aussie needed. In Jerez he overdid the tyre conservation, but here he judged it perfectly and used the full potential of his rear Michelin. An impressive ride and his first points since Qatar.

11 HECTOR BARBERA
Brilliant qualifying followed by the same race as most Ducati riders, that is severe drop-off in rear-tyre grip that saw him lap five seconds slower than on Saturday.

LAP CHART

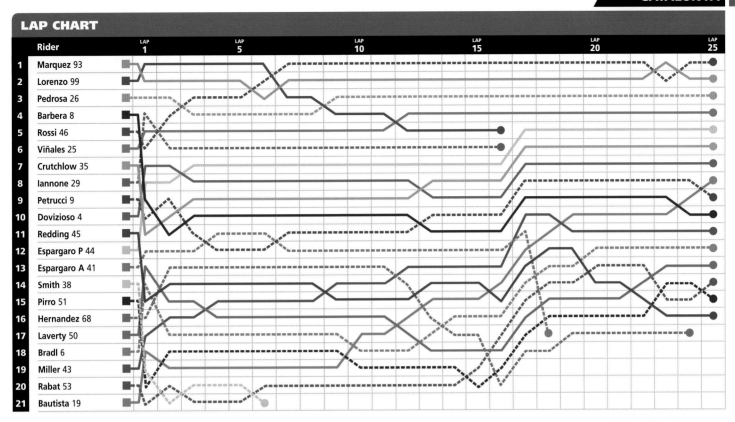

	Rider				
1	Marquez 93				
2	Lorenzo 99				
3	Pedrosa 26				
4	Barbera 8				
5	Rossi 46				
6	Viñales 25				
7	Crutchlow 35				
8	Iannone 29				
9	Petrucci 9				
10	Dovizioso 4				
11	Redding 45				
12	Espargaro P 44				
13	Espargaro A 41				
14	Smith 38				
15	Pirro 51				
16	Hernandez 68				
17	Laverty 50				
18	Bradl 6				
19	Miller 43				
20	Rabat 53				
21	Bautista 19				

RACE

	Rider	Motorcycle	Race time	Time +	Fastest lap	Avg. speed	Tyres
1	Rossi	Yamaha	44m 37.589s		1m 46.102s	97.2mph	H/H
2	Marquez	Honda	44m 40.241s	2.652s	1m 46.040s	97.1mph	H/H
3	Pedrosa	Honda	44m 43.902s	6.313s	1m 46.308s	96.9mph	H/M
4	Viñales	Suzuki	45m 01.977s	24.388s	1m 45.971s	96.3mph	H/H
5	Espargaro P	Yamaha	45m 07.135s	29.546s	1m 46.858s	96.1mph	M/M
6	Crutchlow	Honda	45m 13.833s	36.244s	1m 46.842s	95.9mph	H/H
7	Dovizioso	Ducati	45m 19.053s	41.464s	1m 47.025s	95.7mph	H/H
8	Bautista	Aprilia	45m 20.564s	42.975s	1m 47.685s	95.6mph	H/H
9	Petrucci	Ducati	45m 22.926s	45.337s	1m 47.385s	95.6mph	H/H
10	Miller	Honda	45m 27.103s	49.514s	1m 47.478s	95.4mph	H/H
11	Barbera	Ducati	45m 24.258s	46.669s	1m 46.909s	95.5mph	H/H
12	Bradl	Aprilia	45m 32.722s	55.133s	1m 48.008s	95.3mph	H/H
13	Laverty	Ducati	45m 35.563s	57.974s	1m 47.944s	95.1mph	H/H
14	Rabat	Honda	45m 37.730s	1m 00.141s	1m 47.750s	95.1mph	H/M
15	Pirro	Ducati	45m 38.018s	1m 00.429s	1m 47.910s	95.1mph	H/H
16	Redding	Ducati	45m 53.858s	1m 16.269s	1m 47.527s	94.5mph	H/H
17	Hernandez	Ducati	44m 56.487s	1 lap	1m 47.128s	92.6mph	H/H
NC	Espargaro A	Suzuki	32m 55.150s	7 laps	1m 46.873s	94.9mph	H/H
NC	Lorenzo	Yamaha	28m 39.709s	9 laps	1m 46.438s	96.9mph	H/H
NC	Iannone	Ducati	28m 40.223s	9 laps	1m 46.796s	96.8mph	H/H
NC	Smith	Yamaha	11m 30.558s	19 laps	1m 48.080s	90.5mph	M/M

CHAMPIONSHIP

	Rider	Nation	Team	Points
1	Marquez	SPA	Repsol Honda Team	125
2	Lorenzo	SPA	Movistar Yamaha MotoGP	115
3	Rossi	ITA	Movistar Yamaha MotoGP	103
4	Pedrosa	SPA	Repsol Honda Team	82
5	Viñales	SPA	Team Suzuki ECSTAR	72
6	Espargaro P	SPA	Monster Yamaha Tech 3	59
7	Espargaro A	SPA	Team Suzuki ECSTAR	49
8	Barbera	SPA	Avintia Racing	48
9	Dovizioso	ITA	Ducati Team	43
10	Iannone	ITA	Ducati Team	41
11	Laverty	IRL	Aspar Team MotoGP	39
12	Smith	GBR	Monster Yamaha Tech 3	29
	Bradl	GER	Aprilia Racing Team Gresini	29
	Bautista	SPA	Aprilia Racing Team Gresini	29
15	Petrucci	ITA	OCTO Pramac Yakhnich	24
16	Crutchlow	GBR	LCR Honda	20
17	Pirro	ITA	OCTO Pramac Yakhnich	19
18	Redding	GBR	OCTO Pramac Yakhnich	16
19	Rabat	SPA	Estrella Galicia 0,0 Marc VDS	13
20	Miller	AUS	Estrella Galicia 0,0 Marc VDS	8
	Baz	FRA	Avintia Racing	8
22	Hernandez	COL	Aspar Team MotoGP	3

12 STEFAN BRADL
Made up six places from his grid slot but was a long way off the pace of his team-mate.

13 EUGENE LAVERTY
Maintained his record of scoring points in every race but, like other Ducati riders, had major tyre issues.

14 TITO RABAT
Fifteen days after breaking his collarbone in Italy, Tito rode his home race and scored points for the third time this year. It was only the second time both Marc VDS riders have scored points.

15 MICHELE PIRRO
Replaced Baz. Same problems as the other Ducati riders.

16 SCOTT REDDING
Caught out by the elevated track temperatures of race day after a promising practice: he was fifth fastest on Friday. Used up his rear tyre quickly, tried to change his riding style to no avail.

17 YONNY HERNANDEZ
Two penalties for exceeding track limits and a pit-stop to change bikes due to tyre wear: the definition of a bad day at the office.

DID NOT FINISH

ALEIX ESPARGARO
Suffered, as usual, from grip problems when the tyre performance dropped off, and when the traction control electronics started exacerbating the problem he retired.

JORGE LORENZO
Started fast as usual but was soon in trouble with the right side of his front tyre; but he was surely on for a fifth or sixth place until rammed by Iannone.

ANDREA IANNONE
Torpedoed Lorenzo at the end of the back straight. It wasn't a clever move, to put it mildly, and he was lucky that the penalty was only to start from the back of the grid at the next GP.

BRADLEY SMITH
Looked to have turned round an awful weekend, in which he was slowest in two free-practice sessions, but retired early with transmission trouble.

DID NOT RACE

LORIS BAZ
Recovering from foot injuries sustained at Mugello, replaced by Pirro.

MOTUL TT ASSEN
TT CIRCUIT ASSEN

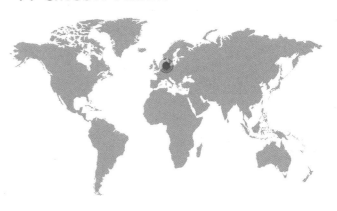

PICTURES AT AN EXHIBITION

Jack Miller kept his head while all about him were losing theirs and won under the trickiest of conditions

If you have the time and stamina, you can watch more than 20 hours of TV coverage over a Grand Prix weekend, but somehow the event is always later defined in the memory by one or two still images. In the case of the first ever Sunday GP at Assen, there were at least three. First, there was Jack Miller's perfect stand-up wheelie over the line. Second, there was Marc Marquez tapping the side of his crash helmet as he finished second. Finally, there was a shot from Valentino Rossi's on-board camera as he slumped despairingly over the tank of his Yamaha unable to get it back on track after crashing.

The background to those mind pictures is a race that had to be restarted, and that saw the field trying to find the limits of unfamiliar Michelin wet-weather front tyres. For the first time in the ten years since the lights-to-flag regulations were introduced, a MotoGP race was red-flagged and restarted. The only reason for not running a complete race is compromised safety, and no-one argued when Race Direction decided there was so much standing water on the track that it was unsafe to continue.

By the time the red flag went out, we had learned a few things. We already knew that Jorge Lorenzo was having a horrible weekend. The spectre of his 2013 collarbone-breaking crash still haunts him. By his own admission, Jorge's feel for and confidence in his front tyre disappears when it rains. That's what put him 11th on the

'I DON'T OFTEN
SAY THIS BUT I'M
LOST FOR WORDS.
I FEEL INCREDIBLY
EMOTIONAL RIGHT
NOW AND IT IS
HARD TO DESCRIBE
THE SENSATION
OF WINNING FOR
THE FIRST TIME
IN MOTOGP'
JACK MILLER

grid. Andrea Dovizioso got pole, Ducati's first since Mugello in 2015, with Rossi second – that's experience for you on a drying track that changed significantly but never quite got dry enough for slicks. The surprise was Scott Redding on last year's Ducati taking his first front-row start in MotoGP.

It was no surprise that old Ducatis went well when the race started. Yonny Hernandez pulled out a big lead before crashing, leaving Dovizioso leading from Danilo Petrucci with Redding fourth when proceedings were halted. Jack Miller was eighth, ten places higher than his qualifying position.

The first 'race' result was used to set the grid for what would be a 12-lap Grand Prix. The new, shorter distance meant that all riders who finished 'Part 1' started the new race on soft wets front and rear. That caught out a few people, notably Rossi and Dovizioso. Dovi went first, from second place, then Rossi disappeared from the lead at the first of the double rights at the far side of the track. The soft, grippier tyre hooked up better and ensured he arrived at Mandeveen 2–3mph more quickly than previously. Not surprisingly, he lost the front.

Then followed an anguished cameo as Rossi tried to get back on track before slumping over the tank with the realisation that he now had a third non-scoring race on his card. No-one has won a MotoGP title this century with three DNFs.

ABOVE The Tech 3 Yamahas led the chase before the conditions got really bad

LEFT Scott Redding qualified on the front row and finished on the rostrum, his first for Ducati

ABOVE Cal Crutchlow slides off his Honda after the restart at Assen

BELOW Yonny Hernandez built up a big lead before the red flag but fell before it came out, thereby missing the restart

OPPOSITE Jack Miller celebrates in *parc fermé* before introducing MotoGP to the concept of the 'shoey'

Those crashes handed the lead to Marquez, who only held it for one lap. Surprisingly, he had declared himself unimpressed with the equipment he had tested after the Catalan GP and was using the same bike as in the previous race. He knew that Miller was closing, and he knew that his team had told him beforehand '40 times' to finish the race. He later admitted that his first thought had been of the infamous Miller/Crutchlow incident at Silverstone the previous season, to which Miller shot back, 'You were lucky!' Although there's no doubt that Marquez was yet again thinking long-term, he crossed the line looking at his team and tapping the side of his crash helmet furiously, indicating that he had indeed done what his team told him. That morphed into the sort of celebration normally reserved for winning a last-lap duel. Marc understood what was happening. He'd extended his championship lead to 24 points and seen both works Yamaha riders suffer badly – and the next track was one of his best.

There is equal certainty that Miller was riding brilliantly. Ex-dirt trackers always seem comfortable in low-grip conditions and the Australian is no exception. He took the lead at the chicane and pulled away steadily to take the first win by a non-factory rider since Toni Elias at Estoril in 2006 and the first win by a 'non-Alien' (ie, not Rossi, Pedrosa, Marquez, Lorenzo or Stoner) since Ben Spies in 2011, also at Assen.

Third place went to Scott Redding after he

caught Pol Espargaro late in the race, the Spaniard again impressing although this time in conditions where he hasn't usually shone. For Redding, his second career rostrum was compensation for the technical problems that had beset him this season as well as reward for a very strong weekend.

There was much to admire in Miller's win apart from the stylish stand-up wheelie over the line, his emotion during the anthem (Jack just held it together), and the slightly less conventional celebration that involved drinking cava from his boot. It has taken some serious strength of mind to deal with the pressures and the doubts brought on by the lack of instant success on a difficult motorcycle, something he addressed in post-race interviews. 'See, I'm not a moron,' was his opening line, followed by the suggestion that Marquez must have thought he'd inherit the lead. On a more serious note, there were heartfelt thanks to Honda and his team for keeping faith. A remark from Marc VDS manager Michael Bartholémy underlined the importance of such a victory: 'Many people have worked all of their life to experience a day like today and to win in MotoGP.'

When Miller jumped from Moto3 to MotoGP, he may have wondered if he'd ever win another race, or at least how long it would take to do so. That is difficult to take for someone who has been used to going out with the belief that he can win. Maybe he avoided that dark thought, who knows, but it never has to cross his mind again.

RAPID REACTIONS

Consider this. In Free Practice Marc Marquez locked his front wheel under braking for Assen's first corner.

Enough smoke came off the tyre for most people to assume that the motor had seized and locked the rear wheel. The bike slewed and the forks hit the lock stops. He saved it. He saved a 'crash' that left a 20-metre black line the shape of a question mark on the tarmac and set off the airbag.

Consider this too. The algorithm that controls deployment of the airbag has been developed to detect the start of a crash and trigger the bag before the rider hits the ground. In the early days this couldn't be used in wet weather because the bike moved around too much and the software wasn't sufficiently sophisticated to tell the difference between a crash and a wobble. Nowadays, however, the accelerometers, gyros and ECU have your collarbones safely wrapped in a bouncy castle before your brain has registered the fact that you're no longer on a motorcycle.

Effectively, Marquez's reactions were quick enough to be outside the parameters that AlpineStars' engineers spent many years and millions of bytes calculating. Consider that.

Later in the day, Marquez crashed in qualifying. He was running to the fence before the bike stopped moving and when he got there he noticed a scooter with the keys in the ignition. He asked the photographer it belonged to if he could take it, but later admitted that he'd have taken it anyway. Happily, it was a Honda.

MOTUL TT ASSEN
TT CIRCUIT ASSEN
ROUND 8
JUNE 26

OFFICIAL TIMEKEEPER

RACE RESULTS

CIRCUIT LENGTH 2.822 miles

NO. OF LAPS 12 (restarted)

RACE DISTANCE 33.87 miles

WEATHER Wet, 17°C

TRACK TEMPERATURE 20°C

WINNER Jack Miller

FASTEST LAP 1m 48.339s, 93.8mph, Danilo Petrucci

LAP RECORD 1m 33.617s, 108.4mph, Marc Marquez (2015)

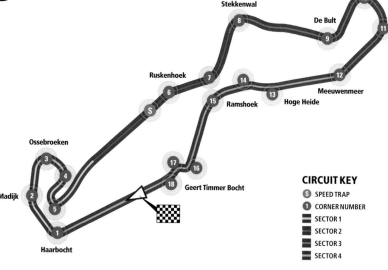

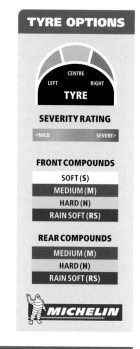

TYRE OPTIONS

SEVERITY RATING

<MILD   SEVERE>

FRONT COMPOUNDS

| SOFT (S) |
| MEDIUM (M) |
| HARD (H) |
| RAIN SOFT (RS) |

REAR COMPOUNDS

| MEDIUM (M) |
| HARD (H) |
| RAIN SOFT (RS) |

MICHELIN

CIRCUIT KEY
- **S** SPEED TRAP
- **1** CORNER NUMBER
- SECTOR 1
- SECTOR 2
- SECTOR 3
- SECTOR 4

QUALIFYING

	Rider	Nation	Motorcycle	Team	Time	Pole +
1	Dovizioso	ITA	Ducati	Ducati Team	1m 45.246s	
2	Rossi	ITA	Yamaha	Movistar Yamaha MotoGP	1m 45.961s	0.715s
3	Redding	GBR	Ducati	OCTO Pramac Yakhnich	1m 46.312s	1.066s
4	Marquez	SPA	Honda	Repsol Honda Team	1m 46.430s	1.184s
5	Crutchlow	GBR	Honda	LCR Honda	1m 46.568s	1.322s
6	Hernandez	COL	Ducati	Aspar Team MotoGP	1m 46.828s	1.582s
7	Espargaro P	SPA	Yamaha	Monster Yamaha Tech 3	1m 46.997s	1.751s
8	Espargaro A	SPA	Suzuki	Team Suzuki ECSTAR	1m 47.118s	1.872s
9	Iannone	ITA	Ducati	Ducati Team	1m 47.567s	2.321s
10	Petrucci	ITA	Ducati	OCTO Pramac Yakhnich	1m 47.601s	2.355s
11	Lorenzo	SPA	Yamaha	Movistar Yamaha MotoGP	1m 47.897s	2.651s
12	Viñales	SPA	Suzuki	Team Suzuki ECSTAR	1m 48.415s	3.169s
13	Barbera	SPA	Ducati	Avintia Racing	1m 48.830s	*0.348s
14	Smith	GBR	Yamaha	Monster Yamaha Tech 3	1m 48.909s	*0.427s
15	Bautista	SPA	Aprilia	Aprilia Racing Team Gresini	1m 49.163s	*0.681s
16	Pedrosa	SPA	Honda	Repsol Honda Team	1m 49.364s	*0.882s
17	Laverty	IRL	Ducati	Aspar Team MotoGP	1m 49.678s	*1.196s
18	Bradl	GER	Aprilia	Aprilia Racing Team Gresini	1m 49.685s	*1.203s
19	Miller	AUS	Honda	Estrella Galicia 0,0 Marc VDS	1m 49.775s	*1.293s
20	Rabat	SPA	Honda	Estrella Galicia 0,0 Marc VDS	1m 49.779s	*1.297s
21	Pirro	ITA	Ducati	Avintia Racing	1m 50.204s	*1.722s

* Gap with the fastest rider in the Q1 session

1 JACK MILLER
His first win in MotoGP, the first by a non-factory rider for nearly ten years, and the first Australian since Casey Stoner in 2012. Took the lead on the fourth lap and held his nerve in appalling conditions.

2 MARC MARQUEZ
Crossed the line celebrating like he'd won another title. His crew had told him repeatedly to just finish the race and Marc's repeated jabbing of finger at crash helmet told the story: he'd used his brain and come away with a 24-point championship lead.

3 SCOTT REDDING
Qualified third, his first front row in MotoGP, and rode with pace and control in the race, taking third off Pol Espargaro with three laps to go. At one point he was lapping two seconds quicker than the leaders. Scott's second rostrum.

4 POL ESPARGARO
Probably his best ever wet-weather ride and the first time he's been comfortable on a MotoGP bike in rain. Only lost third three laps from home but understood that Redding was much faster and acted accordingly. Again, impressive all weekend, and first Yamaha home.

5 ANDREA IANNONE
Crashed as the red flag came out, so was able to restart, albeit from the back of the grid. Worked his way through well – impressive for a rider never noted for his wet-weather form – and rescued some respectability.

6 HECTOR BARBERA
The soft wet tyre transformed his bike and for the first time in the weekend he was happy with it. Took some time to understand it when he discovered some feeling but it was an impressive ride as Hector has never been a wet-weather specialist.

7 EUGENE LAVERTY
Crashed on the first warm-up lap and started from back of grid on his second bike. Had a less eventful second race and continued his run of scoring points in every race.

8 STEFAN BRADL
Had to start the second race with his second bike due to an electronics problem that made itself felt in the interval between races.

9 MAVERICK VIÑALES
Great in the dry sessions, lost in the wet. Pointed to a lack of experience and therefore set-up data in wet conditions with what is still a new bike.

10 JORGE LORENZO
Thoroughly spooked by the conditions, as he has been at Assen since his collarbone-breaking crash in 2013. The only positive was that he scored five points and therefore gained some ground on Rossi.

11 TITO RABAT
Much more confident than usual in the wet; crashed trying to get past Bautista but remounted for useful points.

LAP CHART

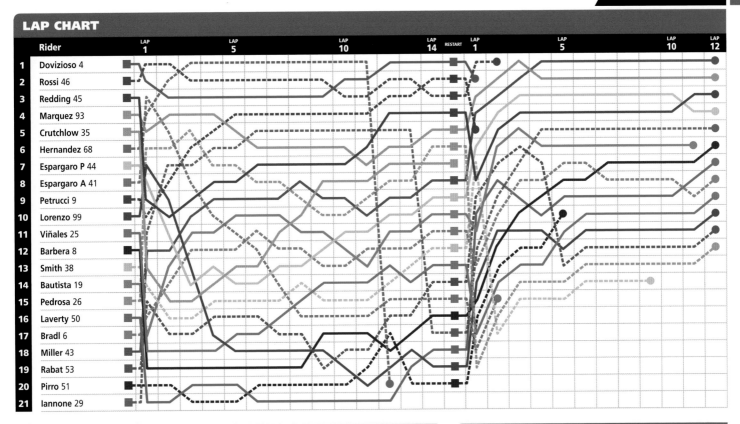

	Rider	LAP 1	LAP 5	LAP 10	LAP 14	RESTART	LAP 1	LAP 5	LAP 10	LAP 12
1	Dovizioso 4									
2	Rossi 46									
3	Redding 45									
4	Marquez 93									
5	Crutchlow 35									
6	Hernandez 68									
7	Espargaro P 44									
8	Espargaro A 41									
9	Petrucci 9									
10	Lorenzo 99									
11	Viñales 25									
12	Barbera 8									
13	Smith 38									
14	Bautista 19									
15	Pedrosa 26									
16	Laverty 50									
17	Bradl 6									
18	Miller 43									
19	Rabat 53									
20	Pirro 51									
21	Iannone 29									

RACE

	Rider	Motorcycle	Race time	Time +	Fastest lap	Avg. speed	Tyres
1	Miller	Honda	22m 17.447s		1m 50.296s	91.2mph	RS/RS
2	Marquez	Honda	22m 19.438s	1.991s	*1m 48.409s	91.0mph	RS/RS
3	Redding	Ducati	22m 23.353s	5.906s	*1m 48.897s	90.7mph	RS/RS
4	Espargaro P	Yamaha	22m 27.259s	9.812s	*1m 49.200s	90.5mph	RS/RS
5	Iannone	Ducati	22m 35.282s	17.835s	*1m 48.607s	89.9mph	RS/RS
6	Barbera	Ducati	22m 36.139s	18.692s	*1m 51.143s	89.9mph	RS/RS
7	Laverty	Ducati	22m 40.052s	22.605s	1m 50.716s	89.6mph	RS/RS
8	Bradl	Aprilia	22m 41.050s	23.603s	*1m 50.395s	89.5mph	RS/RS
9	Viñales	Suzuki	22m 43.595s	26.148s	*1m 49.881s	89.4mph	RS/RS
10	Lorenzo	Yamaha	22m 45.051s	27.604s	*1m 50.848s	89.3mph	RS/RS
11	Rabat	Honda	23m 39.277s	1m 21.830s	*1m 51.686s	85.9mph	RS/RS
12	Pedrosa	Honda	24m 11.816s	1m 54.369s	*1m 50.325s	83.9mph	RS/RS
13	Smith	Yamaha	23m 34.917s	3 laps	*1m 50.927s	64.6mph	RS/RS
NC	Bautista	Aprilia	20m 44.021s	1 lap	*1m 50.393s	89.8mph	RS/RS
NC	Pirro	Ducati	9m 35.702s	7 laps	*1m 50.151s	88.2mph	RS/RS
NC	Rossi	Yamaha	3m 45.283s	10 laps	*1m 48.647s	90.2mph	RS/RS
NC	Espargaro A	Suzuki	3m 59.019s	10 laps	1m 52.019s	85.0mph	RS/RS
NC	Dovizioso	Ducati	1m 56.097s	11 laps	*1m 48.635s	87.4mph	RS/RS
NC	Petrucci	Ducati	1m 57.722s	11 laps	*1m 48.339s	86.2mph	RS/RS
NC	Crutchlow	Honda	–	–	*1m 48.536s	–	RS/RS
NC	Hernandez	Ducati	–	–	*1m 48.745s	–	RS/RS

Results are for the 12-lap race that followed the red-flagged 14-lap 'Part 1' and for which full championship points were awarded; grid order for the race was determined by finishing positions in 'Part 1'; * indicates those riders who set their fastest lap in 'Part 1'

CHAMPIONSHIP

	Rider	Nation	Team	Points
1	Marquez	SPA	Repsol Honda Team	145
2	Lorenzo	SPA	Movistar Yamaha MotoGP	121
3	Rossi	ITA	Movistar Yamaha MotoGP	103
4	Pedrosa	SPA	Repsol Honda Team	86
5	Viñales	SPA	Team Suzuki ECSTAR	79
6	Espargaro P	SPA	Monster Yamaha Tech 3	72
7	Barbera	SPA	Avintia Racing	58
8	Iannone	ITA	Ducati Team	52
9	Espargaro A	SPA	Team Suzuki ECSTAR	49
10	Laverty	IRL	Aspar Team MotoGP	48
11	Dovizioso	ITA	Ducati Team	43
12	Bradl	GER	Aprilia Racing Team Gresini	37
13	Miller	AUS	Estrella Galicia 0,0 Marc VDS	33
14	Redding	GBR	OCTO Pramac Yakhnich	32
	Smith	GBR	Monster Yamaha Tech 3	32
16	Bautista	SPA	Aprilia Racing Team Gresini	29
17	Petrucci	ITA	OCTO Pramac Yakhnich	24
18	Crutchlow	GBR	LCR Honda	20
19	Pirro	ITA	OCTO Pramac Yakhnich	19
20	Rabat	SPA	Estrella Galicia 0,0 Marc VDS	18
21	Baz	FRA	Avintia Racing	8
22	Hernandez	COL	Aspar Team MotoGP	3

12 DANI PEDROSA
A horrible weekend. Used the soft rear in both 'races'; crashed on the first lap after the restart but remounted to score four points.

13 BRADLEY SMITH
Crashed and remounted after a good start to the race. Reckoned his first lap was the most competitive of his season so far.

DID NOT FINISH

ALVARO BAUTISTA
Crashed out of sixth place at the start of the last lap when he couldn't resist trying to dive inside Iannone.

MICHELE PIRRO
Crashed late enough in the first race to start the second, but crashed again.

DANILO PETRUCCI
Lying second and looking like a winner when the red flag came out, then had his engine stop in the second race.

VALENTINO ROSSI
Pushed too hard and lost the front while leading. As he admitted, it was rider error. His despair as he tried to restart the M-1 showed what a third non-scoring race meant to his championship chances.

ANDREA DOVIZIOSO
Pole setter for only the fourth time in his MotoGP career. Crashed on the second lap of the restart while lying second.

ALEIX ESPARGARO
On the outside at the first corner and therefore on the receiving end of domino-effect pushing and shoving that sent him off track. Was looking good and making up places when he crashed on lap three.

CAL CRUTCHLOW
The first victim of the extra grip of the soft rear tyre overpowering the front.

YONNY HERNANDEZ
Crashed out of the first 'race' while holding a handy lead; remounted and started the second race only to crash again.

DID NOT RACE

LORIS BAZ
Still recovering from his foot injury sustained at Mugello, again replaced by Pirro.

GoPro MOTORRAD
GRAND PRIX DEUTSCHLAND
SACHSENRING

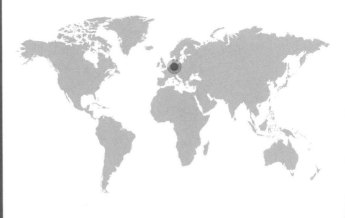

AN INSPIRED GAMBLE

Marc Marquez took a crushing victory as the Yamahas struggled; Crutchlow and Dovizioso completed the rostrum

Marc Marquez made three major mistakes in this race, all before the bike change on a drying track, but then rode the most astonishing half-dozen laps you're ever likely to see.

If you want an example of what makes Marquez so astounding, so special, then this race was it. For the start he chose the softer of the two wet choices of front tyre (mistake number one) and when he went into the pits to change bikes he was far behind the leaders in 14th place. After his out lap he was 18th and riding on slicks on a cold track that was only beginning to develop a dry line. That dry line can't have been more than half a metre wide going into some fast corners, such as Turn 8, where he'd had a massive crash in warm-up (mistake number two) and run off track during the race (mistake number three).

Marquez was the first to change to slicks although Andrea Iannone and Loris Baz had gone in earlier and tried intermediates (in the Frenchman's case with a slick rear), a choice they and others would have cause to regret. Marc won the race in a set of blazing laps that from the 20th lap to the 24th reduced the best lap time from 1m 33s (set by Iannone on inters) to the 1m 26s bracket. On one lap Marquez took seven seconds out of the leaders. A 36-second deficit became a 21-second lead within seven laps.

Those numbers are not typos.

Was luck involved? Probably only in warm-up when the only injury he received was a grazed

'IT WAS AN OPTION TO USE INTERMEDIATES, BUT FOR ME IT IS BETTER TO GO DIRECTLY TO A SLICK AND I CHOSE THE BEST STRATEGY'

MARC MARQUEZ

chin. His team refused to countenance the use of inters and Marc understood that in the wet but drying conditions at the Sachsenring that day you usually have to change bikes early and then be very brave during the early laps on the new tyres. He and his team were right on both counts.

Second-placed Cal Crutchlow made up for what he considered to be, with some justification, an injustice of qualifying (he was fourth fastest overall but didn't get out of Q1) by using the harder front wet before changing to slicks when Andrea Dovizioso led the leading group into pitlane at the end of lap 23. Cal, Dovi, Valentino Rossi and Hector Barbera emerged from pitlane in a tight group only to find themselves tangled up with Scott Redding and a long way behind Jack Miller, who was still on wets, and a charging Marquez. Crutchlow used his slicks bravely, while Dovi – with an inter-front/slick-rear combo – was able to mug Redding on the last lap.

Germany was always going to be a challenge for Michelin, with precious little testing and uncooperative weather, but the company had the foresight to bring along a new super-soft wet-weather front tyre. Friday was dry but cold, with track temperatures barely over ten degrees. The result was an early crash at the fearsome Turn 11 for Jorge Lorenzo. Everyone remembers the 2013 crash that has haunted his Assen efforts, but most forget that his next act was to crash at the Sachsenring and bend the metalwork in his

OPPOSITE Danilo Petrucci led for a couple of laps before crashing and setting fire to his Ducati

LEFT The whole field started the race on wets

ABOVE Hector Barbera qualified second, equalling his career-best

collarbone. The ghosts had travelled with him. Jorge became a shadow of his usual self and didn't even manage to get seeded directly into the final qualifying session. The problem was getting heat into, and feel from, the front tyre. Jorge wasn't alone. Rossi took the discretionary route on Friday but qualified on the front row when the weather was much kinder on Saturday. He did make the point, though, that if it was cold on Sunday he would be in 'big, big trouble as we cannot ride the bike'.

And that's what happened.

Knowing he'd take far too long to get his front slick working after a bike change, Valentino and his team decided to fit the second bike with intermediates front and rear. Like the others, he found that it took time to understand the inters. Rossi dropped off the pace of the leading group with which he had pitted and ended up eighth, mugged by Miller on the last lap.

The Aussie stayed out when the leaders went in – he was the last man to change bikes – and led for two laps. He had clawed his way up to the leading group on wets and his pace when he emerged from the pits was seriously impressive. Andrea Dovizioso's compromise tyre choice was good enough for him to overhaul Scott Redding, who was on inters, on the last lap, but there was no way he could hold off Crutchlow. It's worth noting that Redding came within a corner of taking back-to-back rostrum finishes. It was slicks

ABOVE The Yamaha crew waited for Rossi to pit; and waited, and waited…

BELOW Scott Redding looked to be heading for his second rostrum in a row but was mugged by Dovizioso and Crutchlow in the final laps

FUTURE PERFECT

Following on from the Assen announcement of the renewal of the contract between IRTA and Dorna for another five years, in Germany it was the turn of the independent teams to resolve their place in MotoGP.

This affected seven teams: Tech 3, Marc VDS, Gresini, LCR, Pramac, Aspar and Avintia. The money they would receive from IRTA would double for 2017 and the cost of leasing would be capped at €2.2 million (two bikes for one rider). Should any factory charge more, the difference would be deducted from their fees and handed over to the customer team.

Just as importantly, Dorna guaranteed that the grid would not grow beyond 24 bikes, with Lucio Ceccinello's LCR team having the option to take up the last slot (presently, they only run one bike). Should a new manufacturer wish to enter the series, they would have to do so with one of the independent teams – as Aprilia have done with Team Gresini.

Rough calculations suggested that the IRTA/Dorna arrangement would cover around half of a team's costs, still leaving a lot of work to do to raise sponsorship to cover the expense of leasing bikes and transporting them and approximately 40 staff around the world. Nevertheless, this was an important step for the teams involved and a significant factor in keeping the championship stable.

Stand by for the third (and final?) part of the grand plan. This is to have all the factories – Honda, Yamaha, Suzuki, Ducati, Aprilia and KTM – fielding one works team and supplying one satellite squad.

all round on the rostrum, with the exception of Dovi's front intermediate.

Andrea thought he stayed out for too long, concentrating instead on leading the race. The rest of the group waited for him to make his move and followed suit – the usual tactic of doing what your competitor does. That's why Marquez swapped from soft to super-soft front tyres on the grid – because that's what the other top men had done. That's why for at least three laps Rossi, much to his team's frustration, ignored his pit board telling him to come in.

Marquez's victory at the Sachsenring, his seventh consecutive win from pole, was down to the clear thinking of his team as much as the brilliance of the rider himself. They knew inters were a distraction and that getting on slicks early was the key to victory. That combination saw him finish the first half of the season with a very comfortable 48-point lead as he headed for the beach. If anybody understands how he did that on a motorcycle that doesn't accelerate and is more than a little difficult to ride, would you please let the factory Yamaha team know.

RIGHT Marc Marquez won for the first time in six races – and, just as importantly, his main title challengers had bad days

GoPro MOTORRAD GRAND PRIX DEUTSCHLAND
SACHSENRING

ROUND 9
JULY 17

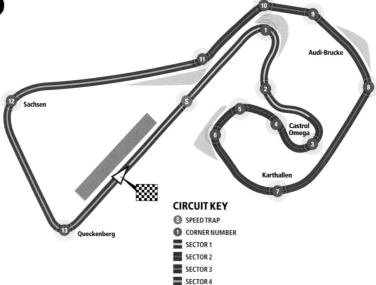

OFFICIAL TIMEKEEPER

RACE RESULTS

CIRCUIT LENGTH 2.281 miles

NO. OF LAPS 30

RACE DISTANCE 68.432 miles

WEATHER Wet, 21°C

TRACK TEMPERATURE 24°C

WINNER Marc Marquez

FASTEST LAP 1m 25.019s, 96.6mph, Cal Crutchlow

LAP RECORD 1m 21.530s, 100.7mph, Marc Marquez (2015)

CIRCUIT KEY
- (S) SPEED TRAP
- (1) CORNER NUMBER
- SECTOR 1
- SECTOR 2
- SECTOR 3
- SECTOR 4

TYRE OPTIONS

TYRE

SEVERITY RATING
<MILD   SEVERE>

FRONT COMPOUNDS
| SOFT (S) |
| MEDIUM (M) |
| INTERMEDIATE (I) |
| RAIN SUPER SOFT (RSS) |
| RAIN SOFT (RS) |

REAR COMPOUNDS
| MEDIUM (M) |
| INTERMEDIATE (I) |
| RAIN SOFT (RS) |

MICHELIN

QUALIFYING

	Rider	Nation	Motorcycle	Team	Time	Pole +
1	Marquez	SPA	Honda	Repsol Honda Team	1m 21.160s	
2	Barbera	SPA	Ducati	Avintia Racing	1m 21.572s	0.412s
3	Rossi	ITA	Yamaha	Movistar Yamaha MotoGP	1m 21.666s	0.506s
4	Petrucci	ITA	Ducati	OCTO Pramac Yakhnich	1m 21.666s	0.506s
5	Espargaro P	SPA	Yamaha	Monster Yamaha Tech 3	1m 21.738s	0.578s
6	Viñales	SPA	Suzuki	Team Suzuki ECSTAR	1m 21.784s	0.624s
7	Dovizioso	ITA	Ducati	Ducati Team	1m 21.858s	0.698s
8	Espargaro A	SPA	Suzuki	Team Suzuki ECSTAR	1m 21.883s	0.723s
9	Iannone	ITA	Ducati	Ducati Team	1m 21.890s	0.730s
10	Pedrosa	SPA	Honda	Repsol Honda Team	1m 21.892s	0.732s
11	Lorenzo	SPA	Yamaha	Movistar Yamaha MotoGP	1m 22.088s	0.928s
12	Hernandez	COL	Ducati	Pull & Bear Aspar Team	1m 22.346s	1.186s
13	Crutchlow	GBR	Honda	LCR Honda	1m 21.783s	*0.071s
14	Smith	GBR	Yamaha	Monster Yamaha Tech 3	1m 21.994s	*0.282s
15	Redding	GBR	Ducati	OCTO Pramac Yakhnich	1m 22.236s	*0.524s
16	Miller	AUS	Honda	Estrella Galicia 0,0 Marc VDS	1m 22.382s	*0.670s
17	Bradl	GER	Aprilia	Aprilia Racing Team Gresini	1m 22.493s	*0.781s
18	Laverty	IRL	Ducati	Pull & Bear Aspar Team	1m 22.567s	*0.855s
19	Bautista	SPA	Aprilia	Aprilia Racing Team Gresini	1m 22.670s	*0.958s
20	Baz	FRA	Ducati	Avintia Racing	1m 22.860s	*1.148s
21	Rabat	SPA	Honda	Estrella Galicia 0,0 Marc VDS	1m 23.075s	*1.363s

* Gap with the fastest rider in the Q1 session

1 MARC MARQUEZ
A remarkable victory after a big crash in warm-up and choosing the wrong front tyre for the start. After he switched to slicks earlier than his championship rivals, he rode the very narrow dry line with such astonishing speed and precision that at one point his lead was over 20 seconds.

2 CAL CRUTCHLOW
First rostrum of the year, a reward for bravery on the harder front wet and then on slicks. Changed bikes with the lead group and beat them all, setting the fastest lap of the race on the way. A remarkable ride anyway and even better

seeing as he was 13th on the grid having gambled on saving a tyre for the second qualifying session.

3 ANDREA DOVIZIOSO
Retook the lead when Petrucci crashed and led to the bike change. Realised he may have stayed out two laps too long to stand a chance of winning but still content with a rostrum.

4 SCOTT REDDING
Fought back after a bad start, pitted seventh and was second starting the last lap. The team sent him out with inters and he couldn't hold off first Crutchlow and

then Dovizioso. So nearly two rostrums in succession.

5 ANDREA IANNONE
The first top man to change bikes and go out on intermediates front and rear. Managed to improve his position in the second part of the race and gained on the three men above him in the points table.

6 DANI PEDROSA
Not as fast as he expected in the wet first half following a very quick warm-up, but was really compromised by having to stay out longer than he wanted when his second bike wouldn't start.

7 JACK MILLER
If he'd come in to change to slicks when his team told him to, he would probably have stood on the rostrum again. Caught the leaders and led when they pitted, then blazingly fast on slicks. Took two places on the last lap and nearly got Pedrosa too.

8 VALENTINO ROSSI
Great qualifying and in the leading group when they pitted – albeit later than his team wanted. Used intermediates as he knew the front slick would take time to come in but found them very difficult due to total lack of feeling.

9 HECTOR BARBERA
A brilliant second in qualifying (he reminded everyone he was top Ducati rider in the championship and on a two-year-old bike). In the top three for nine laps before bike change but lost out on the dry bike with an inter on the front and a rear slick.

10 ALVARO BAUTISTA
Used a new swing arm and induction tracts. A late changer to intermediates, but a very solid result that saw him finish considerably closer than usual to the other factory bikes.

LAP CHART

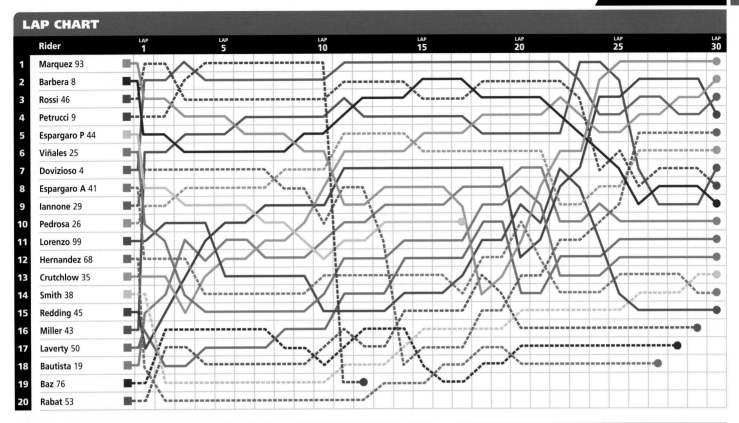

	Rider	LAP 1	LAP 5	LAP 10	LAP 15	LAP 20	LAP 25	LAP 30
1	Marquez 93							
2	Barbera 8							
3	Rossi 46							
4	Petrucci 9							
5	Espargaro P 44							
6	Viñales 25							
7	Dovizioso 4							
8	Espargaro A 41							
9	Iannone 29							
10	Pedrosa 26							
11	Lorenzo 99							
12	Hernandez 68							
13	Crutchlow 35							
14	Smith 38							
15	Redding 45							
16	Miller 43							
17	Laverty 50							
18	Bautista 19							
19	Baz 76							
20	Rabat 53							

RACE

	Rider	Motorcycle	Race time	Time +	Fastest lap	Avg. speed	Tyres
1	Marquez	Honda	47m 03.239s		1m 26.750s	87.2mph	RSS/RS
2	Crutchlow	Honda	47m 13.096s	9.857s	1m 25.019s	86.9mph	RS/RS
3	Dovizioso	Ducati	47m 14.852s	11.613s	1m 25.446s	86.9mph	RSS/RS
4	Redding	Ducati	47m 15.231s	11.992s	1m 26.882s	86.9mph	RS/RS
5	Iannone	Ducati	47m 25.994s	22.755s	1m 26.713s	86.6mph	RSS/RS
6	Pedrosa	Honda	47m 29.159s	25.920s	1m 27.190s	86.4mph	RSS/RS
7	Miller	Honda	47m 29.282s	26.043s	1m 26.510s	86.4mph	RS/RS
8	Rossi	Yamaha	47m 29.688s	26.449s	1m 27.022s	86.4mph	RSS/RS
9	Barbera	Ducati	47m 29.853s	26.614s	1m 26.760s	86.4mph	RSS/RS
10	Bautista	Aprilia	47m 34.513s	31.274s	1m 28.208s	86.2mph	RS/RS
11	Laverty	Ducati	47m 44.447s	41.208s	1m 28.187s	86.0mph	RSS/RS
12	Viñales	Suzuki	47m 45.397s	42.158s	1m 26.821s	85.9mph	RSS/RS
13	Smith	Yamaha	48m 06.368s	1m 03.129s	1m 26.893s	85.3mph	RSS/RS
14	Espargaro A	Suzuki	48m 09.330s	1m 06.091s	1m 28.361s	85.3mph	RSS/RS
15	Lorenzo	Yamaha	48m 20.933s	1m 17.694s	1m 29.176s	84.9mph	RSS/RS
16	Rabat	Honda	47m 49.257s	1 lap	1m 28.212s	83.0mph	RS/RS
17	Baz	Ducati	48m 01.949s	2 laps	1m 29.954s	79.7mph	RSS/RS
18	Hernandez	Ducati	47m 30.750s	3 laps	1m 31.793s	77.7mph	RSS/RS
NC	Espargaro P	Yamaha	27m 13.252s	13 laps	1m 34.988s	85.4mph	RSS/RS
NC	Petrucci	Ducati	20m 54.124s	18 laps	1m 33.865s	78.5mph	RS/RS

CHAMPIONSHIP

	Rider	Nation	Team	Points
1	Marquez	SPA	Repsol Honda Team	170
2	Lorenzo	SPA	Movistar Yamaha MotoGP	122
3	Rossi	ITA	Movistar Yamaha MotoGP	111
4	Pedrosa	SPA	Repsol Honda Team	96
5	Viñales	SPA	Team Suzuki ECSTAR	83
6	Espargaro P	SPA	Monster Yamaha Tech 3	72
7	Barbera	SPA	Avintia Racing	65
8	Iannone	ITA	Ducati Team	63
9	Dovizioso	ITA	Ducati Team	59
10	Laverty	IRL	Pull & Bear Aspar Team	53
11	Espargaro A	SPA	Team Suzuki ECSTAR	51
12	Redding	GBR	OCTO Pramac Yakhnich	45
13	Miller	AUS	Estrella Galicia 0,0 Marc VDS	42
14	Crutchlow	GBR	LCR Honda	40
15	Bradl	GER	Aprilia Racing Team Gresini	37
16	Smith	GBR	Monster Yamaha Tech 3	35
17	Bautista	SPA	Aprilia Racing Team Gresini	35
18	Petrucci	ITA	OCTO Pramac Yakhnich	24
19	Pirro	ITA	OCTO Pramac Yakhnich	19
20	Rabat	SPA	Estrella Galicia 0,0 Marc VDS	18
21	Baz	FRA	Avintia Racing	8
22	Hernandez	COL	Pull & Bear Aspar Team	3

11 EUGENE LAVERTY
The only man other than Marquez to score points in every race of the season so far. Serious traction-control problems on his first bike. Nevertheless, stayed out a little too long, then very fast on his second bike with inters.

12 MAVERICK VIÑALES
After Assen, the team tried to develop some strategies for damp conditions. Unfortunately, there was no real improvement and while Mack can adjust his riding to find traction in the dry, that seems to be impossible in the wet.

13 BRADLEY SMITH
Lost a knee slider – a serious disadvantage in the wet – when Hernandez side-swiped him on the first lap. Pitted at the right time and made up a couple of places.

14 ALEIX ESPARGARO
Too much spinning in warm-up turned into too much traction control in the race. Wet-weather performance was clearly a major problem for Suzuki.

15 JORGE LORENZO
A continuation of the nightmare of Assen. Fell at Turn 11 in FP1 and never went fast again. Never generated any confidence in the front tyre in cool or wet conditions, or when it was hot on Saturday, or on inters on his second bike in the race.

16 TITO RABAT
Crashed at the final corner and remounted just after half distance.

17 LORIS BAZ
Second man into the pits. Left with an inter front and a slick rear but came straight back in for a rear inter too.

18 YONNY HERNANDEZ
Crashed on the second lap and lost two laps getting back to the pits.

NEROGIARDINI MOTORRAD
GRAND PRIX VON ÖSTERREICH
RED BULL RING – SPIELBERG

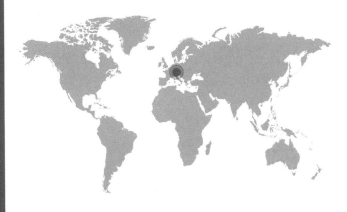

THE HILLS ARE ALIVE

Ducati won at last and Lorenzo also had a good day as MotoGP made a triumphant return to the Alpine circuit

It's almost impossible to overestimate the pressure that had accumulated on the Ducati team by this stage of the season. With no win since Casey Stoner's 2010 Phillip Island masterclass, the Bologna revolution that brought in Gigi Dall'Igna had yet to deliver. But now the Desmosedicis came to a circuit that clearly played to their strengths. Opportunities had been thrown away earlier in the year and here was one they had to win. Testing showed that Ducati, according to the factory Yamaha riders, had a second in hand on everybody. If the red bikes couldn't win here, then where?

The Red Bull Ring – formerly the A1 Ring, before that the Osterreichring and originally Zeltweg – is very fast, with fewer corners than any other circuit on the calendar, and just to complicate matters only three of its ten corners are left-handers. If you couldn't get the power down out of Turn 1 and blast uphill through the left-hand kink of Turn 2 to the tight third corner at the top of the circuit, you weren't going to have a pleasant weekend. No Honda rider had a pleasant weekend.

Marc Marquez came within an inch of serious injury in free practice when he nearly torpedoed team-mate Dani Pedrosa after his bike snapped sideways as he braked for Turn 3. He just managed to miss Dani, who had already gone wide and was off line, but crashed hard on to his right shoulder. How violent was the impact?

His other shoulder was pulled out of joint by the handlebars. Fortunately, that shoulder – it was the third time it had been dislocated – went back in of its own accord during the scooter ride back to the pits. Under the circumstances, Marc regarded fifth place in the race as a very acceptable result.

Jack Miller tempted fate a little too much by saying he was 100 per cent fit for the first time in the season. A massive crash in warm-up at Turn 8 put him out of the race. Turn 8 gave rise to significant safety concerns, but Jack's injuries came from tumbling through the gravel trap rather than hitting anything. Nevertheless, for 2017 the riders will require the barrier at the exit to be moved as it comes in too close. There were similar concerns over Turn 10 but Race Direction took action before practice by effectively taking three metres off its radius. This was done with paint, so there was no longer a kerb, but it was universally agreed to be a good move.

There was one question after practice. Could anyone give the Ducatis a race? The answer appeared to be that Valentino Rossi could. His wheelies after the first practice sessions were a clue – remember Jerez? – and then he split the Ducatis in qualifying for his seventh front-row start of the year. It didn't quite work out that way in the race. The Yamahas were a lot closer than anyone expected but it was difficult to dispel the impression that the Ducatis were controlling the

'I AM REALLY
VERY HAPPY,
BECAUSE IN MY
OPINION WE DID
AN INCREDIBLE
RACE'
ANDREA IANNONE

NeroGiardini NeroGiardini NeroGiardini NeroGiardini NeroGiardini

NeroGiardini

NeroGiardini NeroGiardini

NeroGiardini

14:00:39

contest while conserving their fuel and tyres.

So Ducati finally won. And they did it with clever management of their resources. They resisted the temptation to try and blast away from the factory Yamahas, using a fuel-conserving ignition map off the start and switching to a racier setting at around half distance. That helped conserve the tyres as well. Given their speed at the test in Austria, it was no surprise that the Ducatis finished first and second. But given the planning and self-control needed to take advantage of their strengths, maybe it was a surprise that the winner was Andrea Iannone rather than Andrea Dovizioso. Iannone had enough left in his soft rear in the closing stages to keep Dovizioso at bay. Dovi complained of not having the same grip in the many right-handers and, although better on the brakes, couldn't get close enough to make a pass.

As this is Maniac Joe we are talking about, there was a bit of trickery involved. Alone among the top men, Iannone chose to race with the softer rear tyre. He planned to do this but indulged in a little subterfuge, telling the post-qualifying press conference that he thought he could race with either rear tyre – then come race day changed wheels on the grid. At his post-race conference, Rossi simply refused to believe that Iannone had raced with the softer tyre. Not surprisingly, Dovi wasn't exactly overjoyed. He did his best to sound happy about Ducati winning for the first time in nearly six years, about the 1–2 result, about

ABOVE Jack Miller's warm-up crash put him out of the race with back and hand injuries and affected him for the next four races

BELOW Jorge Lorenzo's Yamaha splits the factory Ducatis early in the race

KTM JOINS THE FUN

The first Austrian GP since 1997 was an undoubted success. Facilities for paddock people and fans were excellent, everything worked smoothly, and the scenery is breathtaking.

National pride was upheld by a KTM 1–2 in the Moto3 race, and then the enormous crowd was treated to the public début of the bike with which KTM will enter the MotoGP class in 2017 – the RC16.

Mika Kallio, who would ride the bike as a wild card at Valencia, and Alex Hofmann turned a few laps before the MotoGP race. First impressions were, as you would expect, very good. The RC16 sounded similar to the Honda RCV, not surprisingly as it is a high-revving V4. There the similarity with mainstream MotoGP design ends. As on the company's Moto3 machines, the frame is tubular steel and the suspension is supplied by WP, a subsidiary company of KTM. The bike looked good as well as sounding sharp. Unofficial timing from the private test at the Red Bull Ring indicated that it was at least as fast as would be expected from a project at this point in its development.

With Bradley Smith and Pol Espargaro signed to ride in 2017 and KTM's desire to compete – and win – in every championship they can, this is a motorcycle the Japanese and Italian factories will be keeping a very close eye on.

The Austrian factory is also entering Moto2 next year with a bike built along the same principles with Brad Binder and Miguel Oliveira as riders.

the vindication of Gigi Dall'Igna's work – about everything really. But none of it rang true.

It was easy to overlook the third man on the rostrum. A grinning Jorge Lorenzo reminded us that he has had tough times in his career before and come through. We should have known better than to forget about the reigning world champion, but Lorenzo hadn't stood on a rostrum since Mugello. This time, he ran the Ducatis closer than anyone thought possible, took five points out of Marquez's points lead and beat his team-mate. That's as good a weekend as he could have hoped for.

It's worth noting that Maverick Viñales was somewhat disappointed in his sixth place close behind Marquez. He had been closer to the front on Friday and Saturday but the higher track temperatures on race day again saw the Suzuki tyres slipping rather than gripping. A Suzuki rider disappointed with a close sixth place? How times change.

What didn't change was the sight of Marc Marquez having a difficult weekend but leaving on Sunday night smiling, having increased his championship lead.

RIGHT Andrea Iannone was delighted with his first MotoGP victory; Jorge Lorenzo was nearly as happy with third

NEROGIARDINI MOTORRAD GRAND PRIX VON ÖSTERREICH

RED BULL RING – SPIELBERG

ROUND 10
AUGUST 14

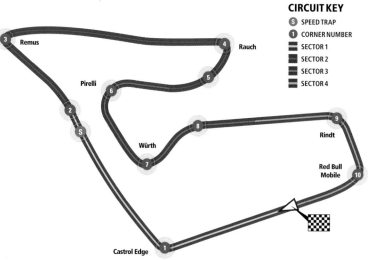

CIRCUIT KEY
- S SPEED TRAP
- 1 CORNER NUMBER
- ▬ SECTOR 1
- ▬ SECTOR 2
- ▬ SECTOR 3
- ▬ SECTOR 4

RACE RESULTS

CIRCUIT LENGTH 2.683 miles
NO. OF LAPS 28
RACE DISTANCE 75.126 miles
WEATHER Dry, 27°C
TRACK TEMPERATURE 46°C
WINNER Andrea Iannone
FASTEST LAP 1m 24.561s, 114.2mph, Andrea Iannone (record)
PREVIOUS LAP RECORD Not applicable

QUALIFYING

	Rider	Nation	Motorcycle	Team	Time	Pole +
1	Iannone	ITA	Ducati	Ducati Team	1m 23.142s	
2	Rossi	ITA	Yamaha	Movistar Yamaha MotoGP	1m 23.289s	0.147s
3	Dovizioso	ITA	Ducati	Ducati Team	1m 23.298s	0.156s
4	Lorenzo	SPA	Yamaha	Movistar Yamaha MotoGP	1m 23.361s	0.219s
5	Marquez	SPA	Honda	Repsol Honda Team	1m 23.475s	0.333s
6	Viñales	SPA	Suzuki	Team Suzuki ECSTAR	1m 23.584s	0.442s
7	Crutchlow	GBR	Honda	LCR Honda	1m 23.597s	0.455s
8	Redding	GBR	Ducati	OCTO Pramac Yakhnich	1m 23.777s	0.635s
9	Espargaro A	SPA	Suzuki	Team Suzuki ECSTAR	1m 23.813s	0.671s
10	Barbera	SPA	Ducati	Avintia Racing	1m 23.822s	0.680s
11	Laverty	IRL	Ducati	Pull & Bear Aspar Team	1m 24.218s	1.076s
12	Pedrosa	SPA	Honda	Repsol Honda Team	1m 24.263s	1.121s
13	Petrucci	ITA	Ducati	OCTO Pramac Yakhnich	1m 24.123s	*0.162s
14	Smith	GBR	Yamaha	Monster Yamaha Tech 3	1m 24.126s	*0.165s
15	Espargaro P	SPA	Yamaha	Monster Yamaha Tech 3	1m 24.265s	*0.304s
16	Hernandez	COL	Ducati	Pull & Bear Aspar Team	1m 24.472s	*0.511s
17	Pirro	ITA	Ducati	Ducati Team	1m 24.593s	*0.632s
18	Rabat	SPA	Honda	Estrella Galicia 0,0 Marc VDS	1m 24.665s	*0.704s
19	Bautista	SPA	Aprilia	Aprilia Racing Team Gresini	1m 24.673s	*0.712s
20	Miller	AUS	Honda	Estrella Galicia 0,0 Marc VDS	1m 24.852s	*0.891s
21	Bradl	GER	Aprilia	Aprilia Racing Team Gresini	1m 24.895s	*0.934s
22	Baz	FRA	Ducati	Avintia Racing	1m 25.192s	*1.231s

* Gap with the fastest rider in the Q1 session

1 ANDREA IANNONE
Swapped to the softer rear tyre on the grid and was able to hold off his team-mate when the pair switched to more powerful maps after half distance. Had a plan, and was restrained enough to make it work for his maiden win.

2 ANDREA DOVIZIOSO
Couldn't stay with his team-mate and tried to pretend he was delighted by a Ducati 1–2. His harder rear tyre lost Dovi ground in right-handers towards the end of the race, but he was never troubled by the Yamahas.

3 JORGE LORENZO
It looked like the old Jorge on the rostrum and in the race. He was cocky beforehand, dealt with his team-mate in the race, and took a few points off Marquez. It was, he said, the best result he could have hoped for.

4 VALENTINO ROSSI
Really happy on Friday and when he got on the front row on Saturday, splitting the Ducatis. However, the race was more difficult. Valentino did lead over the line once but ran on at Turn 1 and dropped to fifth. Got back past Marquez, but couldn't get on terms with the rostrum men.

5 MARC MARQUEZ
Dislocated shoulder in nasty accident in practice, took a few risks at the start of the race but soon realised that he had to think of the championship.

6 MAVERICK VIÑALES
Slightly disappointed with sixth, although he was with the leading group throughout. Used new winglets, which he liked, but still lacked in acceleration out of slow corners; despite that his rear tyre was well worn by the finish.

7 DANI PEDROSA
Another depressing weekend. Confidence-

sapping crash on cold tarmac on Friday, had to go through the first qualifying session, only 12th on the grid. Next to that, race day wasn't as bad.

8 SCOTT REDDING
First independent after having to juggle engine maps to conserve fuel; held off Smith's challenge over the closing stages.

9 BRADLEY SMITH
Lucky not to react to the jump starts all around him. Very fast in the middle part of the race but had to put some serious stress on the tyres and didn't have a lot left to fight for top independent with Redding.

10 POL ESPARGARO
His least competitive race of the season, but Pol did manage to increase the gap on his direct rivals for the top independent rider in the championship.

11 DANILO PETRUCCI
Gained a place on the last corner when he knocked Laverty off, so received a grid penalty for Silverstone.

12 MICHELE PIRRO
Wild-card entry. Didn't make his target of the top ten but consoled himself with the thought that his work had contributed to Ducati's success.

LAP CHART

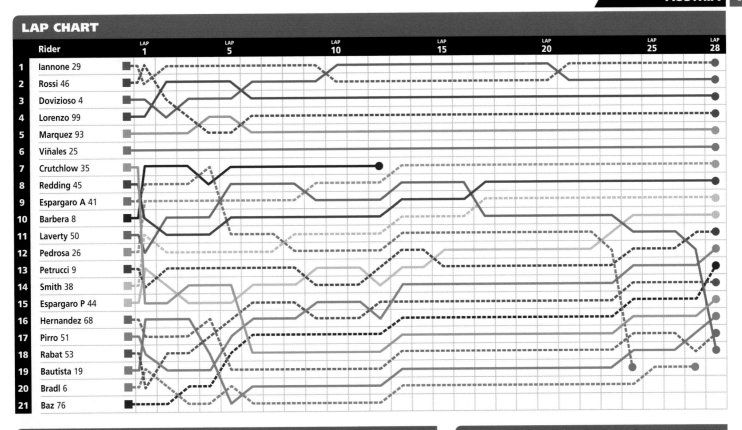

	Rider	LAP 1		LAP 5		LAP 10		LAP 15		LAP 20		LAP 25	LAP 28
1	Iannone 29												
2	Rossi 46												
3	Dovizioso 4												
4	Lorenzo 99												
5	Marquez 93												
6	Viñales 25												
7	Crutchlow 35												
8	Redding 45												
9	Espargaro A 41												
10	Barbera 8												
11	Laverty 50												
12	Pedrosa 26												
13	Petrucci 9												
14	Smith 38												
15	Espargaro P 44												
16	Hernandez 68												
17	Pirro 51												
18	Rabat 53												
19	Bautista 19												
20	Bradl 6												
21	Baz 76												

RACE

	Rider	Motorcycle	Race time	Time +	Fastest lap	Avg. speed	Tyres
1	Iannone	Ducati	39m 46.255s		1m 24.561s	113.3mph	S/M
2	Dovizioso	Ducati	39m 47.193s	0.938s	1m 24.686s	113.3mph	M/H
3	Lorenzo	Yamaha	39m 49.644s	3.389s	1m 24.786s	113.2mph	M/H
4	Rossi	Yamaha	39m 50.070s	3.815s	1m 24.854s	113.2mph	M/H
5	Marquez	Honda	39m 58.068s	11.813s	1m 25.117s	112.8mph	M/H
6	Viñales	Suzuki	40m 00.596s	14.341s	1m 25.073s	112.7mph	M/H
7	Pedrosa	Honda	40m 03.318s	17.063s	1m 25.206s	112.5mph	M/H
8	Redding	Ducati	40m 15.692s	29.437s	1m 25.508s	111.9mph	M/H
9	Smith	Yamaha	40m 16.040s	29.785s	1m 25.521s	111.9mph	S/H
10	Espargaro P	Yamaha	40m 23.349s	37.094s	1m 25.878s	111.6mph	M/H
11	Petrucci	Ducati	40m 26.020s	39.765s	1m 25.875s	111.5mph	M/H
12	Pirro	Ducati	40m 26.021s	39.766s	1m 25.859s	111.5mph	M/H
13	Baz	Ducati	40m 30.539s	44.284s	1m 26.024s	111.2mph	M/H
14	Rabat	Honda	40m 31.259s	45.004s	1m 25.969s	111.2mph	H/H
15	Crutchlow	Honda	40m 49.501s	1m 03.246s	1m 25.479s	110.4mph	M/H
16	Bautista	Aprilia	40m 58.703s	1m 12.448s	1m 25.342s	110.0mph	M/H
17	Hernandez	Ducati	41m 00.772s	1m 14.517s	1m 25.809s	109.9mph	S/H
18	Laverty	Ducati	41m 22.765s	1m 36.510s	1m 25.651s	108.9mph	S/H
19	Bradl	Aprilia	40m 53.077s	1 lap	1m 25.934s	106.3mph	M/H
NC	Espargaro A	Suzuki	35m 27.366s	4 laps	1m 25.580s	108.9mph	M/H
DQ	Barbera	Ducati	–	–	1m 25.368s	–	M/H

CHAMPIONSHIP

	Rider	Nation	Team	Points
1	Marquez	SPA	Repsol Honda Team	181
2	Lorenzo	SPA	Movistar Yamaha MotoGP	138
3	Rossi	ITA	Movistar Yamaha MotoGP	124
4	Pedrosa	SPA	Repsol Honda Team	105
5	Viñales	SPA	Team Suzuki ECSTAR	93
6	Iannone	ITA	Ducati Team	88
7	Dovizioso	ITA	Ducati Team	79
8	Espargaro P	SPA	Monster Yamaha Tech 3	78
9	Barbera	SPA	Avintia Racing	65
10	Redding	GBR	OCTO Pramac Yakhnich	53
	Laverty	IRL	Pull & Bear Aspar Team	53
12	Espargaro A	SPA	Team Suzuki ECSTAR	51
13	Miller	AUS	Estrella Galicia 0,0 Marc VDS	42
	Smith	GBR	Monster Yamaha Tech 3	42
15	Crutchlow	GBR	LCR Honda	41
16	Bradl	GER	Aprilia Racing Team Gresini	37
17	Bautista	SPA	Aprilia Racing Team Gresini	35
18	Petrucci	ITA	OCTO Pramac Yakhnich	29
19	Pirro	ITA	OCTO Pramac Yakhnich	23
20	Rabat	SPA	Estrella Galicia 0,0 Marc VDS	20
21	Baz	FRA	Avintia Racing	11
22	Hernandez	COL	Pull & Bear Aspar Team	3

13 LORIS BAZ
Still not fully fit. Suffered from the front brake locking at the end of every straight for the first half of the lap, but made fewer mistakes than Rabat in the second half.

14 TITO RABAT
Happier with his set-up, lapping at the pace of some top-ten men for most of the race, but outbraked himself to let Baz through at the end.

15 CAL CRUTCHLOW
The new father was the only one penalised for a jump start who made it into the points despite the ride-through penalty.

Thought he was harshly treated and would have finished between Marquez and Viñales.

16 ALVARO BAUTISTA
Outside the points after a jump start, just like his team-mate. Aprilia management were furious as the bike, they said, was the best it has been.

17 YONNY HERNANDEZ
Yonny's chances of points were ruined by a jump start and subsequent ride-through penalty.

18 EUGENE LAVERTY
Career-best qualifying in 11th, all set to extend his points-scoring run when sideswiped out of 11th place by Petrucci. Eugene picked the bike up to finish, but he was outside the points for the first time this season.

19 STEFAN BRADL
Jumped the start, then came in and stopped at his pit due to erroneous dashboard message, so had to do ride through later. Aprilia management were not amused.

DID NOT FINISH

ALEIX ESPARGARO
Forced to stop late in the race when his broken finger couldn't cope with the extra stress of the bike moving around on used tyres.

HECTOR BARBERA
Black-flagged for ignoring signal to come in for a ride-through penalty after jumping the start.

DID NOT RACE

JACK MILLER
Victim of a massive crash coming out of Turn 8 during warm-up. Cracked vertebra and broken wrist.

HJC HELMETS GRAND PRIX
ESKÉ REPUBLIKY
AUTOMOTODROM BRNO

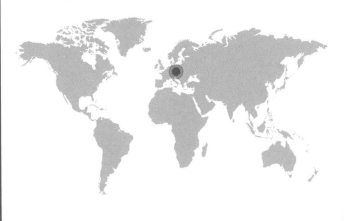

THE WAIT
IS OVER

This was the first British win for 35 years thanks to Cal Crutchlow, who made the right call on tyres

For Cal Crutchlow it was exactly the right set of circumstances, one in which a rider had to make a call and trust his judgment rather than go with the consensus. Said rider then had to execute the plan without panicking as he waited for the track to come to him and his tyres. Note that this plan requires bravery, nerves of steel, self-belief and skill in roughly equal proportions. In other words, a perfect state of affairs for Cal.

For the first time since MotoGP went to the purpose-built Brno circuit, the track was wet for the big race. There had been a wet start to a Moto3 race previously, in 2012, but on that occasion the track dried for the MotoGP race. However, temperatures were considerably lower this year and race day was both cold and wet, with the rain hammering down during warm-up. The field used Michelin's soft rain tyres for warm-up and, despite standing water in places, lap times were impressive. The forecast said the rain would ease for the race but not cease completely, and it was right.

That presented the MotoGP field with a dilemma. Clearly, they would all have to start on wets, but the question was which ones – hard or soft? If you were gambling on the track drying quickly and a lights-to-flag race, then you fitted softs with the intention of probably changing bikes, and this was the choice of most of the field. Only three brave men – Crutchlow, Tito Rabat and Loris Baz – went for hard wets at both ends, Baz

ABOVE Loris Baz redeemed his season with a superb fourth place

OPPOSITE TOP Cal Crutchlow gained vital tyre information in the soaking wet Sunday-morning warm-up

RIGHT Dovizioso overhauls his team-mate Iannone after his front tyre threw the centre of its tread

because of his weight. The two factory Yamaha men, Jorge Lorenzo and Valentino Rossi, used a soft front with a hard rear.

Inevitably the men on soft tyres made the running in the early laps as Crutchlow dropped from tenth on the grid to 15th for the first three laps, and Rossi wasn't doing much better in 12th. At the front Marc Marquez and a host of Ducatis vied for the lead with Andrea Iannone, who had swapped to a soft rear on the grid, emerging from the group to open up a significant lead.

There was no quick drying of the track because it was simply too cold; a few dry patches appeared going into corners but nothing that resembled a dry line. As Rossi and Crutchlow embarked on their steady progress through the field, those on soft front tyres began to suffer.

Dovizioso was the first to be affected, pitting when he lost the entire centre strip of tread on his soft front, and then a similar fate befell Bradley Smith and Jorge Lorenzo. These three had their races ruined when they arrived in pitlane and found their spare bikes on the wrong tyres for the conditions. Iannone and Redding suffered the same problems but stayed out and persevered, as did fellow soft-tyre men Marquez and Hector Barbera. In Iannone's case, he not only lost the central strip of the front tyre but also big chunks from its edges. His lap times only went up by six seconds, but how he managed to stay in control, let alone finish, is difficult to comprehend.

'I WAS PLAYING WITH THEM IN THE END. I KNEW I HAD MADE THE RIGHT TYRE CHOICE ON THE GRID AND PUSHED WHEN I NEEDED TO PUSH. I'M ECSTATIC'

CAL CRUTCHLOW

ABOVE Crutchlow closes in on Iannone, with Barbera – who managed his soft wet tyres brilliantly – right with them

BELOW Hector Barbera on the grid; he went on to have his best race of the season

As for Marquez, he was down in fifth place with three laps to go but had been so gentle on his soft tyres that he was able to push past Barbera as well as the stricken Iannone for another rostrum finish. Add that minor miracle to his record-obliterating pole position and the save of the century in FP3 and it was a quiet weekend by the boy wonder's standards.

It's also worth noting Barbera's performance, as well as the fact that he was followed home by two more 14.2 model Ducatis – all on different combinations of tyre but all notably lacking in wings. Loris Baz on the second Avintia Ducati and with hard tyres looked for a moment as if he might pinch third off Marquez but had to settle for taking his team-mate on the last lap. The team were delighted with their best-ever result.

Crutchlow had passed Rossi on the seventh lap of 22, while the Italian was still in 12th place. Valentino then followed Cal towards the front, although he never closed the gap to much under four seconds. When Cal took the lead with five laps to go, it looked as if Valentino might get to him. The gap was under three seconds, but next time round it was nearly five. As Cal said without irony, 'I had so much grip out there; I was toying with them.' He had never really contemplated racing with the softs, which he described as, 'Honestly, like chewing gum. I said never to put them on my rims.' He had to use the softs in morning warm-up but even in the

ABOUT TIME

Much was made of the fact that Cal Crutchlow's win was the first by a British rider in the top class for 35 years, since Barry Sheene at Anderstorp in Sweden in 1981. That was the 300th 500cc GP race and the 138th victory by a Briton in the class. Between that race and Brno 2016 there had been 532 successive GPs without a British winner in the top class.

That astonishing time elapse has been reflected across the GP classes. John McPhee's win in Moto3 on the same day as Cal's success and Sam Lowes's Moto2 victory at Jerez mean that 2016 was the first time in 43 years that Brits won in all three classes. Back in 1973 the men were Phil Read in 500s, Charlie Williams in 250s, and Tommy Robb and Chas Mortimer in 125s.

Unlike most of his rivals, Cal didn't come up through the ubiquitous route of the Spanish Championship, Moto3 and Moto2. In fact he's only the sixth MotoGP winner never to have raced full-time in the smaller classes. Instead, he emerged from the British Superbike Championship, followed by a year in the Supersport World Championship, which he won, and then another year in World Superbikes. He joined the Tech 3 satellite Yamaha team in MotoGP in 2011, when he was Rookie of the Year thanks to fourth place in the final race.

As Rossi said, when you win a MotoGP race you join a special club. Cal has always been popular in the

paddock as well as very fast, but after the win he seemed to become more at ease, more sure of himself around the other top men. That could also be explained by the birth of his daughter a few days before the Czech GP. For someone who occasionally likes to be the argumentative tough guy, Cal really is at heart a doting family man.

wettest conditions imaginable his team had noticed a little graining on the front tyre. Cal also calculated that he wouldn't be at any significant disadvantage on hard wets in a lights-to-flag race.

The measure of Crutchlow's domination is best shown by the number of laps – ten – he did in the 2m 8s bracket. Only one other rider, Rossi, got his pace to that level, and then only on three laps. When you consider, too, Cal's fastest lap of the race at the drying Sachsenring five weeks earlier, you can see who's now the fastest man in the world in mixed conditions. According to Cal himself, the fastest man in fully wet conditions is Scott Redding, and as Scott was over a second quicker than anyone in warm-up you can't really argue with that.

The real question was this: why didn't anyone else fit hard tyres? Was it the usual safety-first tendency of championship contenders to do what their rivals do? Cal had a different theory. Flashing a grin that made him look like Jack Nicholson in *The Shining*, he thought about it for a second then pronounced: 'They're a bunch of wimps!'

RIGHT Yonny Hernandez celebrates 11th place, his first points score since Jerez and his best result of the season

HJC HELMETS GRAND PRIX ĚSKÉ REPUBLIKY
AUTOMOTODROM BRNO
ROUND 11
AUGUST 21

RACE RESULTS

CIRCUIT LENGTH 3.357 miles

NO. OF LAPS 22

RACE DISTANCE 73.860 miles

WEATHER Wet, 17°C

TRACK TEMPERATURE 18°C

WINNER Cal Crutchlow

FASTEST LAP 2m 08.216s, 94.3mph, Cal Crutchlow

LAP RECORD 1m 56.027s, 104.1mph, Dani Pedrosa (2014)

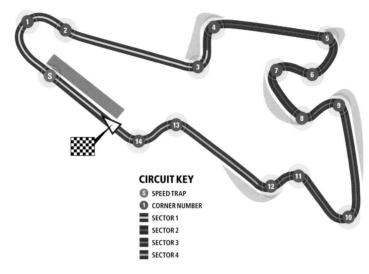

CIRCUIT KEY
- S SPEED TRAP
- 1 CORNER NUMBER
- ▬ SECTOR 1
- ▬ SECTOR 2
- ▬ SECTOR 3
- ▬ SECTOR 4

TYRE OPTIONS

LEFT — CENTRE — RIGHT
TYRE

SEVERITY RATING
<MILD   SEVERE>

FRONT COMPOUNDS
RAIN SOFT (RS)
RAIN HARD (RH)

REAR COMPOUNDS
RAIN SOFT (RS)
RAIN HARD (RH)

MICHELIN

QUALIFYING

	Rider	Nation	Motorcycle	Team	Time	Pole +
1	Marquez	SPA	Honda	Repsol Honda Team	1m 54.596s	
2	Lorenzo	SPA	Yamaha	Movistar Yamaha MotoGP	1m 54.849s	0.253s
3	Iannone	ITA	Ducati	Ducati Team	1m 55.227s	0.631s
4	Espargaro A	SPA	Suzuki	Team Suzuki ECSTAR	1m 55.324s	0.728s
5	Barbera	SPA	Ducati	Avintia Racing	1m 55.437s	0.841s
6	Rossi	ITA	Yamaha	Movistar Yamaha MotoGP	1m 55.509s	0.913s
7	Dovizioso	ITA	Ducati	Ducati Team	1m 55.748s	1.152s
8	Viñales	SPA	Suzuki	Team Suzuki ECSTAR	1m 55.787s	1.191s
9	Pedrosa	SPA	Honda	Repsol Honda Team	1m 55.841s	1.245s
10	Crutchlow	GBR	Honda	LCR Honda	1m 55.930s	1.334s
11	Smith	GBR	Yamaha	Monster Yamaha Tech 3	1m 56.115s	1.519s
12	Espargaro P	SPA	Yamaha	Monster Yamaha Tech 3	1m 56.522s	1.926s
13	Petrucci	ITA	Ducati	OCTO Pramac Yakhnich	1m 56.148s	0.355s
14	Redding	GBR	Ducati	OCTO Pramac Yakhnich	1m 56.263s	0.470s
15	Laverty	IRL	Ducati	Pull & Bear Aspar Team	1m 56.535s	0.742s
16	Bradl	GER	Aprilia	Aprilia Racing Team Gresini	1m 56.718s	0.925s
17	Baz	FRA	Ducati	Avintia Racing	1m 56.797s	1.004s
18	Hernandez	COL	Ducati	Pull & Bear Aspar Team	1m 56.805s	1.012s
19	Bautista	SPA	Aprilia	Aprilia Racing Team Gresini	1m 57.062s	1.269s
20	Rabat	SPA	Honda	Estrella Galicia 0,0 Marc VDS	1m 57.606s	1.813s

* Gap with the fastest rider in the Q1 session

1 CAL CRUTCHLOW
His first MotoGP win and the first by a Brit since Sheene in 1981. Went with hard tyres front and rear, suffered in the opening laps, then cruised past the field, revelling in the grip he had and they didn't. Cal claimed he was 'toying with them'. He was right. The reward for a brave decision.

2 VALENTINO ROSSI
Went with a hard rear and soft front combination that saw him running round in 12th in the early laps before he followed Crutchlow through the field. Valentino knew he had to conserve his tyres and managed the situation superbly.

3 MARC MARQUEZ
The only man on the podium with soft tyres front and rear. Led the first lap but then engulfed by Ducatis and ran fifth. Managed his tyres brilliantly to get yet another rostrum.

4 LORIS BAZ
The big Frenchman had to fit hard tyres because of his weight. He used them well, coming from 17th at the end of the first lap to pass his team-mate with a lap to go and equal his best previous result, at Misano the previous year.

5 HECTOR BARBERA
A very clever ride on soft tyres. Had a non-tyre problem over the last ten laps that he says slowed him but it didn't show. Only lost fourth place to his team-mate on the last lap.

6 EUGENE LAVERTY
Another strong result, but Eugene was devastated to surrender a big chunk of time on the first lap when he went sideways at Turn 3 and lost several places. That delay cost him a chance of racing the Avintia Ducatis – or better.

7 DANILO PETRUCCI
Quick at the start, suffered as the soft tyres went off, then was able to grab places off Iannone and Viñales at the close. Happy to make the top ten.

8 ANDREA IANNONE
Victim of the front tyre delamination. He finished with the central strip of tread rubber completely missing and big chunks out of the shoulders. How he finished the final seven laps, let alone well in the points, is a minor miracle.

9 MAVERICK VIÑALES
Looked like another mediocre Suzuki performance in the wet, but it was a lot better than that. Very quick in warm-up and also the race until suffering the same problem as the rest on soft tyres. Rider and team very happy with the progress.

10 TITO RABAT
One of only three riders to use hard tyres front and rear. Persevered to score his best result since the third race of the season.

11 YONNY HERNANDEZ
Best result of the season, but Yonny started with a very soft engine map. When he switched to a different map, 'the lap times dropped almost by themselves'.

LAP CHART

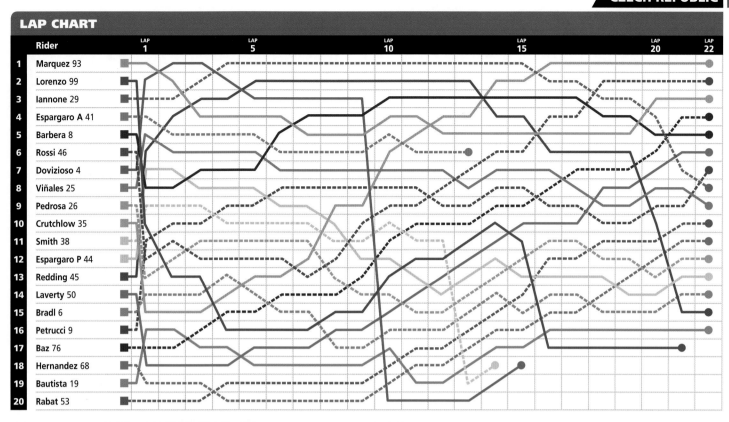

	Rider	LAP 1	LAP 5	LAP 10	LAP 15	LAP 20	LAP 22
1	Marquez 93						
2	Lorenzo 99						
3	Iannone 29						
4	Espargaro A 41						
5	Barbera 8						
6	Rossi 46						
7	Dovizioso 4						
8	Viñales 25						
9	Pedrosa 26						
10	Crutchlow 35						
11	Smith 38						
12	Espargaro P 44						
13	Redding 45						
14	Laverty 50						
15	Bradl 6						
16	Petrucci 9						
17	Baz 76						
18	Hernandez 68						
19	Bautista 19						
20	Rabat 53						

RACE

	Rider	Motorcycle	Race time	Time +	Fastest lap	Avg. speed	Tyres
1	Crutchlow	Honda	47m 44.290s		2m 08.216s	92.8mph	RH/RH
2	Rossi	Yamaha	47m 51.588s	7.298s	2m 08.867s	92.6mph	RS/RH
3	Marquez	Honda	47m 53.877s	9.587s	2m 09.507s	92.4mph	RS/RS
4	Baz	Ducati	47m 56.848s	12.558s	2m 09.166s	92.4mph	RH/RH
5	Barbera	Ducati	47m 57.383s	13.093s	2m 09.090s	92.4mph	RS/RS
6	Laverty	Ducati	47m 58.102s	13.812s	2m 09.304s	92.3mph	RS/RS
7	Petrucci	Ducati	48m 07.704s	23.414s	2m 09.829s	92.0mph	RS/RS
8	Iannone	Ducati	48m 08.852s	24.562s	2m 09.203s	92.0mph	RS/RS
9	Viñales	Suzuki	48m 08.871s	24.581s	2m 09.958s	92.0mph	RS/RS
10	Rabat	Honda	48m 21.421s	37.131s	2m 10.297s	91.6mph	RH/RH
11	Hernandez	Ducati	48m 24.201s	39.911s	2m 09.958s	91.5mph	RS/RS
12	Pedrosa	Honda	48m 25.387s	41.097s	2m 09.513s	91.5mph	RS/RS
13	Espargaro P	Yamaha	48m 27.492s	43.202s	2m 10.707s	91.4mph	RS/RS
14	Bradl	Aprilia	48m 29.977s	45.687s	2m 10.713s	91.3mph	RS/RS
15	Redding	Ducati	48m 46.491s	1m 02.201s	2m 09.418s	90.8mph	RS/RS
16	Bautista	Aprilia	49m 03.131s	1m 18.841s	2m 09.555s	90.3mph	RS/RS
17	Lorenzo	Yamaha	47m 49.179s	1 lap	2m 08.507s	88.4mph	RS/RH
NC	Dovizioso	Ducati	35m 47.906s	7 laps	2m 09.904s	84.4mph	RS/RS
NC	Smith	Yamaha	32m 20.512s	8 laps	2m 10.277s	87.2mph	RS/RS
NC	Espargaro A	Suzuki	28m 20.553s	9 laps	2m 09.850s	92.3mph	RS/RS

CHAMPIONSHIP

	Rider	Nation	Team	Points
1	Marquez	SPA	Repsol Honda Team	197
2	Rossi	ITA	Movistar Yamaha MotoGP	144
3	Lorenzo	SPA	Movistar Yamaha MotoGP	138
4	Pedrosa	SPA	Repsol Honda Team	109
5	Viñales	SPA	Team Suzuki ECSTAR	100
6	Iannone	ITA	Ducati Team	96
7	Espargaro P	SPA	Monster Yamaha Tech 3	81
8	Dovizioso	ITA	Ducati Team	79
9	Barbera	SPA	Avintia Racing	76
10	Crutchlow	GBR	LCR Honda	66
11	Laverty	IRL	Pull & Bear Aspar Team	63
12	Redding	GBR	OCTO Pramac Yakhnich	54
13	Espargaro A	SPA	Team Suzuki ECSTAR	51
14	Miller	AUS	Estrella Galicia 0,0 Marc VDS	42
	Smith	GBR	Monster Yamaha Tech 3	42
16	Bradl	GER	Aprilia Racing Team Gresini	39
17	Petrucci	ITA	OCTO Pramac Yakhnich	38
18	Bautista	SPA	Aprilia Racing Team Gresini	35
19	Rabat	SPA	Estrella Galicia 0,0 Marc VDS	26
20	Baz	FRA	Avintia Racing	24
21	Pirro	ITA	OCTO Pramac Yakhnich	23
22	Hernandez	COL	Pull & Bear Aspar Team	8

12 DANI PEDROSA
The front brake was locking under the slightest provocation, so Dani had to rely on engine braking – not the way to a fast lap. A disappointing weekend, to put it mildly.

13 POL ESPARGARO
Strangely subdued all weekend. Was improving on his qualifying but when the track started drying he was shuffled back.

14 STEFAN BRADL
Far from an easy race, but stuck with the first bike on rain tyres to score points for the first time in three races.

15 SCOTT REDDING
Another Ducati rider who suffered front-tyre delamination in the final laps.

16 ALVARO BAUTISTA
Unhappy on the wet tyres, and found little improvement when he switched to the second bike on intermediates.

17 JORGE LORENZO
On the weekend he finally declared himself at ease with Michelins, Jorge was a victim of front-tyre delamination. With the same tyre choice as his team-mate, Jorge was making rapid progress when the front tyre failed.

DID NOT FINISH

ANDREA DOVIZIOSO
First man to run into the catastrophic front-tyre problem. Pitted with the central strip missing only to find his second bike was fitted with intermediates, which were never going to work. Retired after a few laps on it.

BRADLEY SMITH
Thought he had gearbox problems so pitted and changed to his second bike, which was on slicks. Came in again and retired. The team then found that the electronics had reacted to the tyre problem and cut power.

ALEIX ESPARGARO
Found a major improvement at the end of warm-up and looked very comfortable in the race until stopped by an engine problem.

DID NOT RACE

JACK MILLER
Passed fit to race by the medics but withdrawn by Honda. Everyone thought it a good decision – except Jack when he saw the rain on Sunday morning.

OCTO BRITISH GRAND PRIX
SILVERSTONE

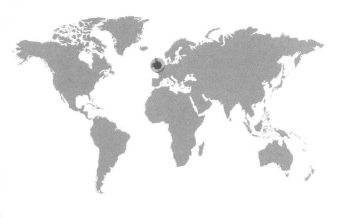

THE NEED FOR SPEED

Viñales won for Suzuki in front of a record crowd that was delighted to see Crutchlow second and Rossi third

It would be easy to imagine that Suzuki's first dry-weather victory since 2000 and Maverick Viñales's first came out of the blue. He was, after all, the seventh different winner in seven races, so surely this must have been a random effect of the new tyres and electronics. Well, no, not really. No-one could say that Viñales hadn't been riding well, even brilliantly, but the Suzuki still had weak points. Getting grip in the wet or on hot tracks was problematic, as was the tendency to lose ground at the start.

Things started to change in the Czech Republic a couple of weeks before the British GP. There were hints of wet-weather improvement in warm-up at Brno and then on the Monday the test turned up a major fix, one that became part of the base setting. Maverick, or 'Mack' as he prefers to be known, hit the ground running at Silverstone. By Saturday evening he was exuding such confidence that it was difficult to imagine anyone else winning, assuming he could get a good start. He could: twice.

After the race had to be restarted following a frightening first-lap coming-together between Pol Espargaro and Loris Baz, Viñales got away with the leaders for a second time, hit the front going into Stowe and was never headed thereafter. How in control was he? His first ten flying laps were in the 2m 2s bracket; the rest, apart from the final one, were 2m 3s. That looked like a switch of engine mapping halfway through

'AFTER THE LAST
RACES WE FELT WE
HAD THE POTENTIAL'
MAVERICK VIÑALES

and doubtless a planned situation. Second-placed Cal Crutchlow and third-placed Valentino Rossi managed two and three laps respectively in the lower bracket; Marc Marquez did seven but they were randomly scattered through an eventful race that involved a gloves-off dice with Rossi.

It may be that Silverstone's comparative lack of slow corners and the mixed weather played to Suzuki's strengths – or rather didn't play to the bike's weaknesses. The variable conditions and temperatures in the run-up to race day certainly meant that many teams had to indulge in a little creative guesswork for race set-up. Just about every tyre combination was used, but it was noticeable that Suzuki and Viñales knew from a very early stage that they were going with the hard rubber. Indeed, the controlled nature of Viñales's race suggests that he may have had a little in hand.

We never found out. The Suzuki pulled away steadily, leaving Crutchlow, Rossi, Andrea Iannone, Marquez and a faster-that-expected Dani Pedrosa to brawl over the lower rostrum places. The highlight was a startling duel between Marquez and Rossi, made even more fascinating by the fact that this was the first time they had come together on track since the events of Sepang 2015. It was serious stuff, as tough as it gets, but it stayed just the right side of acceptability. Both men afterwards claimed it had all been fair and fun, although Valentino did opine to the Italian media

ABOVE Scott Redding spins out behind Aleix Espargaro; he remounted but finished outside the points

OPPOSITE TOP Alex Lowes had his first taste of MotoGP when he replaced the injured Bradley Smith

LEFT The second start was a carbon-copy of the first: Viñales went straight into the lead

ABOVE Viñales pulls away, leaving the rest to fight for the remaining rostrum positions

BELOW Sam Lowes visited the Monster Yamaha pit to give his twin Alex some brotherly advice

that 'Marquez always saves something for me'. Indeed, Marc did come out on top in that tussle but that only meant he then had to deal with crowd favourite Crutchlow in the closing stages.

Sure enough, Marc closed Cal down but on the penultimate lap the Spaniard arrived at the end of the Hangar Straight way too fast and clipped Cal's right knee with the Honda's aerofoil as he rushed up the inside and on to the run-off. That finished Marc's chances of a rostrum position.

Cal's second place was his third rostrum in four GPs, further proof that he was very much the man in form after the summer break. In previous years, the home race hasn't been kind to him but this time Cal was a different animal: a GP winner, a father, and giving every impression of once more being at home racing with the best in the world. He even seemed more delighted with this second place at home than with his win in the Czech Republic.

While the race was massively entertaining, it didn't alter the championship status quo to any great extent. Rossi took just three points out of Marquez's 50-point advantage at the top of the table, but not because Marc was thinking about the championship. This was the Marc of 2014, willing to risk everything for the win and to attack at every corner. His race may have been compromised by the hard front tyre he selected, but this was Marquez at his most combative. It was thrilling to see again but spectators were permanently aware that the Honda could betray him at any time.

Jorge Lorenzo's race hardly merits a mention. He gambled on a hard set-up that had worked at Silverstone in previous years, but that was on Bridgestones, and he was never involved in the fight. The Ducatis were, especially Iannone, who looked like he might be the one who could challenge Viñales as he charged to the front of the pursuing pack. The Italian crashed but it would be too easy to dismiss it as just another hot-headed error. Like his team-mate, Andrea Dovizioso, Iannone again found it very hard work to get the Ducati to change direction and developed arm pump early in the race. The Desmosedici has always been long and low and relatively slow-steering, but it was tempting to wonder if the ever-increasing acreage of wings was now a factor.

The final word goes to Rossi, who, when asked about the prospect of Viñales as his team-mate in 2017, admitted he had been nervous before but was now seriously worried. He didn't sound like he was joking.

RIGHT Valentino Rossi shares a joke with Cal Crutchlow in *parc fermé*

TOP GUN

Maverick Viñales's win was Suzuki's first with the in-line four GSX-RR.

The company's only other winner under the MotoGP formula came with the V4 GSV-R in 2007, when Chris Vermeulen won the French GP at a soaking wet Le Mans. The factory's last dry-weather win was back in 2000, the year that Kenny Roberts Junior won the 500cc title. As for the British GP, the previous Suzuki winner was Franco Uncini in 1982, his championship year.

That this victory came in only the second year of the new project represents a massive achievement by Davide Brivio and his team in a short period of time. It was also a vindication of Dorna's and IRTA's forcing through of the new unified software regulations. It's very difficult to tempt new factories into the championship if they have to develop software to match the highly sophisticated engine-management systems of Honda and Yamaha.

From their début at the start of the 2015 season, it was obvious that Suzuki's tiny race department had produced a motorcycle that made life easy for its rider: easy handling, plenty of edge grip, and, said riders who saw it at close quarters, the ability to handle more power. Lack of data, of course, meant that it took time to work through obvious problems such as lack of grip in very hot or wet conditions and the inability to start well.

That the smallest of the Japanese factories has gone from zero to winner in a season and a half is a major achievement. It helped, of course, that they had the foresight to hire one of the outstanding young talents of recent years, although it's also worth recalling that most people thought Maverick was making a career-stifling move when he signed. For 2017, he will be Rossi's team-mate in the factory Yamaha team.

OFFICIAL TIMEKEEPER

OCTO BRITISH GRAND PRIX
SILVERSTONE
ROUND **12**
SEPTEMBER 4

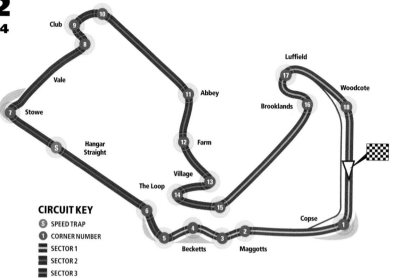

RACE RESULTS

CIRCUIT LENGTH 3.660 miles

NO. OF LAPS 19

RACE DISTANCE 69.549 miles

WEATHER Dry, 18°C

TRACK TEMPERATURE 18°C

WINNER Maverick Viñales

FASTEST LAP 2m 02.339s, 107.9mph, Maverick Viñales

LAP RECORD 2m 01.941s, 108.2mph, Dani Pedrosa (2013)

CIRCUIT KEY
- **S** SPEED TRAP
- **1** CORNER NUMBER
- SECTOR 1
- SECTOR 2
- SECTOR 3
- SECTOR 4

TYRE OPTIONS

CENTRE
LEFT RIGHT
TYRE

SEVERITY RATING

<MILD   SEVERE>

FRONT COMPOUNDS

SOFT (S)
MEDIUM (M)
HARD (H)

REAR COMPOUNDS

SOFT (S)
MEDIUM (M)

MICHELIN

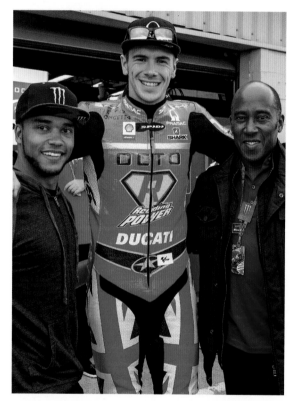

QUALIFYING

	Rider	Nation	Motorcycle	Team	Time	Pole +
1	Crutchlow	GBR	Honda	LCR Honda	2m 19.265s	
2	Rossi	ITA	Yamaha	Movistar Yamaha MotoGP	2m 20.263s	0.998s
3	Viñales	SPA	Suzuki	Team Suzuki ECSTAR	2m 20.514s	1.249s
4	Pedrosa	SPA	Honda	Repsol Honda Team	2m 20.742s	1.477s
5	Marquez	SPA	Honda	Repsol Honda Team	2m 20.779s	1.514s
6	Laverty	IRL	Ducati	Pull & Bear Aspar Team	2m 20.821s	1.556s
7	Redding	GBR	Ducati	OCTO Pramac Yakhnich	2m 21.074s	1.809s
8	Iannone	ITA	Ducati	Ducati Team	2m 21.446s	2.181s
9	Lorenzo	SPA	Yamaha	Movistar Yamaha MotoGP	2m 21.687s	2.422s
10	Dovizioso	ITA	Ducati	Ducati Team	2m 22.420s	3.155s
11	Espargaro A	SPA	Suzuki	Team Suzuki ECSTAR	2m 25.285s	6.020s
12	Miller	AUS	Honda	Estrella Galicia 0,0 Marc VDS	2m 18.531s	*0.338s
13	Baz	FRA	Ducati	Avintia Racing	2m 18.552s	*0.359s
14	Petrucci	ITA	Ducati	OCTO Pramac Yakhnich	2m 18.657s	*0.464s
15	Espargaro P	SPA	Yamaha	Monster Yamaha Tech 3	2m 18.871s	*0.678s
16	Lowes	GBR	Yamaha	Monster Yamaha Tech 3	2m 18.900s	*0.707s
17	Bradl	GER	Aprilia	Aprilia Racing Team Gresini	2m 19.115s	*0.922s
18	Barbera	SPA	Ducati	Avintia Racing	2m 19.125s	*0.932s
19	Bautista	SPA	Aprilia	Aprilia Racing Team Gresini	2m 20.299s	*2.106s
20	Hernandez	COL	Ducati	Pull & Bear Aspar Team	2m 21.255s	*3.062s
21	Rabat	SPA	Honda	Estrella Galicia 0,0 Marc VDS	2m 21.774s	*3.581s

* Gap with the fastest rider in the Q1 session

1 MAVERICK VIÑALES
His first win, Suzuki's first since 2007 and its first in the dry since 2000. Maverick is the first man to win in Moto3, Moto2 and MotoGP. Fast all weekend, in control from the start, and robot-like in his precision. He didn't give the rest a chance.

2 CAL CRUTCHLOW
Standing on the rostrum in front of his home crowd was, he said, as good as winning. He looked totally comfortable with the bike (a new chassis helped) and won a fine fight with Rossi, Marquez and Iannone. The man in form.

3 VALENTINO ROSSI
Another front row, another rostrum. Knew he'd have tyre trouble in a dry race and, sure enough, the rear started sliding eight laps in. Still managed to have a very hard fight with Marquez and happy to take three points out of his championship lead.

4 MARC MARQUEZ
Looked more like his old win-or-bust self, especially when racing with Rossi. Raced with the soft front tyre, which turned out to be a mistake, and lost his chance of a rostrum when he clouted Crutchlow while braking for Stowe and ran off-track.

5 DANI PEDROSA
Happier than he's been for a while, even if he doesn't get on with the track nor liked the conditions on the day. Used the soft tyres and thought it was the right choice, despite issues in the final laps.

6 ANDREA DOVIZIOSO
Looked like he might be a factor early on, but had a lonely race limited by serious arm pump, which also afflicted his team-mate.

7 ALEIX ESPARGARO
His best finish since Le Mans. Happy with the gap to the winner and said the right things about his team-mate.

8 JORGE LORENZO
Gambled on a stiff suspension set-up that worked a couple of years ago but there was no time to test it, and it proved to cause a major vibration at the rear with consequent lack of grip.

9 DANILO PETRUCCI
Beaten up from a scooter crash on the road and content to register a top-ten finish.

10 ALVARO BAUTISTA
His race was a big improvement on practice. When he passed Hernandez, he switched to a more aggressive map and gapped him. Conversely, Alvaro needs to find pace with new tyres in qualification and the race.

11 YONNY HERNANDEZ
Made up ten places on his qualifying position and equalled his best finish of the year, helped by major changes to engine electronics and mapping.

12 EUGENE LAVERTY
Career-best qualifying, second when the race was red-flagged, then involved in Bradl's crash and other comings-together after the clutch didn't feel as good for the second start.

LAP CHART

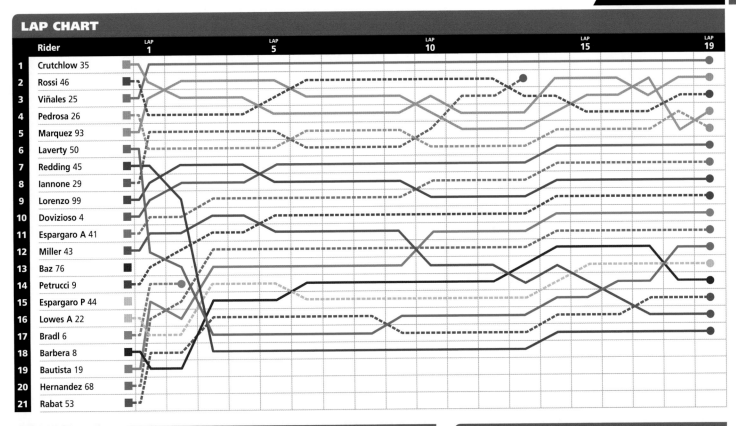

	Rider	LAP 1	LAP 5	LAP 10	LAP 15	LAP 19
1	Crutchlow 35					
2	Rossi 46					
3	Viñales 25					
4	Pedrosa 26					
5	Marquez 93					
6	Laverty 50					
7	Redding 45					
8	Iannone 29					
9	Lorenzo 99					
10	Dovizioso 4					
11	Espargaro A 41					
12	Miller 43					
13	Baz 76					
14	Petrucci 9					
15	Espargaro P 44					
16	Lowes A 22					
17	Bradl 6					
18	Barbera 8					
19	Bautista 19					
20	Hernandez 68					
21	Rabat 53					

RACE

	Rider	Motorcycle	Race time	Time +	Fastest lap	Avg. speed	Tyres
1	Viñales	Suzuki	39m 03.559s		2m 02.339s	106.9mph	H/M
2	Crutchlow	Honda	39m 07.039s	3.480s	2m 02.659s	106.8mph	H/M
3	Rossi	Yamaha	39m 07.622s	4.063s	2m 02.745s	106.8mph	H/M
4	Marquez	Honda	39m 09.551s	5.992s	2m 02.815s	106.7mph	S/M
5	Pedrosa	Honda	39m 09.940s	6.381s	2m 02.721s	106.7mph	S/S
6	Dovizioso	Ducati	39m 15.862s	12.303s	2m 02.837s	106.4mph	S/S
7	Espargaro A	Suzuki	39m 20.231s	16.672s	2m 02.680s	106.2mph	H/M
8	Lorenzo	Yamaha	39m 22.991s	19.432s	2m 03.171s	106.1mph	S/M
9	Petrucci	Ducati	39m 29.177s	25.618s	2m 03.883s	105.8mph	S/S
10	Bautista	Aprilia	39m 35.643s	32.084s	2m 04.061s	105.5mph	S/S
11	Hernandez	Ducati	39m 39.690s	36.131s	2m 04.244s	105.3mph	S/S
12	Laverty	Ducati	39m 42.689s	39.130s	2m 04.457s	105.2mph	S/S
13	Lowes	Yamaha	39m 43.702s	40.143s	2m 04.429s	105.1mph	S/S
14	Barbera	Ducati	39m 44.915s	41.356s	2m 04.384s	105.1mph	S/S
15	Rabat	Honda	39m 45.502s	41.943s	2m 04.500s	105.1mph	H/M
16	Miller	Honda	39m 51.169s	47.610s	2m 03.720s	104.8mph	S/M
17	Redding	Ducati	40m 59.736s	1m 56.177s	2m 03.939s	101.9mph	S/S
NC	Iannone	Ducati	26m 45.452s	6 laps	2m 02.790s	106.8mph	S/S
NC	Bradl	Aprilia	4m 14.323s	17 laps	2m 04.849s	103.8mph	H/S
NS	Baz	Ducati	–	–	–	–	H/S
NS	Espargaro P	Yamaha	–	–	–	–	S/S

CHAMPIONSHIP

	Rider	Nation	Team	Points
1	Marquez	SPA	Repsol Honda Team	210
2	Rossi	ITA	Movistar Yamaha MotoGP	160
3	Lorenzo	SPA	Movistar Yamaha MotoGP	146
4	Viñales	SPA	Team Suzuki ECSTAR	125
5	Pedrosa	SPA	Repsol Honda Team	120
6	Iannone	ITA	Ducati Team	96
7	Dovizioso	ITA	Ducati Team	89
8	Crutchlow	GBR	LCR Honda	86
9	Espargaro P	SPA	Monster Yamaha Tech 3	81
10	Barbera	SPA	Avintia Racing	78
11	Laverty	IRL	Pull & Bear Aspar Team	67
12	Espargaro A	SPA	Team Suzuki ECSTAR	60
13	Redding	GBR	OCTO Pramac Yakhnich	54
14	Petrucci	ITA	OCTO Pramac Yakhnich	45
15	Miller	AUS	Estrella Galicia 0,0 Marc VDS	42
16	Smith	GBR	Monster Yamaha Tech 3	42
17	Bautista	SPA	Aprilia Racing Team Gresini	41
18	Bradl	GER	Aprilia Racing Team Gresini	39
19	Rabat	SPA	Estrella Galicia 0,0 Marc VDS	27
20	Baz	FRA	Avintia Racing	24
21	Pirro	ITA	OCTO Pramac Yakhnich	23
22	Hernandez	COL	Pull & Bear Aspar Team	13
23	Lowes	GBR	Monster Yamaha Tech 3	3

13 ALEX LOWES
An excellent début replacing the injured Smith. Did everything right and, considering the race was the first time he'd run a full tank or full distance, a result that justified the faith shown in him following his Eight Hours win and the test at Brno that was his reward.

14 HECTOR BARBERA
Described the weekend as 'a complete disaster'. No positives at all – move on.

15 TITO RABAT
A very difficult weekend, one he described as the worst of his career. Happy to score points for the third race in a row and look ahead to the next round.

16 JACK MILLER
Cleared to race despite new fractures found in his right hand. Going well but after five laps lost grip on the right side of the rear tyre.

17 SCOTT REDDING
Well up in the red-flagged race but never had the same feeling after the restart. Crashed two laps in but remounted and finished for his fans.

DID NOT FINISH

ANDREA IANNONE
Racing with the group chasing Viñales and making progress when he crashed. Blamed serious arm pump – 'I was riding with one arm.' His team-mate also suffered from the same problem.

STEFAN BRADL
Crashed when he collided with Eugene Laverty.

LORIS BAZ
Crashed with Pol Espargaro on first lap, bringing out the red flag. Briefly unconscious but thought to be otherwise unhurt until fractures discovered in the foot he'd injured at Mugello. Didn't make the restart.

POL ESPARGARO
Crashed with Baz in the incident that brought out the red flag. Hit by both bikes, very lucky to escape with heavy bruising. Didn't make the restart.

DID NOT RACE

BRADLEY SMITH
Out for at least two races following knee-ligament damage in practice for a World Endurance ride for Yamaha. Replaced by Alex Lowes.

GP TIM DI SAN MARINO E DELLA RIVIERA DI RIMINI
MISANO WORLD CIRCUIT MARCO SIMONCELLI

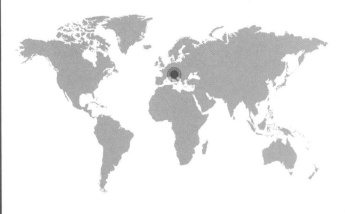

RECORD BREAKER

For the first time ever, there was an eighth different winner in eight GPs as Pedrosa spoiled Rossi's party

Valentino was fed up, really fed up, about failing to win his home race. And by home race, I mean any closer to his property and the racing would have been in his back garden. It had all been set up so nicely: Marc Marquez had problems and then had to use the hard tyre, Valentino had the best home-race crash-helmet design for a while, and the overwhelming majority of the spectators appeared to be card-carrying members of his fan club.

There were enough yellow shirts in the stands to show just how much money the VR-46 merchandising operation must turn over. The crowd on race day was over 100,000 and well over 90 per cent of them were wearing at least one piece of Rossi merchandise. At a conservative estimate, that was a couple of million euros of profit right there. As we've come to expect, Jorge Lorenzo and Marc Marquez were roundly booed before the race, although it must be said that it felt more like kids greeting a pantomime villain than the tribal nastiness of a British soccer match. Could still do without it, though.

The man who spoiled Rossi's party was Dani Pedrosa. He overhauled nearly every other works bike and then hunted down Valentino, who had taken the lead off Lorenzo on the second lap, to the delight of the fans. Rossi held the lead for 20 more laps but never stretched it to much more than a second, and Dani was across the gap and past in four laps. His win was greeted with quiet

respect as Valentino tried to get the crowd going by drinking the rostrum cava from his boot – or *à la* Miller as it's known in better restaurants.

Valentino's mood wasn't helped by Marc Marquez's distant fourth-place finish. Yes, Rossi took points put of the Spaniard's championship lead but it should have been five more. Perhaps more tellingly, Marquez did exactly what he'd been saying he'd do since the start of the year and rode for points rather than the win. The contrast with Silverstone couldn't have been more stark.

Dani has won a race in each of the ten years of his MotoGP career and was coming off his longest run without a rostrum since his 125 rookie year – five races. Maybe we shouldn't have been surprised. He'd looked much more like his old self at Silverstone thanks to a good test at Brno and now had a genuinely warm race track to operate on. He didn't have to spend time trying to force energy into the Michelins, and the soft tyre with a new, stiffer construction was fine for his weight and style on race day. As Dani is short, he can't move around on the bike to find grip. If he hasn't got it on Friday, it tends to stay that way.

He had it on Friday, lost it on Saturday – which meant a third-row start – but rediscovered it in time for Sunday. The win wasn't down to one of his disappearing acts, as used to be the case. He had to pass Viñales, Dovizioso, Marquez, Lorenzo and, finally, Valentino himself. The moves on both his team-mate and Lorenzo were as clean and

ABOVE Valentino Rossi leads in front of his home fans as Dani Pedrosa prepares his attack

OPPOSITE TOP Michele Pirro got a late call-up after Andrea Iannone's injury and was impressive, qualifying top Ducati rider and following Dovi home

RIGHT Aprilia had a good home race; Alvaro Bautista made it to the second qualifying session and finished the race in tenth place

'IT WAS A GREAT RACE, AND IT HAS BEEN A LONG TIME SINCE I HAVE HAD THESE FEELINGS. THE PERFORMANCE I PUT IN TODAY SURPRISED EVEN MYSELF'

DANI PEDROSA

precise as you could hope to see. The one to take the lead from Rossi involved barging up the inside at a slow corner, Rio, and running seriously wide, taking his victim with him. Remember Aragón last year? A bit like that. You'd have trouble finding another win that involved passing that many factory riders and pulling away.

Pedrosa's third-row start should have finished his chances but this was as dominant a victory as it's possible to imagine. It never occurred to anybody watching that any of the champions he passed would be able to go with him let alone repass. It was good to be reminded that Dani is still a force. Interestingly, unlike the opposition, his Honda sported no wings. He doesn't like them and only raced with them once – in Austria.

As usual, Pedrosa conducted himself impeccably but his patience must have been tried by the post-race press conference, where he sat between the factory Yamaha riders as they engaged in a domestic dispute. Lorenzo started his story of the race by complaining about Rossi's pass on him. Valentino was surprised enough to interrupt his flow. There followed a rather petty exchange best characterised by another football phrase – handbags.

As usual, the Italian factories put some extra effort into their home race. Aprilia had a new frame that helped Alvaro Bautista finish in the top ten. His team-mate Stefan Bradl impressed too, but wrecked his new frame in practice.

ABOVE Javier Fores replaced Loris Baz at Avintia and found the going tough

BELOW Dani Pedrosa produced a series of strong overtaking moves; the one on Jorge Lorenzo was as clean as a whistle

WINGS

The powers that be finally delivered their definitive verdict on wings and other aerodynamic devices. The decision was to ban them in MotoGP from the 2017 season, in line with the existing ban in the Moto2 and Moto3 classes.

IRTA and Dorna tasked the MSMA with proving that such devices weren't dangerous – an interesting problem given that philosophers aren't even sure that proving a negative is possible. Not that the MSMA's own internal vote would have been unanimous. Ducati have been the driving force behind the wings and strakes appearing on every factory's bikes this year. Clearly, Gigi Dall'Igna set great store by them.

Opposition came from other factories and IRTA on the grounds of cost, and from other quarters, including some riders, on the grounds of safety. If the MSMA had voted unanimously to retain wings, the Grand Prix Commission couldn't have overturned the decision. Thus it was clear that at least one factory voted to do away with them.

The regulations for the 2017 season effectively give the MotoGP Technical Director the power to ban anything he considers to be an aerodynamic device – not a bad thing given the propensity of engineers for circumventing written regulations.

But what did wings actually do? Honda riders reported having to use much less rear brake to counter the tendency to wheelie under acceleration and Casey Stoner reported a positive effect in fast corners. Honda have used a variety of sizes, whereas Yamaha riders used a large, single wing for most of the year and Suzuki favoured a triple-decker. It took a while, but most riders finally came round to the advantages of using wings.

The exception was Dani Pedrosa, who notably didn't use any wings to win at Misano. There may have been a correlation between Ducati riders reporting arm pump this year and diminutive Dani not wanting his bike to be more resistant to changes of direction.

Ducati lost Andrea Iannone to a back injury and transferred the impressive Michele Pirro from wild-card duties to the factory team. That meant we only saw his test bike on Saturday, which was a shame as it had a very interesting carbon-fibre lenticular wheel insert not unlike those used in track cycle racing. What was it for? Obviously it was meant to improve aerodynamics in some way. Smoothing airflow over the back of the bike? Probably. Helping airflow through radiators and out of fairing ducts? Maybe. Keeping rear tyre temperature constant? Unlikely. Ducati racing chief Gigi Dall'Igna winding up the opposition who curtailed his use of wings (see inset story)? Almost certainly.

The extra effort didn't really have an effect. Andrea Dovizioso and Pirro finished 20 seconds behind Pedrosa. It wasn't really an enjoyable home race for any Italians.

RIGHT Dani Pedrosa maintained his record of winning a race in every year of his MotoGP career – which has now extended to 11 seasons

GP TIM DI SAN MARINO E DELLA RIVIERA DI RIMINI
MISANO WORLD CIRCUIT MARCO SIMONCELLI
ROUND 13
SEPTEMBER 11

TYRE OPTIONS

TYRE

SEVERITY RATING

<MILD   SEVERE>

FRONT COMPOUNDS

| SOFT (S) |
| MEDIUM (M) |
| HARD (H) |

REAR COMPOUNDS

| MEDIUM (M) |
| HARD (H) |

MICHELIN

RACE RESULTS

CIRCUIT LENGTH 2.626 miles

NO. OF LAPS 28

RACE DISTANCE 73.526 miles

WEATHER Dry, 28°C

TRACK TEMPERATURE 43°C

WINNER Dani Pedrosa

FASTEST LAP 1m 32.979s, 101.7mph, Dani Pedrosa (record)

PREVIOUS LAP RECORD 1m 33.273s, 101.3mph, Jorge Lorenzo (2015)

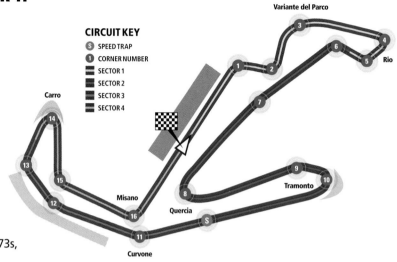

CIRCUIT KEY
- (S) SPEED TRAP
- (1) CORNER NUMBER
- SECTOR 1
- SECTOR 2
- SECTOR 3
- SECTOR 4

QUALIFYING

	Rider	Nation	Motorcycle	Team	Time	Pole +
1	Lorenzo	SPA	Yamaha	Movistar Yamaha MotoGP	1m 31.868s	
2	Rossi	ITA	Yamaha	Movistar Yamaha MotoGP	1m 32.216s	0.348s
3	Viñales	SPA	Suzuki	Team Suzuki ECSTAR	1m 32.381s	0.513s
4	Marquez	SPA	Honda	Repsol Honda Team	1m 32.443s	0.575s
5	Pirro	ITA	Ducati	Ducati Team	1m 32.467s	0.599s
6	Dovizioso	ITA	Ducati	Ducati Team	1m 32.677s	0.809s
7	Crutchlow	GBR	Honda	LCR Honda	1m 32.743s	0.875s
8	Pedrosa	SPA	Honda	Repsol Honda Team	1m 32.859s	0.991s
9	Espargaro A	SPA	Suzuki	Team Suzuki ECSTAR	1m 32.918s	1.050s
10	Espargaro P	SPA	Yamaha	Monster Yamaha Tech 3	1m 33.002s	1.134s
11	Barbera	SPA	Ducati	Avintia Racing	1m 33.301s	1.433s
12	Bautista	SPA	Aprilia	Aprilia Racing Team Gresini	1m 33.929s	2.061s
13	Bradl	GER	Aprilia	Aprilia Racing Team Gresini	1m 33.399s	*0.340s
14	Lowes	GBR	Yamaha	Monster Yamaha Tech 3	1m 33.635s	*0.576s
15	Petrucci	ITA	Ducati	OCTO Pramac Yakhnich	1m 33.716s	*0.657s
16	Laverty	IRL	Ducati	Pull & Bear Aspar Team	1m 33.772s	*0.713s
17	Miller	AUS	Honda	Estrella Galicia 0,0 Marc VDS	1m 33.847s	*0.788s
18	Redding	GBR	Ducati	OCTO Pramac Yakhnich	1m 33.989s	*0.930s
19	Rabat	SPA	Honda	Estrella Galicia 0,0 Marc VDS	1m 34.302s	*1.243s
20	Hernandez	COL	Ducati	Pull & Bear Aspar Team	1m 34.465s	*1.406s
21	Fores	SPA	Ducati	Avintia Racing	1m 35.161s	*2.102s

* Gap with the fastest rider in the Q1 session

1 DANI PEDROSA

The eighth different winner in as many races, and Dani's first since Malaysia 2015. Qualified on the third row than passed Viñales, Dovizioso, Marquez, Lorenzo and Rossi. Only Dani and Pirro used the soft front tyre, and the track was hot enough for it to work.

2 VALENTINO ROSSI

Couldn't hide his disappointment at failing to win his real home race. Had to console himself with taking another seven points out of Marquez's championship lead.

3 JORGE LORENZO

Blazingly fast in qualifying, got the holeshot but couldn't pull away as he hoped. Not happy with Rossi's pass, although that had more to do with his disappointment than reality.

4 MARC MARQUEZ

Had to go with the hard front tyre owing to his riding style. When Pedrosa came past, Marc quickly realised he would crash if he tried to chase and settled for fourth.

5 MAVERICK VIÑALES

A decent result given the heat in the track, which has been a Suzuki bugbear, and the fact Mack was penalised for exceeding track limits and had to give up a place. Qualified superbly, dropped back in early laps then fought back.

6 ANDREA DOVIZIOSO

Top Ducati finisher in a disappointing race for the Bologna factory. The big problem, again, was the bike's disinclination to turn and the energy the rider needs to expend in the early laps to persuade it to do so.

7 MICHELE PIRRO

Promoted to the factory team from wild-card entry after Iannone's injury. Top Ducati qualifier: started from the second row, lost places off the start but got past Crutchlow to follow his team-mate home.

8 CAL CRUTCHLOW

Lost out to Pirro early on but held off Pol Espargaro only to temporarily lose a position due to a penalty for exceeding track limits – but that was rescinded when data showed he had slowed to give up any time gained. So, top independent finisher.

9 POL ESPARGARO

A difficult weekend. Slow start to the race, struggled with a full fuel load but was able to challenge Crutchlow in the closing laps.

10 ALVARO BAUTISTA

Put the Aprilia direct into Q2 for the first time. Used the new frame to good effect but lost places after getting sideswiped by Redding on the second lap. Passed his team-mate and Petrucci, and pulled away from them.

11 DANILO PETRUCCI

Like the other non-factory Ducati riders, Danilo had difficulty in making the front tyre work in practice and qualifying. Started the race well, but hit problems again after half distance and could only hold off one of the Aprilias.

LAP CHART

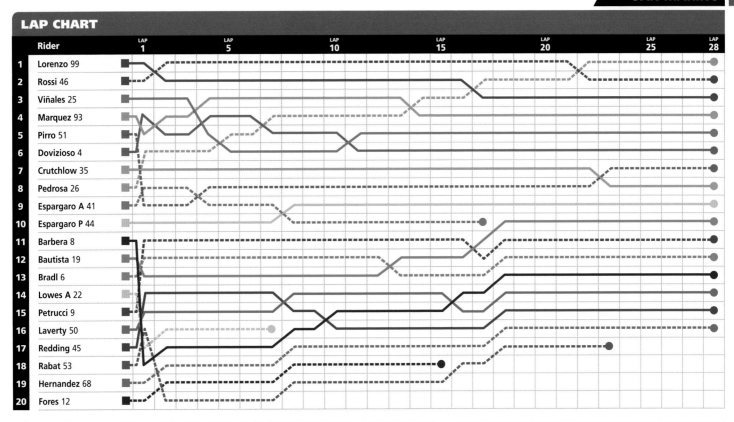

	Rider	LAP 1	LAP 5	LAP 10	LAP 15	LAP 20	LAP 25	LAP 28
1	Lorenzo 99							
2	Rossi 46							
3	Viñales 25							
4	Marquez 93							
5	Pirro 51							
6	Dovizioso 4							
7	Crutchlow 35							
8	Pedrosa 26							
9	Espargaro A 41							
10	Espargaro P 44							
11	Barbera 8							
12	Bautista 19							
13	Bradl 6							
14	Lowes A 22							
15	Petrucci 9							
16	Laverty 50							
17	Redding 45							
18	Rabat 53							
19	Hernandez 68							
20	Fores 12							

RACE

	Rider	Motorcycle	Race time	Time +	Fastest lap	Avg. speed	Tyres
1	Pedrosa	Honda	43m 43.524s		1m 32.979s	100.8mph	S/M
2	Rossi	Yamaha	43m 46.361s	2.837s	1m 33.025s	100.7mph	M/M
3	Lorenzo	Yamaha	43m 47.883s	4.359s	1m 33.260s	100.7mph	M/M
4	Marquez	Honda	43m 53.093s	9.569s	1m 33.319s	100.5mph	H/M
5	Viñales	Suzuki	43m 58.991s	15.467s	1m 33.493s	100.3mph	H/M
6	Dovizioso	Ducati	44m 03.200s	19.676s	1m 33.696s	100.1mph	M/M
7	Pirro	Ducati	44m 06.460s	22.936s	1m 33.822s	100.0mph	S/M
8	Crutchlow	Honda	44m 09.226s	25.702s	1m 33.689s	99.9mph	M/M
9	Espargaro P	Yamaha	44m 10.679s	27.155s	1m 33.911s	99.9mph	M/M
10	Bautista	Aprilia	44m 17.492s	33.968s	1m 34.008s	99.5mph	M/M
11	Petrucci	Ducati	44m 22.730s	39.206s	1m 34.090s	99.4mph	M/M
12	Bradl	Aprilia	44m 23.491s	39.967s	1m 34.286s	99.4mph	M/M
13	Barbera	Ducati	44m 26.521s	42.997s	1m 34.437s	99.2mph	M/M
14	Laverty	Ducati	44m 32.974s	49.450s	1m 34.733s	99.0mph	M/M
15	Redding	Ducati	44m 38.403s	54.879s	1m 34.604s	98.8mph	M/M
16	Hernandez	Ducati	44m 48.596s	1m 05.072s	1m 35.200s	98.4mph	M/M
17	Rabat	Honda	44m 23.911s	5 laps	1m 34.896s	81.6mph	M/M
NC	Espargaro A	Suzuki	26m 52.205s	11 laps	1m 34.094s	99.7mph	H/M
NC	Fores	Ducati	24m 23.949s	13 laps	1m 36.455s	96.8mph	M/M
NC	Lowes	Yamaha	11m 14.356s	21 laps	1m 34.706s	98.1mph	M/M

CHAMPIONSHIP

	Rider	Nation	Team	Points
1	Marquez	SPA	Repsol Honda Team	223
2	Rossi	ITA	Movistar Yamaha MotoGP	180
3	Lorenzo	SPA	Movistar Yamaha MotoGP	162
4	Pedrosa	SPA	Repsol Honda Team	145
5	Viñales	SPA	Team Suzuki ECSTAR	136
6	Dovizioso	ITA	Ducati Team	99
7	Iannone	ITA	Ducati Team	96
8	Crutchlow	GBR	LCR Honda	94
9	Espargaro P	SPA	Monster Yamaha Tech 3	88
10	Barbera	SPA	Avintia Racing	81
11	Laverty	IRL	Pull & Bear Aspar Team	69
12	Espargaro A	SPA	Team Suzuki ECSTAR	60
13	Redding	GBR	OCTO Pramac Yakhnich	55
14	Petrucci	ITA	OCTO Pramac Yakhnich	50
15	Bautista	SPA	Aprilia Racing Team Gresini	47
16	Bradl	GER	Aprilia Racing Team Gresini	43
17	Miller	AUS	Estrella Galicia 0,0 Marc VDS	42
	Smith	GBR	Monster Yamaha Tech 3	42
19	Pirro	ITA	OCTO Pramac Yakhnich	32
20	Rabat	SPA	Estrella Galicia 0,0 Marc VDS	27
21	Baz	FRA	Avintia Racing	24
22	Hernandez	COL	Pull & Bear Aspar Team	13
23	Lowes	GBR	Monster Yamaha Tech 3	3

12 STEFAN BRADL
Couldn't use Aprilia's new evolution chassis because of crash damage for some of the weekend, so raced on the standard frame. Not necessarily the right choice as he lost out on the brakes, an area the new chassis definitely improved.

13 HECTOR BARBERA
Lost a lot of time to the group ahead in the first five laps when the front kept tucking. Feeling improved a lot as fuel load went down, but too far back to improve his position.

14 EUGENE LAVERTY
Continued his run of finishing every race this season but really suffered in the tight sections where he found the bike difficult to turn. Consistent pace but couldn't follow Petrucci or Barbera.

15 SCOTT REDDING
Front tyre woes meant Scott ran wide every time he tried to push. That consigned him to awful qualifying and just one point in the race. A very frustrating weekend on a track where he'd expected his Ducati to be fast.

16 YONNY HERNANDEZ
Failed to score points for the first time in three races. Couldn't find any feeling in practice then tyre performance dropped off in the race.

17 TITO RABAT
Crashed on the second lap and returned to the pit for repairs. Rejoined and raced with the Petrucci and Bradl, matching their lap times. A useful test rather than a race.

DID NOT FINISH

ALEIX ESPARGARO
Crashed three times during the weekend, each time off the front. He was pushing hard when it happened in the race.

JAVIER FORES
Replaced Loris Baz for his MotoGP début; pulled out with arm pump.

ALEX LOWES
Again replaced Bradley Smith; crashed out when he lost the front at Turn 1 but still impressed.

DID NOT RACE

ANDREA IANNONE
After some unsavoury politicking between local medics and the Clinica Mobile, Andrea was ruled out with a cracked vertebra from a crash in FP1.

LORIS BAZ
Sidelined after his big Silverstone crash that broke bones in his foot.

BRADLEY SMITH
Out for this and at least one more race as he recovered from an operation on his injured knee.

GRAN PREMIO MOVISTAR DE ARAGÓN
MOTORLAND ARAGÓN

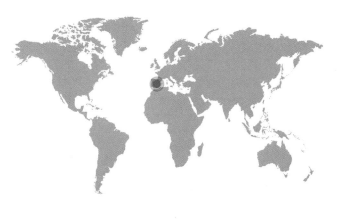

FAMILY HOME

It was a good weekend for the Marquez family, and Lorenzo won the war between the Yamaha riders

You know that old cliché, 'Every race is a home race for Valentino Rossi'? Well, it isn't quite true. Aragón isn't the nearest circuit to the Marquez family home but it's the closest in terms of regional identity and character. It showed. For once there were no banks of yellow stands around the track, instead the red and orange of the Marquez brothers was everywhere. And both of them had a very good day.

The younger one, Alex, finished second in Moto2, a career best, and big brother won his 54th GP. Frankly, it would have been a surprise if Marc hadn't won given his amazing advantage in qualifying, but he did have a good go at throwing it away on lap three of the race when he saved a major front-end moment. And it was major by Marc's standards, if not by those of ordinary men or even ordinary GP winners. The save took him off-track and put him behind both factory Yamahas plus Maverick Viñales and Andrea Dovizioso. He overhauled them all in ten laps and pulled away. It wasn't an easy win.

After practice, everyone thought the tyres would drop in performance and the Hondas would cope best on worn rubber, but it wasn't quite that simple. Marquez set the fastest lap of the race after half distance while Dani Pedrosa and Dovizioso had serious problems with the medium front tyre. Rossi and Viñales both outbraked themselves to lose their chance of victory, thus letting in Jorge Lorenzo for second

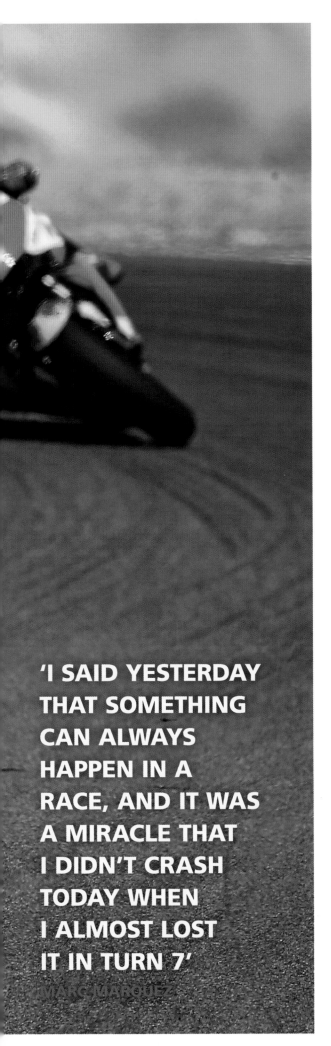

'I SAID YESTERDAY THAT SOMETHING CAN ALWAYS HAPPEN IN A RACE, AND IT WAS A MIRACLE THAT I DIDN'T CRASH TODAY WHEN I ALMOST LOST IT IN TURN 7'

MARC MARQUEZ

place, which was his best result since Mugello. That explains why Jorge was looking so pleased afterwards – that and the fact that he probably put the tin hat on Valentino's chances of the championship. Marquez was now over 50 points ahead with four races to go.

There was, as usual, a fair amount of tyre talk. Cold morning sessions saw a lot of crashes, including for Rossi and Marquez. Trouble was, the tyre allocation was a little on the soft side, so the softer rear was gone in under five laps and the harder one was prone to spinning. None of which ever compromised Marquez's love for what is his true home track. As only he can, Marc was able to put in startling laps seemingly at will. The only session in which he was beaten was FP2, when Pedrosa was half a tenth quicker. In FP4 Marc was three-quarters of a second quicker, and in qualifying over half a second faster than the rest. And he set the fastest lap of the race.

At previous races Marquez showed that he is willing to subjugate his urge to win in the search to regain his championship, and he even managed to smile while doing it, but this was the Marquez of old, the Marquez of 2014. His incident at the seventh turn of the third lap showed how near the edge he was and, typically, the brush with disaster did nothing to slow his charge. Once he was back in front he steadily stretched his advantage to over three and a half seconds.

Lorenzo's stealthier progress to second place

LEFT The top four early in the race: Viñales leads Rossi, Marquez and Lorenzo

BELOW Nicky Hayden returned to MotoGP in place of Jack Miller

ABOVE Lorenzo, with special shark helmet, leads Rossi in front of Motorland's landmark wall

BELOW Pol Espargaro got over a couple of big practice crashes to finish a creditable eighth

was almost as impressive. He said that there was no way he could be on the rostrum then had a heavy crash in warm-up. That turned out to be a good thing. Jorge did two warm-up laps, one on each tyre, and realised he liked the stability of the harder rear tyre, so swapped to it on the grid. That was crucial. He had the edge grip he needs and was always in contention. Crucially, he didn't make a mistake and when Rossi did, Jorge was safe in second. It was his best result in eight races. No wonder he looked pleased, although that may also have had something to do with beating Rossi and reigniting the fight for runner-up spot in the championship.

As for Marquez, he had triumphed in front of his own fans, beaten Valentino for the first time in five races, and taken back most of the points Rossi gained in the process. It was one of those weekends when the bloke in third place struggles to put a positive spin on events.

There was no challenge from Ducati or Dani Pedrosa, victor last time out and second at this track the previous season. Both had no feeling from their tyres, Dani saying that his never felt like new tyres should. Pedrosa's front chunked badly towards the end of the race, letting Cal Crutchlow through, and Dovi had similar problems. There were mutterings about Michelin's quality control over the weekend but the French company did point out that some riders had decided to ignore their advice.

If Ducati's form continued to underwhelm, then Aprilia's continued its upward trend. Stefan Bradl made it straight through to the second qualifying session for the first time and looked more than comfortable doing it. No-one was getting through the final corner better than the German. Both Aprilias made it into the top ten, beating all the Ducatis as they did at the previous round. The nature of the Motorland track suggests that it wasn't just the chassis that had been improved but that the extra power promised back at Mugello had finally arrived.

In the great scheme of things the swing to Marquez in the title chase wasn't enormous, but it felt like it because it took his lead to over 50 points – more than two race wins. More than that, it was the manner of Marc's win that meant the paddock headed off to the trio of Asian and Australian races with the belief that he was going to win his third world title in the top class.

RIGHT This was Marquez's first dry-weather win since Texas; his management kept telling him to be patient because 'Aragón is coming'

HEAD TO HEAD AT PRAMAC

In Saturday morning's free practice Danilo Petrucci suffered a nasty crash entirely not of his making. He was coming out of pitlane when he was scooped up by Pol Espargaro's sliding Yamaha. The Italian took a heavy fall, notably banging his head hard. He got back on his spare bike and later went out in qualifying. However, when talking to both press and TV cameras later he said that he was unable to remember the crash and indeed most of the rest of the session. Danilo also raced on Sunday, fortunately without further incident.

As Petrucci and his team-mate Scott Redding are in competition for the single 2017-specification Desmosedici the team will have for the 2017 season, Danilo had even more than the usual racer's motivation to get out on track rather than watch from the pits. The team are counting points from Brno onwards (with one result dropped) to decide who gets the new bike.

None of which explains why a rider who was clearly confused was allowed straight back out on track. MotoGP does use one of the accepted medical protocols to screen potential concussion victims but that wasn't carried out until Sunday morning. Given the attention that sports like rugby and American football as well as other motorsports are now paying to the potential damage caused by concussion, especially repeated concussions, the cavalier manner in which Danilo's accident was treated was rather concerning. As more evidence comes to light on what is now a highly researched condition, MotoGP is going to have to show it's doing at least as much as other sports to look after its riders.

GRAN PREMIO MOVISTAR DE ARAGÓN
MOTORLAND ARAGÓN
ROUND **14**
SEPTEMBER 25

CIRCUIT KEY
- **S** SPEED TRAP
- **1** CORNER NUMBER
- SECTOR 1
- SECTOR 2
- SECTOR 3
- SECTOR 4

RACE RESULTS

CIRCUIT LENGTH 3.155 miles
NO. OF LAPS 23
RACE DISTANCE 72.572 miles
WEATHER Dry, 22°C
TRACK TEMPERATURE 36°C
WINNER Marc Marquez
FASTEST LAP 1m 48.694s, 104.4mph, Marc Marquez
LAP RECORD 1m 48.120s, 105.0mph, Jorge Lorenzo (2015)

TYRE OPTIONS

TYRE

CENTRE
LEFT RIGHT

SEVERITY RATING
<MILD   SEVERE>

FRONT COMPOUNDS
SOFT (S)
MEDIUM (M)
HARD (H)

REAR COMPOUNDS
MEDIUM (M)
HARD (H)

MICHELIN

QUALIFYING

	Rider	Nation	Motorcycle	Team	Time	Pole +
1	Marquez	SPA	Honda	Repsol Honda Team	1m 47.117s	
2	Viñales	SPA	Suzuki	Team Suzuki ECSTAR	1m 47.748s	0.631s
3	Lorenzo	SPA	Yamaha	Movistar Yamaha MotoGP	1m 47.778s	0.661s
4	Dovizioso	ITA	Ducati	Ducati Team	1m 47.819s	0.702s
5	Crutchlow	GBR	Honda	LCR Honda	1m 47.843s	0.726s
6	Rossi	ITA	Yamaha	Movistar Yamaha MotoGP	1m 47.951s	0.834s
7	Pedrosa	SPA	Honda	Repsol Honda Team	1m 48.017s	0.900s
8	Espargaro A	SPA	Suzuki	Team Suzuki ECSTAR	1m 48.230s	1.113s
9	Petrucci	ITA	Ducati	OCTO Pramac Yakhnich	1m 48.236s	1.119s
10	Redding	GBR	Ducati	OCTO Pramac Yakhnich	1m 48.242s	1.125s
11	Espargaro P	SPA	Yamaha	Monster Yamaha Tech 3	1m 48.448s	1.331s
12	Bradl	GER	Aprilia	Aprilia Racing Team Gresini	1m 49.083s	1.966s
13	Barbera	SPA	Ducati	Avintia Racing	1m 48.699s	*0.103s
14	Bautista	SPA	Aprilia	Aprilia Racing Team Gresini	1m 48.904s	*0.308s
15	Hernandez	COL	Ducati	Pull & Bear Aspar Team	1m 48.954s	*0.358s
16	Laverty	IRL	Ducati	Pull & Bear Aspar Team	1m 49.052s	*0.456s
17	Pirro	ITA	Ducati	Ducati Team	1m 49.139s	*0.543s
18	Rabat	SPA	Honda	Estrella Galicia 0,0 Marc VDS	1m 49.319s	*0.723s
19	Hayden	USA	Honda	Estrella Galicia 0,0 Marc VDS	1m 49.490s	*0.894s
20	Baz	FRA	Ducati	Avintia Racing	1m 49.841s	*1.245s
21	Lowes	GBR	Yamaha	Monster Yamaha Tech 3	1m 50.988s	*2.559s

* Gap with the fastest rider in the Q1 session

1 MARC MARQUEZ
Enjoyed his real home race. Survived a major front-end moment at Turn 7 on the third lap, which dropped him to fifth, then took just eight laps to regain the lead. Pulled away to take back the points Rossi gained over him in recent races.

2 JORGE LORENZO
Switched to the hard rear tyre on the grid after a sighting lap on both options. That was prompted by a big crash in warm-up. It proved to be the right choice and Jorge was able to pace himself brilliantly and conserve grip for the later stages.

3 VALENTINO ROSSI
Lucky to escape uninjured from a free-practice crash. Tried, as usual, to set up for race distance but found his rear was spinning in later stages. Couldn't hold off Marquez and then made a mistake on the brakes two laps from home trying to stay with Lorenzo.

4 MAVERICK VIÑALES
Led after Marquez's mistake but had a similar moment himself. Ran into the expected drop-off in rear tyre performance at mid-distance after which he had to give up thoughts of the rostrum and concentrate on finishing.

5 CAL CRUTCHLOW
Top independent yet again. Took time to get the hard rear tyre working then couldn't get past Pedrosa until he hit problems.

6 DANI PEDROSA
Knew from the warm-up lap that he was in tyre trouble. Couldn't get any traction in early stages then felt a vibration from the front later in the race. Finished with some lumps of tread missing from the front tyre.

7 ALEIX ESPARGARO
Still frustrated with his lack of feeling at the front. Nevertheless, was impressive all weekend, matching his team-mate in practice. Couldn't find a way past Crutchlow in the second half of the race then made a mistake to lose sixth.

8 POL ESPARGARO
Victim of a couple of brutal crashes in practice, which made rider and team more satisfied with eighth place than would usually be the case. Ran wide at the end of the back straight early on, which lost Pol contact with the Crutchlow group.

9 ALVARO BAUTISTA
Made up five places from his grid position on Aprilia's best race weekend so far.

Followed Pol Espargaro and closed in on the fifth-place group; didn't drop into the 1m 50s bracket until six laps from home.

10 STEFAN BRADL
Went direct into second qualifying session for the first time. Good pace in the race for which he said improvement in braking and front feeling in general were responsible.

11 ANDREA DOVIZIOSO
Felt a vibration from the front tyre from four laps into the race. Tried to manage the situation but his final half-dozen laps were very difficult and Dovi was passed by both Aprilias.

LAP CHART

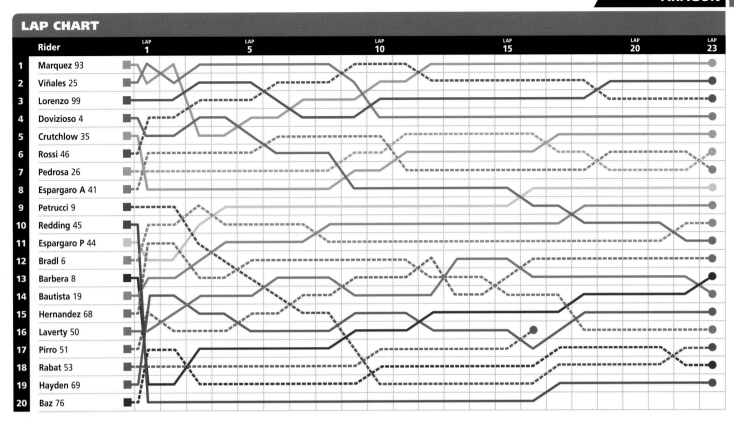

	Rider	LAP 1	LAP 5	LAP 10	LAP 15	LAP 20	LAP 23
1	Marquez 93						
2	Viñales 25						
3	Lorenzo 99						
4	Dovizioso 4						
5	Crutchlow 35						
6	Rossi 46						
7	Pedrosa 26						
8	Espargaro A 41						
9	Petrucci 9						
10	Redding 45						
11	Espargaro P 44						
12	Bradl 6						
13	Barbera 8						
14	Bautista 19						
15	Hernandez 68						
16	Laverty 50						
17	Pirro 51						
18	Rabat 53						
19	Hayden 69						
20	Baz 76						

RACE

	Rider	Motorcycle	Race time	Time +	Fastest lap	Avg. speed	Tyres
1	Marquez	Honda	41m 57.678s		1m 48.694s	103.8mph	H/H
2	Lorenzo	Yamaha	42m 00.418s	2.740s	1m 49.050s	103.6mph	M/H
3	Rossi	Yamaha	42m 03.661s	5.983s	1m 48.729s	103.5mph	M/H
4	Viñales	Suzuki	42m 05.916s	8.238s	1m 49.064s	103.4mph	H/H
5	Crutchlow	Honda	42m 10.899s	13.221s	1m 49.309s	103.2mph	H/H
6	Pedrosa	Honda	42m 14.750s	17.072s	1m 49.509s	103.0mph	M/H
7	Espargaro A	Suzuki	42m 16.200s	18.522s	1m 49.318s	103.0mph	M/H
8	Espargaro P	Yamaha	42m 17.110s	19.432s	1m 49.580s	103.0mph	M/H
9	Bautista	Aprilia	42m 20.749s	23.071s	1m 49.626s	102.8mph	M/M
10	Bradl	Aprilia	42m 25.576s	27.898s	1m 49.752s	102.6mph	M/M
11	Dovizioso	Ducati	42m 30.126s	32.448s	1m 49.422s	102.4mph	M/M
12	Pirro	Ducati	42m 32.711s	35.033s	1m 50.155s	102.3mph	M/M
13	Barbera	Ducati	42m 33.902s	36.224s	1m 49.955s	102.3mph	M/M
14	Laverty	Ducati	42m 35.299s	37.621s	1m 50.236s	102.2mph	M/M
15	Hayden	Honda	42m 38.187s	40.509s	1m 50.362s	102.1mph	M/M
16	Hernandez	Ducati	42m 41.584s	43.906s	1m 50.114s	102.0mph	M/M
17	Petrucci	Ducati	42m 54.418s	56.740s	1m 50.121s	101.5mph	M/M
18	Baz	Ducati	42m 57.359s	59.681s	1m 51.007s	101.3mph	M/M
19	Redding	Ducati	43m 31.804s	1m 34.126s	1m 50.853s	100.0mph	M/M
NC	Rabat	Honda	29m 38.577s	7 laps	1m 50.227s	102.2mph	M/M

CHAMPIONSHIP

	Rider	Nation	Team	Points
1	Marquez	SPA	Repsol Honda Team	248
2	Rossi	ITA	Movistar Yamaha MotoGP	196
3	Lorenzo	SPA	Movistar Yamaha MotoGP	182
4	Pedrosa	SPA	Repsol Honda Team	155
5	Viñales	SPA	Team Suzuki ECSTAR	149
6	Crutchlow	GBR	LCR Honda	105
7	Dovizioso	ITA	Ducati Team	104
8	Iannone	ITA	Ducati Team	96
	Espargaro P	SPA	Monster Yamaha Tech 3	96
10	Barbera	SPA	Avintia Racing	84
11	Laverty	IRL	Pull & Bear Aspar Team	71
12	Espargaro A	SPA	Team Suzuki ECSTAR	69
13	Redding	GBR	OCTO Pramac Yakhnich	55
14	Bautista	SPA	Aprilia Racing Team Gresini	54
15	Petrucci	ITA	OCTO Pramac Yakhnich	50
16	Bradl	GER	Aprilia Racing Team Gresini	49
17	Miller	AUS	Estrella Galicia 0,0 Marc VDS	42
	Smith	GBR	Monster Yamaha Tech 3	42
19	Pirro	ITA	OCTO Pramac Yakhnich	36
20	Rabat	SPA	Estrella Galicia 0,0 Marc VDS	27
21	Baz	FRA	Avintia Racing	24
22	Hernandez	COL	Pull & Bear Aspar Team	13
23	Lowes	GBR	Monster Yamaha Tech 3	3
24	Hayden	USA	Estrella Galicia 0,0 Marc VDS	1

12 MICHELE PIRRO
Stood in for Iannone after he withdrew, so missed Friday. Didn't start well, was then affected by tyre vibration from half-distance but was able to hold his position.

13 HECTOR BARBERA
Lost ground after a collision with Pirro on the first lap but equalled his qualifying position. Won a good dice with Laverty. Like all the Ducati riders, suffered from lack of grip.

14 EUGENE LAVERTY
Not bothered by the rear tyre dropping but caught out by the softer front, which caused him to run off-track late on and lose a couple of positions.

15 NICKY HAYDEN
Replaced Jack Miller and not surprisingly found that it took time to come to terms with the Michelin front. On race day he was racing with people who were two seconds faster than him on Friday. His usual professional job; impressed the team.

16 YONNY HERNANDEZ
Got a superb start and moved up to 11th but was a victim of massive rear tyre performance drop-off at half distance.

17 DANILO PETRUCCI
Given a ride-through penalty for knocking Redding off. Said he was running wide repeatedly because of brake problems and the race was extremely difficult.

18 LORIS BAZ
Back after missing Misano, but far from fit. Treated the race as a training session and managed to finish.

19 SCOTT REDDING
Punted off on the first lap by team-mate Petrucci. Remounted to finish but absolutely furious about the multiple comings-together on the first lap.

DID NOT FINISH

TITO RABAT
Crashed in warm-up so took it easy for the first two laps, only to crash again. That's five front-end crashes in two GPs. A chance of good points lost.

DID NOT RACE

BRADLEY SMITH
Finishing his recovery from knee injury and subsequent operation.

JACK MILLER
Recovering from his crash in Austria.

ANDREA IANNONE
Forced to withdraw by the pain from his back injury, replaced by Pirro.

ALEX LOWES
A big crash on Saturday forced him to withdraw.

MOTUL GRAND PRIX OF JAPAN
TWIN-RING MOTEGI

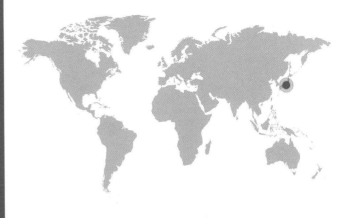

FIVE-STAR PERFORMANCE

Yamaha's nightmare weekend handed Marc Marquez his third MotoGP title and his fifth in all classes at Honda's home track

No-one expected Marc Marquez to wrap up the championship with three races to spare. After all, it was going to take an exceptional set of circumstances to finish the job so early in the season. For starters, he had to win; something he had yet to do in the MotoGP class at Motegi. Secondly, Valentino Rossi had to finish 15th or lower. Thirdly, Jorge Lorenzo had to finish off the rostrum. That was a long-odds bet.

However, the odds shortened before the first practice session when it was announced that Andrea Iannone wasn't going to race. Given that Ducatis tend to go well at the Twin Rings, that was one potential winner out. Ostensibly, the reason was Andrea's back injury from Misano (which raises the question of how he was declared fit for that race and for Aragón), but there were a lot of rumours flying around suggesting that the relationship with Ducati was under severe strain. When he was also pulled out of the Australian race the following weekend, the rumours gained more credence. Hector Barbera was promoted from the customer Avintia team and spent the weekend doing a passable impression of a kid in a sweet shop.

Back at the bookmakers, the odds were shortened again after Friday practice when Dani Pedrosa highsided himself into orbit on an out-lap and broke his collarbone. So the rider who has won three Japanese GPs, including last year's, at Motegi had his name rubbed off the chalk board.

ABOVE The grid rushes down to Turn 1, Lorenzo with the advantage

OPPOSITE TOP Hector Barbera's deal to ride the factory Ducati was done so late he didn't have time to get leathers made in time for qualifying

RIGHT The moment the title was won and lost; Jorge Lorenzo crashes the Yamaha at V-Corner with five laps to go

Lorenzo waited until the second bend of the first flying lap of a Saturday morning run to highside himself just as viciously. He went to hospital in a helicopter, to which he was transported in a wheelchair with a drip in his arm. Astonishingly, he was back just over an hour later and ready to qualify. He was fast enough for the front row, but surely he would have problems over race distance. The odds were trimmed once more.

As for Rossi, he looked a sure bet for the second row of the grid. He hadn't looked happy on track and appeared to be suffering from the worst case of jet lag known to medical science. He promptly took his third pole position of the year. That confused the bookies. In fact it confused everybody. Before Japan the two Yamaha riders had said that the title was gone and they were now racing for second in the championship. In truth they should have said they were racing to be the top Yamaha rider and it wouldn't have mattered if that had been for eighth place – the contest wouldn't have been any less fierce. Now Valentino was adamant he was racing for the win.

He was as good as his word. Fast-starter Lorenzo was mugged by Marquez on the fourth lap but two laps later Rossi was past his team-mate and less than a second behind Marc. The odds on a Marquez championship shot back up, and came crashing back down less than a lap later when Valentino lost the front going into

'IT'S INCREDIBLE!
BEFORE THE
RACE I DIDN'T
EXPECT TO BE
CHAMPION, AND
I SAID THAT HERE
IT WOULD BE
IMPOSSIBLE'
MARC MARQUEZ

Turn 10, the hairpin at the top of the track that's a contender for the slowest corner of the year.

The plot now pivoted on the ability of Lorenzo to keep up the pace as Andrea Dovizioso looked to close in under pressure from Maverick Viñales, both of these pursuers having to deal with a very feisty Aleix Espargaro, who was enjoying his best weekend in Suzuki's colours. Every time Dovi closed the gap, Jorge responded. Right up to lap 19 out of 24 when Lorenzo opened the throttle at the apex of V-Corner a fraction early and lost the front.

Marc learned that he only had to finish the next five laps to be champion again as he crossed the line, and promptly came closer than he had all race to losing it. The fact that he had the title in his hands seemed to shock him. His sector and lap times went haywire for a few minutes as he made mistakes on the brakes, missed apexes and even, he said later, forgot which circuit he was racing on.

Afterwards Marc seemed surprised that the team had the obligatory celebratory T-shirts to hand but was lucid enough to offer a few interesting reflections on the season. He identified the crash at Le Mans as a crucial moment that forced him to think hard. During the 2015 season he failed to score in six races. This time he won the championship by scoring in every race, but had to wait 11 races – eleven – between dry-weather victories. As he grew more

ABOVE Yamaha's veteran factory tester Nakasuga again rode as a wild card and again put in a solid top-ten finish

BELOW No Yamaha rider on the rostrum, so Marc Marquez got to wear another championship T-shirt

DREAMS DO COME TRUE

When the Avintia Ducati team's Hector Barbera was given the chance to ride the factory bike, his team had a problem. Who to put on their bike at short notice? One of Ducati's old heroes, triple World Superbike Champion and MotoGP race winner Troy Bayliss, had the answer – his rider in the Australian Superbike Championship.

Mike Jones, the 22-year-old Australian champ of 2015, moved to Ducati for 2016 but had never ridden Motegi, the Desmosedici, Michelins, or carbon brakes. It's a reflection on what has happened to the status of the Australian championship, not the man himself, that hardly anyone in the paddock had heard of Jones before he turned up on Friday. The most commonly expressed emotion was the hope that he didn't embarrass himself.

There was no need to worry about 'Mad Mike'. Despite arriving on Friday morning after an overnight flight, the Queenslander did everything right, getting faster with each session and even out-qualifying Hiro Aoyama, another late replacement. The team was impressed with the way he learned and his application. In practice his attitude was, 'Fill the tank and I'll come back in when it's empty.' The steepness of his learning curve was clearly demonstrated when he thought there was a fault with the brakes that nearly sent him over the 'bars. It turned out

that he'd grabbed the lever as you would with steel discs.

To finish the race without a crash all weekend was a real achievement and got Jones the reward of a ride in his home GP.

frustrated, his manager, Emilio Alzamora, and race engineer, Santi Hernandez, would reassure him by reminding him, 'Aragón is coming.'

Sure enough, on the track that's closest to his home region and his heart, Marc ripped the rest to shreds, humiliated them, and he did it while looking smooth and controlled, although there was one major moment as usual and the equally usual and inevitable impossible save. With hindsight, that was the moment when Marc put the title out of reach of the Yamaha men. Not mathematically, but psychologically. The last time a Yamaha rider won was back at Catalunya, seven races before Aragón.

And now that the title was safely back in his possession, he announced that he could now cut loose and unleash the old-style Marc Marquez. A thought that was unlikely to give much hope or reassurance to riders of any other make of motorcycle. Or the other Honda riders.

RIGHT Aleix Espargaro came closer than he's ever done to a rostrum finish on the Suzuki

MOTUL GRAND PRIX OF JAPAN
TWIN-RING MOTEGI
ROUND **15**
OCTOBER 16

RACE RESULTS

CIRCUIT LENGTH 2.983 miles

NO. OF LAPS 24

RACE DISTANCE 71.597 miles

WEATHER Dry, 25°C

TRACK TEMPERATURE 36°C

WINNER Marc Marquez

FASTEST LAP 1m 45.576s, 101.7mph, Marc Marquez

LAP RECORD 1m 45.350s, 101.9mph, Jorge Lorenzo (2014)

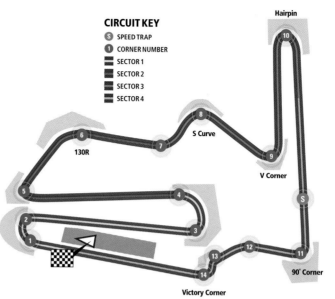

CIRCUIT KEY

- **S** SPEED TRAP
- **1** CORNER NUMBER
- ▬ SECTOR 1
- ▬ SECTOR 2
- ▬ SECTOR 3
- ▬ SECTOR 4

TYRE OPTIONS

CENTRE
LEFT RIGHT
TYRE

SEVERITY RATING

<MILD SEVERE>

FRONT COMPOUNDS
SOFT (S)
MEDIUM (M)
HARD (H)

REAR COMPOUNDS
SOFT (S)
MEDIUM (M)

MICHELIN

QUALIFYING

	Rider	Nation	Motorcycle	Team	Time	Pole +
1	Rossi	ITA	Yamaha	Movistar Yamaha MotoGP	1m 43.954s	
2	Marquez	SPA	Honda	Repsol Honda Team	1m 44.134s	0.180s
3	Lorenzo	SPA	Yamaha	Movistar Yamaha MotoGP	1m 44.221s	0.267s
4	Dovizioso	ITA	Ducati	Ducati Team	1m 44.294s	0.340s
5	Crutchlow	GBR	Honda	LCR Honda	1m 44.402s	0.448s
6	Espargaro A	SPA	Suzuki	Team Suzuki ECSTAR	1m 44.494s	0.540s
7	Viñales	SPA	Suzuki	Team Suzuki ECSTAR	1m 44.539s	0.585s
8	Barbera	SPA	Ducati	Ducati Team	1m 44.980s	1.026s
9	Espargaro P	SPA	Yamaha	Monster Yamaha Tech 3	1m 45.232s	1.278s
10	Petrucci	ITA	Ducati	OCTO Pramac Yakhnich	1m 45.782s	1.828s
11	Redding	GBR	Ducati	OCTO Pramac Yakhnich	1m 45.827s	1.873s
12	Bautista	SPA	Aprilia	Aprilia Racing Team Gresini	1m 45.614s	–
13	Bradl	GER	Aprilia	Aprilia Racing Team Gresini	1m 45.823s	*0.209s
14	Miller	AUS	Honda	Estrella Galicia 0,0 Marc VDS	1m 46.347s	*0.733s
15	Smith	GBR	Yamaha	Monster Yamaha Tech 3	1m 46.593s	*0.979s
16	Nakasuga	JPN	Yamaha	Yamalube Yamaha Factory	1m 46.627s	*1.013s
17	Hernandez	COL	Ducati	Pull & Bear Aspar Team	1m 46.705s	*1.091s
18	Rabat	SPA	Honda	Estrella Galicia 0,0 Marc VDS	1m 46.753s	*1.139s
19	Laverty	IRL	Ducati	Pull & Bear Aspar Team	1m 47.060s	*1.446s
20	Baz	FRA	Ducati	Avintia Racing	1m 47.501s	*1.887s
21	Jones	AUS	Ducati	Avintia Racing	1m 47.631s	*2.017s
22	Aoyama	JPN	Honda	Repsol Honda Team	1m 47.788s	*2.174s

* Gap with the fastest rider in the Q1 session

1 MARC MARQUEZ
Clinched his third MotoGP championship and took his first top-class win at Motegi with a faultless race. The Yamahas crashed trying to match his pace. The only time he faltered was when he saw on his pitboard that Lorenzo was out and therefore he was world champion.

2 ANDREA DOVIZIOSO
A typically clever race. Didn't panic after a bad start that detached him from the front three, but was closing Lorenzo down steadily when the Yamaha man crashed. Knew it would be easy to crash and managed his effort superbly.

3 MAVERICK VIÑALES
Didn't look comfortable until race day, when he started badly. Stayed calm and resisted the temptation to use up his tyres and was, typically, fast in the closing stages when he shadowed Dovizioso.

4 ALEIX ESPARGARO
His best result of the season and the closest Aleix has been to the leaders. Out-qualified his team-mate and gave him a tough time fighting for third.

5 CAL CRUTCHLOW
Top independent and it may have been even better but for an off-track excursion mid-race that lost Cal around eight seconds. He ran the hard front and was planning a late bid for a rostrum position.

6 POL ESPARGARO
Never happy, so surprised with sixth place. Spent most of the race on his own once he'd got the jump on the Pramac Ducatis.

7 ALVARO BAUTISTA
Aprilia's best result so far, aided of course by some crashes but still the result of good work by the team after a tough start on Friday. Alvaro went straight to the final qualifying session for the second time in three races.

8 DANILO PETRUCCI
Slightly disappointed by his race pace, which was limited by the same difficulties under braking as everyone else.

9 SCOTT REDDING
Had the same problems as his team-mate but lost places off the start and couldn't get close enough to attack him once he'd recovered.

10 STEFAN BRADL
A second double top ten for Aprilia, although Stefan was not happy with his performance in qualifying or the race. He just missed going through to Q2 and made a couple of mistakes in the race that could have cost the chance to fight with his team-mate.

11 KATSUYUKI NAKASUGA
Yamaha's veteran All-Japan Champion, double Eight-Hour winner and factory MotoGP tester took a wild-card ride as usual and again did a professional job of testing some parts for 2017 and scoring points.

12 YONNY HERNANDEZ
Had to use the hard rear tyre, which lost him a lot of ground in the early stages.

LAP CHART

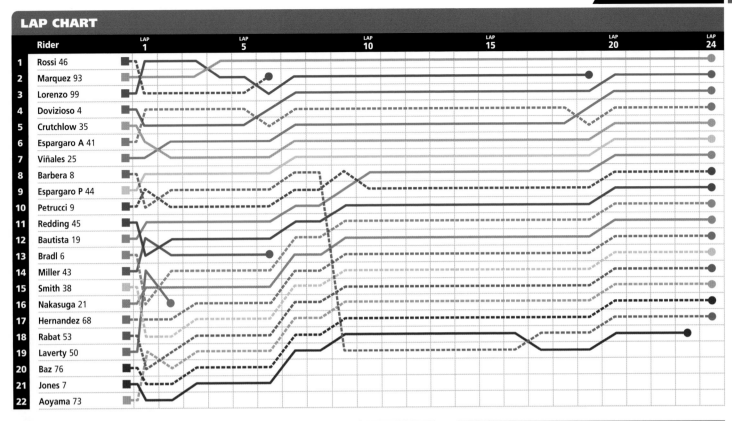

Rider		LAP 1	LAP 5	LAP 10	LAP 15	LAP 20	LAP 24
1	Rossi 46						
2	Marquez 93						
3	Lorenzo 99						
4	Dovizioso 4						
5	Crutchlow 35						
6	Espargaro A 41						
7	Viñales 25						
8	Barbera 8						
9	Espargaro P 44						
10	Petrucci 9						
11	Redding 45						
12	Bautista 19						
13	Bradl 6						
14	Miller 43						
15	Smith 38						
16	Nakasuga 21						
17	Hernandez 68						
18	Rabat 53						
19	Laverty 50						
20	Baz 76						
21	Jones 7						
22	Aoyama 73						

RACE

	Rider	Motorcycle	Race time	Time +	Fastest lap	Avg. speed	Tyres
1	Marquez	Honda	42m 34.610s		1m 45.576s	100.8mph	M/S
2	Dovizioso	Ducati	42m 37.602s	2.992s	1m 45.847s	100.7mph	M/S
3	Viñales	Suzuki	42m 38.714s	4.104s	1m 45.791s	100.7mph	M/S
4	Espargaro A	Suzuki	42m 39.336s	4.726s	1m 45.861s	100.7mph	M/S
5	Crutchlow	Honda	42m 49.659s	15.049s	1m 45.792s	100.3mph	H/S
6	Espargaro P	Yamaha	42m 54.264s	19.654s	1m 46.522s	100.1mph	M/S
7	Bautista	Aprilia	42m 57.642s	23.032s	1m 46.741s	100.0mph	M/S
8	Petrucci	Ducati	43m 03.165s	28.555s	1m 46.865s	99.7mph	M/S
9	Redding	Ducati	43m 03.412s	28.802s	1m 46.752s	99.7mph	M/S
10	Bradl	Aprilia	43m 06.940s	32.330s	1m 46.568s	99.6mph	M/S
11	Nakasuga	Yamaha	43m 17.455s	42.845s	1m 47.512s	99.2mph	M/S
12	Hernandez	Ducati	43m 26.829s	52.219s	1m 47.851s	98.9mph	S/M
13	Smith	Yamaha	43m 28.393s	53.783s	1m 47.881s	98.8mph	S/S
14	Rabat	Honda	43m 29.370s	54.760s	1m 47.966s	98.7mph	M/S
15	Aoyama	Honda	43m 34.765s	1m 00.155s	1m 47.954s	98.5mph	S/S
16	Baz	Ducati	43m 39.050s	1m 04.440s	1m 47.915s	98.4mph	H/S
17	Barbera	Ducati	44m 17.576s	1m 42.966s	1m 46.593s	96.9mph	S/S
18	Jones	Ducati	42m 51.865s	1 lap	1m 50.023s	96.0mph	S/S
NC	Lorenzo	Yamaha	33m 43.286s	5 laps	1m 45.819s	100.8mph	M/S
NC	Rossi	Yamaha	10m 42.812s	18 laps	1m 45.722s	100.2mph	M/S
NC	Miller	Honda	10m 53.385s	18 laps	1m 47.099s	98.6mph	M/S
NC	Laverty	Ducati	3m 45.477s	22 laps	1m 48.688s	95.3mph	M/S

CHAMPIONSHIP

	Rider	Nation	Team	Points
1	Marquez	SPA	Repsol Honda Team	273
2	Rossi	ITA	Movistar Yamaha MotoGP	196
3	Lorenzo	SPA	Movistar Yamaha MotoGP	182
4	Viñales	SPA	Team Suzuki ECSTAR	165
5	Pedrosa	SPA	Repsol Honda Team	155
6	Dovizioso	ITA	Ducati Team	124
7	Crutchlow	GBR	LCR Honda	116
8	Espargaro P	SPA	Monster Yamaha Tech 3	106
9	Iannone	ITA	Ducati Team	96
10	Barbera	SPA	Avintia Racing	84
11	Espargaro A	SPA	Team Suzuki ECSTAR	82
12	Laverty	IRL	Pull & Bear Aspar Team	71
13	Bautista	SPA	Aprilia Racing Team Gresini	63
14	Redding	GBR	OCTO Pramac Yakhnich	62
15	Petrucci	ITA	OCTO Pramac Yakhnich	58
16	Bradl	GER	Aprilia Racing Team Gresini	55
17	Smith	GBR	Monster Yamaha Tech 3	45
18	Miller	AUS	Estrella Galicia 0,0 Marc VDS	42
19	Pirro	ITA	OCTO Pramac Yakhnich	36
20	Rabat	SPA	Estrella Galicia 0,0 Marc VDS	29
21	Baz	FRA	Avintia Racing	24
22	Hernandez	COL	Pull & Bear Aspar Team	17
23	Nakasuga	JPN	Yamalube Yamaha Factory	5
24	Lowes	GBR	Monster Yamaha Tech 3	3
25	Aoyama	JPN	Repsol Honda Team	1
	Hayden	USA	Estrella Galicia 0,0 Marc VDS	1

13 BRADLEY SMITH
Returned from two operations on a nasty knee ligament injury. Looked like he wouldn't be able to race after the first session – his team wasn't sure he'd complete one lap! Yet he rode every session, qualified well and scored points.

14 TITO RABAT
Points on his least-favourite circuit and a good gap to the other independent riders.

15 HIRO AOYAMA
Called in to replace Pedrosa. Didn't ride until Saturday morning, qualified last but made sure he got the bike home.

16 LORIS BAZ
Thought he was now fit after two injuries but found he wasn't when he caught Aoyama and had no energy left to attack.

17 HECTOR BARBERA
Replaced Iannone for his first ride on a factory bike. Crashed trying to pass Pol Espargaro. Picked the bike up and finished.

18 MIKE JONES
The 2015 Australian Superbike Champion was drafted in late to replace Barbera on the Avintia Ducati. With no experience of the track or bike, he did a good job.

DID NOT FINISH

JACK MILLER
Crashed when he got a little too optimistic at Turn 1 but was able to take positives from his fitness, especially the fact that the hand he broke in Austria stood up to Motegi's hard braking efforts.

VALENTINO ROSSI
Qualified on pole and knew he had to try to catch Marquez to keep his title hopes alive. Crashed when he lost the front without warning going into the slowest turn on the track.

EUGENE LAVERTY
Lucky to race after a massive crash on Friday. In the race he crashed at V-Corner on lap three trying to take Nakasuga, ending his run of finishing every race.

JORGE LORENZO
Looked like he was going to keep the title chase alive until he lost the front as he got on the throttle at V-Corner four laps from the flag. Blamed his mistake on choosing the medium front tyre, not the soft.

DID NOT RACE

ANDREA IANNONE
Out because his injury from Misano hadn't healed, said the press release, although there were rumours about a serious falling-out with Ducati.

DANI PEDROSA
Victim of a massive highside on Friday that broke his right collarbone and cracked his left fibula. Flew home for surgery.

AUSTRALIA

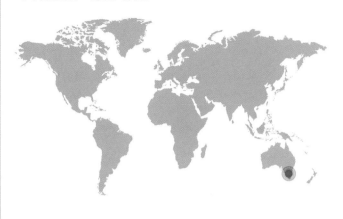

MICHELIN® AUSTRALIAN
MOTORCYCLE GRAND PRIX
PHILLIP ISLAND

DOUBLE?
NO TROUBLE!

**Cal Crutchlow dominated to win his
second race of the year and this time
there could be no arguments**

Cast your mind back to the Italian GP at
Mugello. Cal Crutchlow finished 11th, only
his second points-scoring ride of the year, to
leave himself 19th in the championship, a slight
improvement on the 20th he'd been after
crashing at Le Mans. Did anyone believe that by
the end of the year he'd win two races, stand on
the rostrum two more times and look like the
answer to Honda's prayer?

All of a sudden Cal was without question one
of the finest riders in the world. His win in the
Czech Republic was founded on the right tyre
choice and bravery. This win in Australia involved
closing down Marc Marquez and then beating
Valentino Rossi on an even playing field. That's
a good day's work in anyone's language. More
proof of Cal's new-found status was his visit to
HRC after the Motegi race and the way they have
been pushing things like a new chassis at him to
test. It helps that he is, in his own words, 'normal'.
This means not being Marc Marquez and not
weighing only 50kg like Dani Pedrosa.

It's true that tyre choice played a part in Cal's
victory, but doesn't it always? He went with
the hard front, as did Marquez, Jack Miller and
the Suzuki riders. He saw Marquez crash, and
knew Aleix Espargaro had also lost the front in
a straight line at Honda corner, the right-hand
hairpin that had claimed Cal on the last lap
two years earlier when he was in a safe second
place. Back then, track temperature had dropped

ABOVE Pol Espargaro leads from third on the grid, but inevitably the factory bikes came by

BELOW Jack Miller with his mate Jackass on the grid for his home race

OPPOSITE Nicky Hayden leads the fight for seventh place; he was almost emotional when he saw his number back on a Repsol Honda

dramatically. This time it was just consistently cold, as it tends to be when you hold a race in October this far from the equator and start it at 4pm. Double jeopardy or what?

Marquez's crash wiped enough bits off his bike to prevent him restarting, resulting in his first non-finish of the year. Marc refused to blame the front tyre, saying the error was his.

Not surprisingly, Cal was visited by serious paranoia between Marc's crash and the chequered flag. When the sun peeked out from the cloud cover he relaxed a little and when it went back in he pushed again, knowing only too well that he had to keep some heat in the front tyre. When his pit board told him that it was Rossi who was chasing, he thought, 'From 15th?!' Those 18 laps weren't easy. Not easy at all.

Mind you, it wasn't easy all weekend. Cal had to go through the first qualifying session after horrible weather disrupted free practice. He got a front-row start. The other rostrum finishers, Valentino Rossi and Maverick Viñales, also had to go through Q1 but didn't make it out into Q2. Thus Rossi started from 15th on the grid, which makes second place in the race one of his minor miracles. He hadn't looked quick until the only dry time anyone got, in Sunday morning warm-up. As we've come to expect, Rossi and his team took full advantage of that dry half hour to arrive at a bike that worked. He carved through the field, going fourth on the eighth lap. It took a couple

'I WAS ACTUALLY QUITE CONFIDENT THAT I COULD HAVE CAUGHT MARC TODAY, BUT ONCE HE CRASHED I JUST CARRIED ON AT THE SAME PACE'

CAL CRUTCHLOW

of laps to get past Aleix Espargaro, who was again looking good, and when Valentino did pass he was second and believed he could win. But Crutchlow, having harried Marquez into an error, was able to hold off Rossi's challenge.

Viñales achieved back-to-back rostrums for the first time in MotoGP. He had also started way back on the grid, in 13th spot, and had trouble with both Espargaro brothers and Andrea Dovizioso. When Aleix fell out of third, Maverick was two seconds behind Rossi with four laps left and he halved the gap by the flag.

Lorenzo? Don't ask. It was another weekend when he couldn't find any confidence on a cold track and he finished a distant sixth, which only looks good in relation to his 12th on the grid.

Marquez's crash, of course, didn't affect the riders' championship, and Crutchlow's victory ensured that Honda kept their grip on the constructors' championship. However, with Dani Pedrosa still absent, the teams' championship was definitely up for grabs and HRC hoped that another replacement ride by Nicky Hayden on a circuit where he held the lap record for years would bolster the Repsol Honda team. Nicky was indeed impressive, topping one practice session and going directly to Q2, and being involved in the frantic battle for seventh place that kept the crowd entertained for most of the race.

The man who came out on top in that fight was Scott Redding, but only after Hayden had been

ABOVE Local hero Mike Jones rode the Avintia Ducati for a second time and scored a point

BELOW Aleix Espargaro had another good weekend; here he leads the fight for third

END OF THE INNOCENCE

Maverick Viñales's third place took the Suzuki team over the threshold of six concession points, meaning that the factory henceforth lost the concessions granted to new entrants to MotoGP or those who haven't scored a dry-weather win for two seasons. Suzuki received one concession point for each of Maverick's third places in France, Japan and Australia plus three for his win at Silverstone.

Suzuki immediately lost the right to unlimited testing, not that this would have had an effect at this stage the season, and the other concessions would be cancelled from the start of the 2017 season. That means the Suzukis will have to complete 2017 with seven engines, not the nine they've been allowed so far, and will also have to freeze their engine design.

That puts them on a par with Honda, Yamaha and Ducati, who lost their concessions last year. Of the factories currently competing, only Aprilia go into 2017 with concessions – and so will newcomers KTM.

Dorna and IRTA have been steering the technical regulations to achieve their objective of one type of motorcycle on the grid. Concessions were part of that plan and helped new factories justify entering MotoGP. The strategy has proved to be much better than CRT or Open Class bikes forming a race within a race.

unceremoniously punted off by Jack Miller. Thus the Repsol Honda team scored zero points and the Movistar Yamaha team closed right in with 30. This may seem an issue of little interest to most fans, but it matters a lot to the factories and especially to Honda's long-time sponsor Repsol. Which does make you wonder why the Japanese factories don't have a test rider of the quality of Ducati's Michele Pirro.

Not that Ducati fared well in Australia. Dovizioso was a distant fourth while temporary team-mate Hector Barbera again crashed in the closing stages, this time while in the fight for seventh. The Mike Jones feel-good story continued: the Aussie again replaced Barbera on the Avintia bike and again did a fine job, this time being rewarded with a point that was enthusiastically celebrated by the team.

Phillip Island nearly always provides good racing but this time it mainly provided tension – mostly for Cal Crutchlow. In winning two races in a season, he joined a select group of British riders who have done that in the top class – Les Graham, Geoff Duke, John Surtees, Mike Hailwood, Phil Read and Barry Sheene. World Champions all, and not bad company.

OPPOSITE Cal Crutchlow, a man who now knows he's among the best in the world

MICHELIN® AUSTRALIAN MOTORCYCLE GRAND PRIX

PHILLIP ISLAND

ROUND **16**
OCTOBER 23

RACE RESULTS

CIRCUIT LENGTH 2.764 miles

NO. OF LAPS 27

RACE DISTANCE 74.624 miles

WEATHER Dry, 12°C

TRACK TEMPERATURE 33°C

WINNER Cal Crutchlow

FASTEST LAP 1m 29.494s, 111.2mph, Cal Crutchlow

LAP RECORD 1m 28.108s, 112.9mph, Marc Marquez (2013)

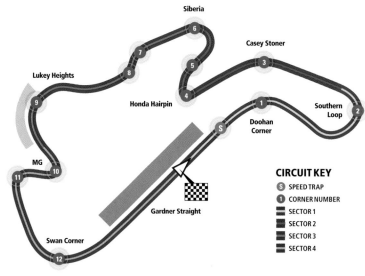

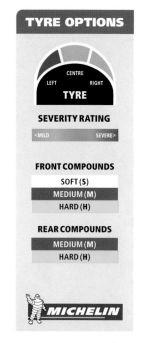

TYRE OPTIONS

TYRE

CENTRE
LEFT   RIGHT

SEVERITY RATING

<MILD   SEVERE>

FRONT COMPOUNDS

SOFT (S)
MEDIUM (M)
HARD (H)

REAR COMPOUNDS

MEDIUM (M)
HARD (H)

MICHELIN

QUALIFYING

	Rider	Nation	Motorcycle	Team	Time	Pole +
1	Marquez	SPA	Honda	Repsol Honda Team	1m 30.819s	
2	Crutchlow	GBR	Honda	LCR Honda	1m 30.981s	0.792s
3	Espargaro P	SPA	Yamaha	Monster Yamaha Tech 3	1m 31.107s	0.918s
4	Espargaro A	SPA	Suzuki	Team Suzuki ECSTAR	1m 31.673s	1.484s
5	Miller	AUS	Honda	Estrella Galicia 0,0 Marc VDS	1m 31.754s	1.565s
6	Petrucci	ITA	Ducati	OCTO Pramac Yakhnich	1m 32.420s	2.231s
7	Hayden	USA	Honda	Repsol Honda Team	1m 32.944s	2.755s
8	Bradl	GER	Aprilia	Aprilia Racing Team Gresini	1m 33.015s	2.826s
9	Dovizioso	ITA	Ducati	Ducati Team	1m 33.090s	2.901s
10	Barbera	ITA	Ducati	Ducati Team	1m 33.914s	3.725s
11	Redding	GBR	Ducati	OCTO Pramac Yakhnich	1m 34.682s	4.493s
12	Lorenzo	SPA	Yamaha	Movistar Yamaha MotoGP	1m 36.840s	6.651s
13	Viñales	SPA	Suzuki	Team Suzuki ECSTAR	1m 40.744s	*2.277s
14	Smith	GBR	Yamaha	Monster Yamaha Tech 3	1m 41.129s	*2.662s
15	Rossi	ITA	Yamaha	Movistar Yamaha MotoGP	1m 41.368s	*2.901s
16	Laverty	IRL	Ducati	Pull & Bear Aspar Team	1m 41.532s	*3.065s
17	Hernandez	COL	Ducati	Pull & Bear Aspar Team	1m 41.766s	*3.299s
18	Bautista	SPA	Aprilia	Aprilia Racing Team Gresini	1m 41.850s	*3.383s
19	Jones	AUS	Ducati	Avintia Racing	1m 42.261s	*3.794s
20	Baz	FRA	Ducati	Avintia Racing	1m 43.128s	*4.661s
21	Rabat	SPA	Honda	Estrella Galicia 0,0 Marc VDS	1m 44.096s	*5.629s

* Gap with the fastest rider in the Q1 session

1 CAL CRUTCHLOW
An even better ride than his win at Brno. Came through Q1 to start on the front row, and went with the hard front tyre. Closing in on Marquez when the champion fell, after which it was 18 laps of worry about keeping heat in that front Michelin.

2 VALENTINO ROSSI
Failed to progress from Q1 so started 15th. Very fast in Sunday warm-up, the first dry period of the weekend, after which Valentino believed he could win. He thought the same when he saw Marquez fall but conceded that Crutchlow was faster on the day.

3 MAVERICK VIÑALES
Used the hard front tyre and, with precious little dry practice, spent the first few laps assessing it after qualifying back in 13th spot. Moved through the field impressively, but spent too much time going from sixth to third to be able to catch Rossi. The result gave him consecutive rostrums for the first time in MotoGP.

4 ANDREA DOVIZIOSO
Happy with fourth and fighting for the rostrum on a track where the Ducati most certainly has good points and bad points – and where Dovi isn't usually happy.

5 POL ESPARGARO
Very brave to qualify third in difficult conditions, his first front row of the year. Started well but had to watch factory bikes go past. Took consolation from beating one or two of them.

6 JORGE LORENZO
Another difficult weekend. Managed the same sort of times in the race as he had in warm-up but suffered from his usual cool-track problem – lack of rear grip that got worse during the race.

7 SCOTT REDDING
Won the ferocious group battle for seventh and gained a couple of points over team-mate Petrucci in the intra-Pramac fight for the right to ride in 2017. Involved with Petrucci, Miller and Hayden for most of the race but was able to pull out a small gap in the last five laps.

8 BRADLEY SMITH
Very careful at the start of the race, got across a five-second gap to the group and then rode round Miller and Petrucci on the last corner for his best result since Mugello. An astonishing achievement given his physical condition.

9 DANILO PETRUCCI
Started well and got up to third but, like many, suffered traction problems as the race progressed. Was preparing to attack his team-mate on the last lap but was punted wide by Miller and then mugged out of the last corner by Smith.

10 JACK MILLER
Hadn't used the hard front tyre until he raced with it. Part of the entertaining group fight for seventh for most of the race. His troubles came from the rear tyre losing performance and sending him wide a few times.

OFFICIAL TIMEKEEPER

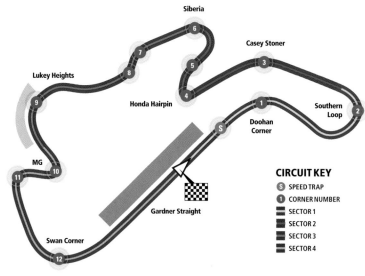

Siberia
Casey Stoner
Lukey Heights
Honda Hairpin
Southern Loop
Doohan Corner
MG
Gardner Straight
Swan Corner

CIRCUIT KEY
- (S) SPEED TRAP
- (1) CORNER NUMBER
- SECTOR 1
- SECTOR 2
- SECTOR 3
- SECTOR 4

LAP CHART

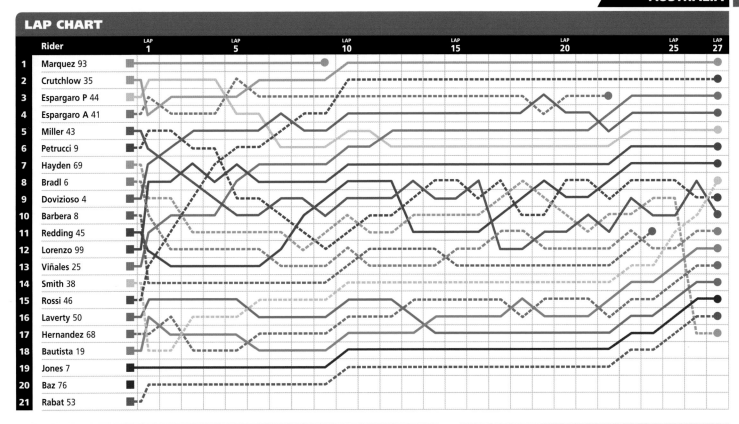

	Rider	LAP 1	LAP 5	LAP 10	LAP 15	LAP 20	LAP 25	LAP 27
1	Marquez 93							
2	Crutchlow 35							
3	Espargaro P 44							
4	Espargaro A 41							
5	Miller 43							
6	Petrucci 9							
7	Hayden 69							
8	Bradl 6							
9	Dovizioso 4							
10	Barbera 8							
11	Redding 45							
12	Lorenzo 99							
13	Viñales 25							
14	Smith 38							
15	Rossi 46							
16	Laverty 50							
17	Hernandez 68							
18	Bautista 19							
19	Jones 7							
20	Baz 76							
21	Rabat 53							

RACE

	Rider	Motorcycle	Race time	Time +	Fastest lap	Avg. speed	Tyres
1	Crutchlow	Honda	40m 48.543s		1m 29.494s	109.7mph	H/M
2	Rossi	Yamaha	40m 52.761s	4.218s	1m 29.726s	109.5mph	S/M
3	Viñales	Suzuki	40m 53.852s	5.309s	1m 29.964s	109.4mph	H/M
4	Dovizioso	Ducati	40m 57.700s	9.157s	1m 30.131s	109.3mph	S/M
5	Espargaro P	Yamaha	41m 02.842s	14.299s	1m 30.264s	109.0mph	S/M
6	Lorenzo	Yamaha	41m 08.668s	20.125s	1m 30.446s	108.8mph	S/M
7	Redding	Ducati	41m 16.912s	28.269s	1m 30.428s	108.4mph	S/M
8	Smith	Yamaha	41m 17.324s	28.781s	1m 30.834s	108.4mph	S/M
9	Petrucci	Ducati	41m 17.335s	28.792s	1m 30.909s	108.4mph	S/M
10	Miller	Honda	41m 17.358s	28.815s	1m 30.836s	108.4mph	H/M
11	Bradl	Aprilia	41m 20.352s	31.809s	1m 30.855s	108.3mph	S/M
12	Bautista	Aprilia	41m 36.277s	47.734s	1m 31.573s	107.6mph	S/M
13	Hernandez	Ducati	41m 36.292s	47.749s	1m 31.749s	107.6mph	S/M
14	Laverty	Ducati	41m 42.854s	54.311s	1m 32.114s	107.3mph	S/M
15	Jones	Ducati	41m 44.418s	55.875s	1m 31.663s	107.2mph	S/M
16	Rabat	Honda	41m 54.938s	1m 06.395s	1m 32.416s	106.8mph	S/M
17	Hayden	Honda	42m 11.147s	1m 22.604s	1m 30.684s	106.1mph	S/M
NC	Barbera	Ducati	36m 42.129s	3 laps	1m 30.746s	108.4mph	S/M
NC	Espargaro A	Suzuki	33m 18.496s	5 laps	1m 30.011s	109.4mph	H/M
NC	Marquez	Honda	13m 35.800s	18 laps	1m 29.583s	109.7mph	H/M
NC	Baz	Ducati	–	–	–	–	S/M

CHAMPIONSHIP

	Rider	Nation	Team	Points
1	Marquez	SPA	Repsol Honda Team	273
2	Rossi	ITA	Movistar Yamaha MotoGP	216
3	Lorenzo	SPA	Movistar Yamaha MotoGP	192
4	Viñales	SPA	Team Suzuki ECSTAR	181
5	Pedrosa	SPA	Repsol Honda Team	155
6	Crutchlow	GBR	LCR Honda	141
7	Dovizioso	ITA	Ducati Team	137
8	Espargaro P	SPA	Monster Yamaha Tech 3	117
9	Iannone	ITA	Ducati Team	96
10	Barbera	SPA	Avintia Racing	84
11	Espargaro A	SPA	Team Suzuki ECSTAR	82
12	Laverty	IRL	Pull & Bear Aspar Team	73
13	Redding	GBR	OCTO Pramac Yakhnich	71
14	Bautista	SPA	Aprilia Racing Team Gresini	67
15	Petrucci	ITA	OCTO Pramac Yakhnich	65
16	Bradl	GER	Aprilia Racing Team Gresini	60
17	Smith	GBR	Monster Yamaha Tech 3	53
18	Miller	AUS	Estrella Galicia 0,0 Marc VDS	48
19	Pirro	ITA	OCTO Pramac Yakhnich	36
20	Rabat	SPA	Estrella Galicia 0,0 Marc VDS	29
21	Baz	FRA	Avintia Racing	24
22	Hernandez	COL	Pull & Bear Aspar Team	20
23	Nakasuga	JPN	Yamalube Yamaha Factory	5
24	Lowes	GBR	Monster Yamaha Tech 3	3
25	Aoyama	JPN	Repsol Honda Team	1
	Hayden	USA	Estrella Galicia 0,0 Marc VDS	1
	Jones	AUS	Avintia Racing	1

11 STEFAN BRADL
Like everyone else, only had the warm-up to find a set-up, but the Aprilia team didn't have any data from test either. Stefan went direct to Q2 but his gearing for the race was short, so he couldn't hold the group slipstream.

12 ALVARO BAUTISTA
A difficult weekend for the same reasons as his team-mate, but Alvaro didn't find anything in warm-up and did well to hold off Hernandez.

13 YONNY HERNANDEZ
Spent most of the race in a dice with Bautista and, in total contrast to his team-mate, enjoyed what he thought was his best race of the year. Conserved his tyre and only lost out to the Aprilia by one hundredth of a second.

14 EUGENE LAVERTY
His toughest race of the year. Happy on the brakes but very much not happy in the fluid parts of the track – which meant most of it.

15 MIKE JONES
Took over from Barbera for the second time

and got to race in his home GP. Did nothing wrong and was rewarded with a point.

16 TITO RABAT
Conditions militated against Tito improving his knowledge of the bike, but his team manager was still moved to say he 'knows he must improve'.

17 NICKY HAYDEN
Replaced Pedrosa and impressed on a track he loves. Nicky reckoned he should have been seventh but was the victim of a Miller barge that put him on the floor.

DID NOT FINISH

LORIS BAZ
Electrical problems saw Loris start from pitlane and retire on the first lap.

MARC MARQUEZ
Crashed out of the lead when he lost the front at Honda.

ALEIX ESPARGARO
Lost the front at Honda while third with only five laps left.

HECTOR BARBERA
Lost the front trying to outbrake Miller.

DID NOT RACE

DANI PEDROSA
Back home recovering from the collarbone break from Japan. Replaced by Nicky Hayden.

ANDREA IANNONE
Still absent following his Misano crash. Replaced by Hector Barbera.

MALAYSIA
ROUND 17

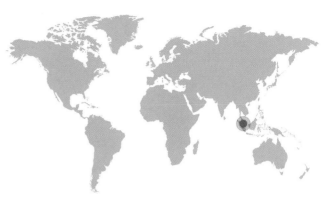

SHELL MALAYSIAN
MOTORCYCLE GRAND PRIX
SEPANG INTERNATIONAL CIRCUIT

DOVI MAKES IT NINE

Andrea Dovizioso made it nine different winners and Rossi's second place secured runner-up position in the championship

Always the professional, Andrea Dovizioso had managed to deal with all the questions about him winning a race this year. Up to Sepang there had been eight different winners; if there was going to be a ninth surely it had to be Dovi? After all, among the factory riders only he and Aleix Espargaro had failed to win so far this season.

Dovi should have won in Austria but was undone by his tyre choice, so as the chances were ticked off the pressure increased. He didn't admit it until after the race, but he was feeling that pressure and had been for a long time. The last time he won a MotoGP race, his only other victory, was at Donington Park in 2009, and his recent expressions of happiness with decent placings raised a few eyebrows.

Here was the perfect response: pole position, the win and the fastest lap. Pole came as a surprise. Dovi had taken the edge off the soft wet and had to make his last run with the hard tyre. He was surprised to go faster. This was an effect of the newly resurfaced track, which was displaying astounding grip levels in the usual monsoon conditions that visit Malaysia at this time of year. The remodelling of the final corner, with steep adverse camber and a ridge, didn't draw instant approval from the riders, but they got used to it.

The weather delayed the race twice, and in fact conditions were only just 'raceable' when the grid set off in a cloud of spray that gave the midfield runners real problems. Dovi sat in third place for

ABOVE Bradley Smith was in the fight for points, an amazing achievement given his physical condition after knee operations

RIGHT Loris Baz and Hector Barbera charged to fourth and fifth, and by the flag Hector had got in front of Loris

the first half of the race as his team-mate Andrea Iannone, finally back from injury, and Valentino Rossi led. Dovi moved past Iannone and into second on lap 12, and next time round Iannone became the third man in the leading group to fall within two laps. Marc Marquez and Cal Crutchlow fell separately; Marc remounted quickly but Cal went down hard on his face, his second crash of the weekend, both slow but both painful. When Iannone also fell, it would have been easy to heap more opprobrium on The Maniac's head, but he was hardly alone in making the tiny error that inevitably led to a crash and he had said that, given he had no interest in championship position, he felt free to attack and to try to win.

This spate of crashes was due to the improving conditions. Rossi, in the lead, suddenly found the right-hand side of his front tyre giving him problems. After a couple of warnings, he went very deep at the slow right of the first corner and let Dovizioso through. The expectation was that Valentino would bite straight back, but it didn't happen. Dovi instantly pulled out a two-second advantage and kept it. Rossi's lap times dropped from 2m 12s to 2m 14s while Dovizioso did a lap in the high 2m 11s bracket followed by a low 12 and a mid 13. In other words, he kept his pace up while the Yamaha couldn't.

There was no threat to Rossi's second place. He could cruise home and try to convince everyone that securing second place in the championship

'IT WAS VERY IMPORTANT FOR ME TO WIN A RACE THIS YEAR: I'VE BEEN TRYING FOR SO LONG AND I'VE COME CLOSE ON SEVERAL OCCASIONS'
ANDREA DOVIZIOSO

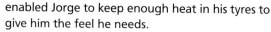

ABOVE Dovizioso watches as Rossi and Iannone fight for the lead; he was never far away

BELOW Jorge Lorenzo was third in a wet race – worth celebrating

actually mattered. Given that Yamaha still hadn't won a race since Catalunya, he may have meant it, but it was also clear that he would have traded just about any position in the table for a race win.

Jorge Lorenzo stayed on his wheels to finish third, albeit nine seconds further back. He was disarmingly honest in saying that he had been lucky with other people's crashes but it was clear that the new surface and the high temperatures

enabled Jorge to keep enough heat in his tyres to give him the feel he needs.

With both Movistar Yamahas on the rostrum, plus Repsol Honda only getting a few points from Marquez's 11th place, the factory Yamahas went to the top of the teams' championship, giving them a good chance of depriving Honda of the triple crown of riders', constructors' and teams' titles they are so fond of.

One team that again had a great day was Avintia Ducati. Back on his regular bike, Hector Barbera looked fast, fluid and relaxed, much more so than on the factory bike. Just as on the wet track at Brno, he and team-mate Loris Baz ended up fighting for fourth and fifth, but this time the Spaniard was in front. Cue much joy among the Ducati customer team and especially Baz, who really needed this boost to his confidence after a season bedevilled by injury.

There was joy at head office, too. The team sent Paolo Ciabatti, long-serving Ducati Corse Sporting Director and MotoGP Project Director at Ducati Motor Holding, up to the rostrum to collect the constructors' trophy. Amazingly, it was the first time Ciabatti had been given that honour. He was happy about it and about achieving what he said was the team's target of two wins in the season. As the man who brought Lorenzo to Ducati, he knows the bar will be set considerably higher in 2017. In the meantime, both Ciabatti and Dovizioso could enjoy a perfect weekend. Next season can wait.

ABOVE Ducati's Paolo Ciabatti savours a perfect weekend for his team

RIGHT The relief shows as Dovi celebrates his first win in seven years

CARBON BRAKES IN THE WET

You might assume that it would be impossible to use carbon brakes in the sort of conditions the Malaysian GP experienced, but that assumption would be wrong. Both Bradley Smith and Marc Marquez ran low-mass carbon front discs protected by shrouds to retain heat and they suited the conditions perfectly. Neither rider reported problems with the brakes dropping below their usual operating temperature once there was some heat in them, which happened more quickly than with the tyres. In fact the low-mass discs would have been overheating in the dry.

The first thing to note is that the Sepang track is a serious challenge for brakes under any conditions. They are applied for 30 per cent of the lap time – that's 37 seconds – and the corners at the end of the two long straights require over 7kg of brake-lever pressure, with decelerations of 1.5g to lose over 150mph and 165mph respectively. Brake manufacturer Brembo rates those two corners as

highly challenging and four more on the Sepang circuit as having standard difficulty. Only at Motegi and Barcelona do brakes have as much to cope with.

This has the counter-intuitive advantage of ensuring that low-mass carbon discs stay up to temperature even in soaking wet conditions, and in fact the steel discs used by most of the

field were close to overheating at the end of the race, when conditions had improved but remained wet. This is what Marquez was waiting for but his crash put him out of the top ten. He was adamant that his choice of carbon brakes had nothing to do with the crash and the fact that it happened in the corner rather than approaching it backs up that statement.

SHELL MALAYSIAN MOTORCYCLE GRAND PRIX
SEPANG INTERNATIONAL CIRCUIT

ROUND **17**
OCTOBER 30

OFFICIAL TIMEKEEPER

RACE RESULTS

CIRCUIT LENGTH 3.444 miles

NO. OF LAPS 19

RACE DISTANCE 65.441 miles

WEATHER Wet, 25°C

TRACK TEMPERATURE 28°C

WINNER Andrea Dovizioso

FASTEST LAP 2m 11.950s
94.0mph, Andrea Dovizioso

LAP RECORD 2m 00.606s
102.8mph, Jorge Lorenzo (2015)

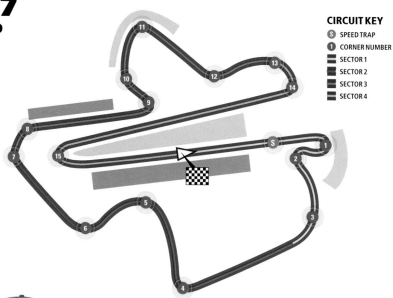

CIRCUIT KEY
- **S** SPEED TRAP
- **1** CORNER NUMBER
- SECTOR 1
- SECTOR 2
- SECTOR 3
- SECTOR 4

QUALIFYING

	Rider	Nation	Motorcycle	Team	Time	Pole +
1	Dovizioso	ITA	Ducati	Ducati Team	2m 11.485s	
2	Rossi	ITA	Yamaha	Movistar Yamaha MotoGP	2m 11.731s	0.246s
3	Lorenzo	SPA	Yamaha	Movistar Yamaha MotoGP	2m 11.787s	0.302s
4	Marquez	SPA	Honda	Repsol Honda Team	2m 11.874s	0.389s
5	Crutchlow	GBR	Honda	LCR Honda	2m 12.558s	1.073s
6	Iannone	ITA	Ducati	Ducati Team	2m 12.598s	1.113s
7	Espargaro A	SPA	Suzuki	Team Suzuki ECSTAR	2m 12.869s	1.384s
8	Viñales	SPA	Suzuki	Team Suzuki ECSTAR	2m 12.981s	1.496s
9	Bautista	SPA	Aprilia	Aprilia Racing Team Gresini	2m 13.325s	1.840s
10	Baz	FRA	Ducati	Avintia Racing	2m 13.452s	1.967s
11	Espargaro P	SPA	Yamaha	Monster Yamaha Tech 3	2m 13.707s	2.222s
12	Barbera	SPA	Ducati	Avintia Racing	2m 13.973s	2.488s
13	Smith	GBR	Yamaha	Monster Yamaha Tech 3	2m 12.898s	*1.307s
14	Miller	AUS	Honda	Estrella Galicia 0,0 Marc VDS	2m 12.907s	*1.316s
15	Petrucci	ITA	Ducati	OCTO Pramac Yakhnich	2m 13.776s	*2.185s
16	Bradl	GER	Aprilia	Aprilia Racing Team Gresini	2m 13.850s	*2.259s
17	Aoyama	JPN	Honda	Repsol Honda Team	2m 14.179s	*2.588s
18	Redding	GBR	Ducati	OCTO Pramac Yakhnich	2m 14.433s	*2.842s
19	Laverty	IRL	Ducati	Pull & Bear Aspar Team	2m 14.769s	*3.178s
20	Hernandez	COL	Ducati	Pull & Bear Aspar Team	2m 14.786s	*3.195s
21	Rabat	SPA	Honda	Estrella Galicia 0,0 Marc VDS	2m 15.894s	*4.303s

* Gap with the fastest rider in the Q1 session

1 ANDREA DOVIZIOSO
Pole, the win and the fastest lap for his second career victory in MotoGP. Sat behind Rossi and Iannone until lap 12, when he went second, then took the lead two laps later and pulled out a gap. A perfect race with consistent pace.

2 VALENTINO ROSSI
Secured second in the championship but lost the chance to win when the water cleared and he had trouble with the right side of the front tyre. Fought for the lead with Iannone then lost it to Dovi when he ran wide at Turn 1.

3 JORGE LORENZO
Front-row start, the holeshot and a rostrum sounds like a welcome return to wet-weather form, but Jorge said he was lucky. However, he felt more confident than any time since Brno, although better in practice than the race.

4 HECTOR BARBERA
A career-best MotoGP finish after two races on the factory bike. Looked like a man back in his favourite chair on the 14.2 Ducati and rode a clever race, making steady progress and then taking advantage of his team-mate's problems.

5 LORIS BAZ
Delighted with the conditions in which he was able to restore some of his lost confidence. Moved through from bad qualifying then fought with his team-mate but had to concede fourth when his rear tyre started overheating on the drying tarmac.

6 MAVERICK VIÑALES
The team's result showed that Suzuki have yet to master the electronics settings for wet conditions. The limiting factor is acceleration and the chance of highsiding.

7 ALVARO BAUTISTA
In the top ten in practice and qualifying as well as the race thanks to a new motor. The worst part was the early stages of the race when Alvaro ran around 14th in the wettest conditions. Then overtook Smith, the Espargaros and Miller when conditions eased. Impressive.

8 JACK MILLER
First Honda home despite never finding a set-up he liked in the rain. Given what happened to the other Hondas, Jack was happy with the result.

9 POL ESPARGARO
Cautious at the start as he struggled to find any markers amid the spray. Then managed his pace and kept an eye on the gap behind him. The result sealed eighth place in the championship, which pleased him more than the finishing position.

10 DANILO PETRUCCI
Couldn't get going until half distance due to the spray and lack of confidence when on the brakes. Glad to escape without a crash.

LAP CHART

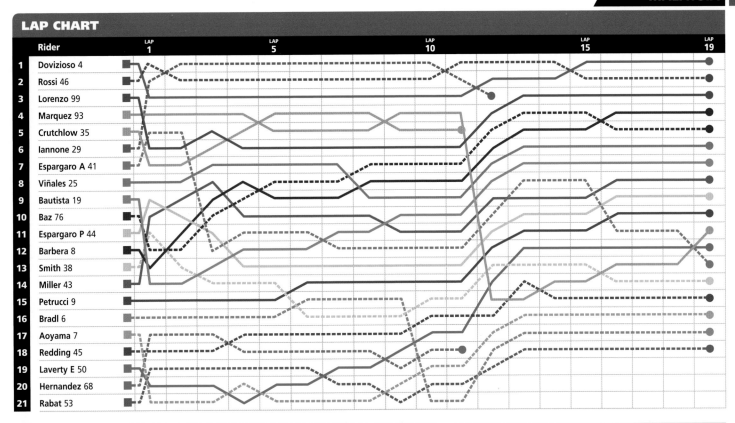

	Rider				
		LAP 1	LAP 5	LAP 10	LAP 15	LAP 19
1	Dovizioso 4					
2	Rossi 46					
3	Lorenzo 99					
4	Marquez 93					
5	Crutchlow 35					
6	Iannone 29					
7	Espargaro A 41					
8	Viñales 25					
9	Bautista 19					
10	Baz 76					
11	Espargaro P 44					
12	Barbera 8					
13	Smith 38					
14	Miller 43					
15	Petrucci 9					
16	Bradl 6					
17	Aoyama 7					
18	Redding 45					
19	Laverty E 50					
20	Hernandez 68					
21	Rabat 53					

RACE

	Rider	Motorcycle	Race time	Time +	Fastest lap	Avg. speed	Tyres
1	Dovizioso	Ducati	42m 27.333s		2m 11.950s	92.4mph	RM/RM
2	Rossi	Yamaha	42m 30.448s	3.115s	2m 12.107s	92.3mph	RM/RM
3	Lorenzo	Yamaha	42m 39.257s	11.924s	2m 13.449s	92.0mph	RM/RM
4	Barbera	Ducati	42m 47.249s	19.916s	2m 13.065s	91.7mph	RM/RM
5	Baz	Ducati	42m 48.686s	21.353s	2m 13.711s	91.7mph	RM/RM
6	Viñales	Suzuki	42m 50.265s	22.932s	2m 13.579s	91.7mph	RM/RM
7	Bautista	Aprilia	42m 53.162s	25.829s	2m 13.790s	91.5mph	RM/RM
8	Miller	Honda	43m 00.079s	32.746s	2m 14.081s	91.3mph	RM/RM
9	Espargaro P	Yamaha	43m 01.037s	33.704s	2m 14.129s	91.2mph	RM/RM
10	Petrucci	Ducati	43m 01.613s	34.280s	2m 14.147s	91.2mph	RM/RM
11	Marquez	Honda	43m 03.813s	36.480s	2m 12.407s	91.2mph	RM/RM
12	Laverty	Ducati	43m 03.971s	36.638s	2m 13.551s	91.2mph	RM/RM
13	Espargaro A	Suzuki	43m 04.230s	36.987s	2m 14.196s	91.2mph	RM/RS
14	Smith	Yamaha	43m 12.942s	45.609s	2m 14.560s	90.8mph	RM/RM
15	Redding	Ducati	43m 17.112s	49.779s	2m 14.954s	90.7mph	RM/RM
16	Aoyama	Honda	43m 19.998s	52.665s	2m 14.608s	90.6mph	RM/RS
17	Bradl	Aprilia	43m 20.117s	52.784s	2m 14.355s	90.6mph	RM/RM
18	Rabat	Honda	43m 22.224s	54.891s	2m 14.598s	90.5mph	RM/RM
NC	Iannone	Ducati	26m 54.777s	7 laps	2m 12.696s	92.1mph	RM/RM
NC	Crutchlow	Honda	24m 43.757s	8 laps	2m 12.830s	91.9mph	RM/RM
NC	Hernandez	Ducati	25m 17.337s	8 laps	2m 15.598s	89.9mph	RS/RM

CHAMPIONSHIP

	Rider	Nation	Team	Points
1	Marquez	SPA	Repsol Honda Team	278
2	Rossi	ITA	Movistar Yamaha MotoGP	236
3	Lorenzo	SPA	Movistar Yamaha MotoGP	208
4	Viñales	SPA	Team Suzuki ECSTAR	191
5	Dovizioso	ITA	Ducati Team	162
6	Pedrosa	SPA	Repsol Honda Team	155
7	Crutchlow	GBR	LCR Honda	141
8	Espargaro P	SPA	Monster Yamaha Tech 3	124
9	Barbera	SPA	Avintia Racing	97
10	Iannone	ITA	Ducati Team	96
11	Espargaro A	SPA	Team Suzuki ECSTAR	85
12	Laverty	IRL	Pull & Bear Aspar Team	77
13	Bautista	SPA	Aprilia Racing Team Gresini	76
14	Redding	GBR	OCTO Pramac Yakhnich	72
15	Petrucci	ITA	OCTO Pramac Yakhnich	71
16	Bradl	GER	Aprilia Racing Team Gresini	60
17	Miller	AUS	Estrella Galicia 0,0 Marc VDS	56
18	Smith	GBR	Monster Yamaha Tech 3	55
19	Pirro	ITA	OCTO Pramac Yakhnich	36
20	Baz	FRA	Avintia Racing	35
21	Rabat	SPA	Estrella Galicia 0,0 Marc VDS	29
22	Hernandez	COL	Pull & Bear Aspar Team	20
23	Nakasuga	JPN	Yamalube Yamaha Factory	5
24	Lowes	GBR	Monster Yamaha Tech 3	3
25	Aoyama	JPN	Repsol Honda Team	1
	Hayden	USA	Estrella Galicia 0,0 Marc VDS	1
	Jones	AUS	Avintia Racing	1

11 MARC MARQUEZ
Fell at Turn 11 while in fourth then remounted. The crash was nothing to do with his decision to use carbon brakes in the wet conditions, more to do with the usual Honda problem of making time up on the brakes.

12 EUGENE LAVERTY
Lost too much time, mainly under braking, in the soaking wet opening to take advantage of his impressive pace in the drier part.

13 ALEIX ESPARGARO
Went with the softer rear tyre in the hope that the rain would persist. Also made a couple of mistakes early on.

14 BRADLEY SMITH
Another remarkable ride given his physical condition. Used the hard rear tyre, with which he has never got on, and suffered accordingly.

15 SCOTT REDDING
Never found any feeling in the wet and had a terrible weekend. Tried to push but never found his rhythm.

16 HIRO AOYAMA
Replaced Pedrosa again but couldn't make much of an impression on a track he likes. Lost ground in the spray of the opening laps and couldn't regain it.

17 STEFAN BRADL
Fell on lap 10 and remounted, but was too far back to score points.

18 TITO RABAT
Had a terrible time in practice and qualifying but made no mistakes in the race and brought the bike home.

DID NOT FINISH

ANDREA IANNONE
Took the lead on the second lap and held it for eight laps. Crashed after being passed by Rossi and Dovizioso.

CAL CRUTCHLOW
Crashed out of fifth following Marquez and had the misfortune to 'faceplant' as well as hurt his foot.

YONNY HERNANDEZ
Used the softer front, which made it impossible to continue when the track started to dry.

DID NOT RACE

DANI PEDROSA
Back in Spain recovering from injuries sustained in Japan.

GRAN PREMIO MOTUL DE LA COMUNITAT VALENCIANA
CIRCUITO RICARDO TORMO

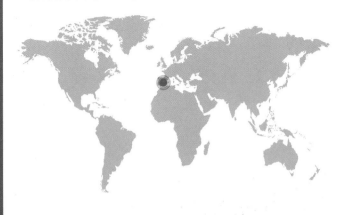

GOLD STANDARD

Jorge Lorenzo left Yamaha with a dominant victory as MotoGP enjoyed its end-of-year party

Valencia 2016 felt and sounded very different from Valencia 2015. In place of the sourness and at times hysterical atmosphere of 12 months previously there was a celebratory end-of-term feel to this year's race. All three championships had been decided so all the racers had to do was go out there and race on a sunny autumn afternoon in front of 110,000 fans who were pleased to see them. It felt like a sporting event should. It felt like fun, both in the paddock and in the packed stands.

That's not to suggest the pressure was off anyone. Yamaha hadn't won since Catalunya, some big names were looking to leave their current employers with a bang, and the entire KTM board of directors had turned up to see their RC16 MotoGP bike make its début. There were also constructors' and teams' championships to sort out plus the usual desire to go into the winter break on a high. The result was a day of superb racing across all three classes with the only similarity to 2015 being that Valentino Rossi again finished fourth.

The man under most pressure was Jorge Lorenzo, facing his last race with Yamaha after nine years with the team – that's his entire MotoGP career and a third of his lifetime as he pointed out in his touching goodbye letter. Then he went out and demolished his own pole-position record. Last year he said his 1m 30.011s effort was a perfect lap. This year he did three

'IT HAS BEEN
AN INCREDIBLE
WEEKEND WITH
A PERFECT FIRST
FEW LAPS, THE
POLE POSITION,
THE FASTEST LAP,
AND THE VICTORY'
JORGE LORENZO

runs of out-lap, flying lap and in-lap, and on each of those three flying laps he was in the 29s, culminating in a pole time of 1m 29.401s. On a track where small gaps are hard won, it was a blinding display of speed and precision. Perfect? Not quite, Jorge ran wide at the first corner on his two flying laps.

It was one of those races where you knew the plot before the start – a rarity in this mixed-up season. As we have so often seen, it was expected that Jorge would bolt from the start and smash in a sequence of robotically rapid and precise laps, opening up a lead. Marc Marquez said he had slightly better race pace, but only on worn tyres once the fuel load had gone down. So the question, assuming no nasty first-lap incidents, was whether Marc would have time to catch Jorge when he found his rhythm? Just to emphasise the difference between the riders, their bikes and their approaches to the race, they also went for different tyres. Michelin had some new '2017' profiles for their fronts and both went for them, but Jorge used the medium compound while Marc was again playing the long game with the hard.

Frankly, no-one thought anyone other than these two was in with a chance, but when Marc suffered clutch problems at the start things got a little more complex.

As expected, Jorge led into the first corner and at the end of the first lap he was the best part of half a second ahead. By lap seven the lead was

OPPOSITE Valentino Rossi started from the front row for the 12th time this season, but had to settle for fourth in the race

LEFT Marc Marquez makes his break from the group dicing for second place

ABOVE Both factory Aprilias turned out in red in support of an AIDS charity fronted by Bono of U2

two and a half seconds, and Jorge kept on going. By lap 20 he was five and a half seconds ahead, but this was a turning point. Marquez had finally gained control of the fight for second place and had a small but significant gap over Valentino Rossi and Andrea Iannone. For a circuit where overtaking is difficult, it was a revelation; lots of passes, most of them by necessity quite tough. It was a fight that also highlighted the Honda's shortcomings. It was no surprise to see the Ducati blast past it out of the last corner but the Yamaha also made it look slow.

Iannone, like Lorenzo, was desperate to say goodbye to his team in the best possible way. He made a stunning start from the third row and was in the mix right from the first corner. Even though he was still in pain and far from fit, he was able to force the Ducati through the tighter turns, apply its power on the front straight, and use his undoubted bravery anywhere he could. There were 21 overtaking moves between Andrea, Valentino and Marc. It looked as if it might have been more as Maverick Viñales and Andrea Dovizioso both shaped to join in but they faded without landing a punch.

Marc broke away from the fight at two-thirds distance and started to close. For once a 2016 race was going to the script: a softer tyre was giving trouble at the end of a race and the harder one was lasting better. Still Jorge stayed in the 1m 31s bracket, but much nearer the 32s than earlier.

ABOVE Dani Pedrosa returned from injury but crashed early in the race

BELOW Mika Kallio gave the KTM RC16 its début but didn't complete the race due to electronic sensor failure

THE LAST WALTZ

This was Jorge Lorenzo's 156th and final race with Yamaha. In nine years he won the world title three times and stood on the rostrum 107 times, 44 of them as the winner. He started from pole position 39 times and set the fastest lap 28 times. By any standards, that's a remarkable record.

Before the Valencia race he wrote a 'goodbye' letter to his team. Here it is.

'I've been riding a Yamaha for nine seasons, but Sunday will be the last day that I get on the M1. It will be a really weird sensation. I've spent a third of my life here. We have lived more than 150 races, we achieved 43 victories and three World Championship titles. We have fallen many times, but we always got up together and experienced amazing feats (including a few while having some anesthesia in blood...). These nine years in Yamaha will be a part of myself forever. Unrepeatable. Unforgettable.

'I want to thank Yamaha and especially you, Lin Jarvis, for having

given me the opportunity to enter the manufacturing team directly when I was only 19 years old and I didn't even obtain my first 250cc World Championship in 2006.

'I would also like to appreciate my mechanics' affection and effort, both those who were there from the first day and also those who arrived later, and the Japanese engineers who always gave me a winner motorbike. It would not have been possible without you. Thank you all!

'I'm leaving Yamaha with my head held high in good conscience for having given my best since my first race in 2008. I'm really proud of everything that I've experienced here, which has made me become a better rider and person.

'From the next year on, I'll be facing new challenges, but we still have a last objective in Yamaha: let's try to win the last race of the season. This would be a very beautiful parting gift for those who have believed in me.

'See you on the track!'

Marc was gaining around 0.4 second per lap. Even the nerveless Lorenzo admitted later that seeing the name 'Marquez' on the pitboard next to a diminishing lead is a disconcerting experience. Yet Jorge only dropped into the 32s twice, two laps from home and on the last lap. Marc also had two laps in the 32s, but much earlier in the race while involved with Iannone and Rossi. Jorge held on to win by a second despite a front tyre that was by now well past its best.

This was Marquez off the leash. He pushed as hard as he could, taking the Honda to the edge of disaster as only he can with the frequency that only he can. There was some tension in the pit, for if Marquez had crashed Honda would have lost the constructors' championship to Yamaha. As it was, the Movistar team had to content themselves with the teams' title.

Marc was in tune with the spirit of the day afterwards. When it was suggested that he would probably have won if the race had been a lap longer, he flashed that smile and pointed out that the race was over 30 laps, not 31, and that Jorge had ridden a superb race. No-one argued.

RIGHT The conclusion of a great weekend – outgoing and incoming world champions embrace in *parc fermé*

GRAN PREMIO MOTUL DE LA COMUNITAT VALENCIANA
CIRCUITO RICARDO TORMO

ROUND 18
NOVEMBER 13

MotoGP
TISSOT SWISS WATCHES SINCE 1853
OFFICIAL TIMEKEEPER

RACE RESULTS

CIRCUIT LENGTH 2.489 miles

NO. OF LAPS 30

RACE DISTANCE 74.658 miles

WEATHER Dry, 22°C

TRACK TEMPERATURE 25°C

WINNER Jorge Lorenzo

FASTEST LAP 1m 31.171s, 98.2mph, Jorge Lorenzo (record)

PREVIOUS LAP RECORD 1m 31.367s, 98.1mph, Jorge Lorenzo (2015)

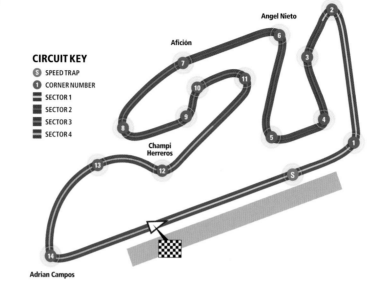

CIRCUIT KEY
- (S) SPEED TRAP
- (1) CORNER NUMBER
- SECTOR 1
- SECTOR 2
- SECTOR 3
- SECTOR 4

Mick Doohan
Angel Nieto
Afición
Champi Herreros
Adrian Campos

TYRE OPTIONS

CENTRE
LEFT   RIGHT
TYRE

SEVERITY RATING

<MILD   SEVERE>

FRONT COMPOUNDS
| MEDIUM (M) |
| NEW MEDIUM (NM) |
| HARD (H) |
| NEW HARD (NH) |

REAR COMPOUNDS
| SOFT (S) |
| MEDIUM (M) |

MICHELIN

QUALIFYING

	Rider	Nation	Motorcycle	Team	Time	Pole +
1	Lorenzo	SPA	Yamaha	Movistar Yamaha MotoGP	1m 29.401s	
2	Marquez	SPA	Honda	Repsol Honda Team	1m 29.741s	0.340s
3	Rossi	ITA	Yamaha	Movistar Yamaha MotoGP	1m 30.128s	0.727s
4	Viñales	SPA	Suzuki	Team Suzuki ECSTAR	1m 30.276s	0.875s
5	Dovizioso	ITA	Ducati	Ducati Team	1m 30.338s	0.937s
6	Espargaro P	SPA	Yamaha	Monster Yamaha Tech 3	1m 30.392s	0.991s
7	Iannone	ITA	Ducati	Ducati Team	1m 30.420s	1.019s
8	Pedrosa	SPA	Honda	Repsol Honda Team	1m 30.574s	1.173s
9	Espargaro A	SPA	Suzuki	Team Suzuki ECSTAR	1m 30.885s	1.484s
10	Smith	GBR	Yamaha	Monster Yamaha Tech 3	1m 30.949s	1.548s
11	Crutchlow	GBR	Honda	LCR Honda	1m 31.030s	1.629s
12	Petrucci	ITA	Ducati	OCTO Pramac Yakhnich	1m 31.203s	1.802s
13	Barbera	SPA	Ducati	Avintia Racing	1m 30.894s	*0.350s
14	Redding	GBR	Ducati	OCTO Pramac Yakhnich	1m 31.406s	*0.862s
15	Miller	AUS	Honda	Estrella Galicia 0,0 Marc VDS	1m 31.686s	*1.142s
16	Baz	FRA	Ducati	Avintia Racing	1m 31.749s	*1.205s
17	Bradl	GER	Aprilia	Aprilia Racing Team Gresini	1m 31.813s	*1.269s
18	Bautista	SPA	Aprilia	Aprilia Racing Team Gresini	1m 31.847s	*1.303s
19	Laverty	IRL	Ducati	Pull & Bear Aspar Team	1m 31.956s	*1.412s
20	Kallio	FIN	KTM	Red Bull KTM Factory Racing	1m 32.092s	*1.548s
21	Rabat	SPA	Honda	Estrella Galicia 0,0 Marc VDS	1m 32.181s	*1.637s
22	Hernandez	COL	Ducati	Pull & Bear Aspar Team	1m 32.240s	*1.696s

Gap with the fastest rider in the Q1 session

1 JORGE LORENZO
A stunning farewell to Yamaha: pole and the win, leading every lap and with a new lap record in there too. This was Jorge at his best, and, although he had to nurse a worn front tyre at the end, he had enough of a lead to hold off Marquez.

2 MARC MARQUEZ
Knew he'd be fastest on worn tyres but at the start he was tangled up with Rossi and Iannone. By the time Marc got clear of the scrap he was over five seconds from Lorenzo with 10 of the 30 laps to go. If it had been 11, he might have won.

3 ANDREA IANNONE
Still in pain, still not fit, but able to fight tooth and nail with Rossi and Marquez to give Ducati the present he wanted as he prepares to join Suzuki for 2017. Emotional after the race.

4 VALENTINO ROSSI
Valencia has never been too kind to Valentino. Fourth last year in controversial circumstances from the back of the grid, fourth again this year from the front row. Good fight with Marquez and Iannone.

5 MAVERICK VIÑALES
Started brilliantly, ran in third but suffered when the tyres dropped off and he faded away from the fight for second.

6 POL ESPARGARO
A strong weekend to finish his time with Tech 3 Yamaha. Right from FP1 he was fast, and top independent team finisher for the fifth time in the season.

7 ANDREA DOVIZIOSO
Looked like he could be involved in the fight for the rostrum but his lap times dropped off suddenly when he hit front-tyre issues.

8 ALEIX ESPARGARO
Lost places at the start and while he fought back was conscious that he had to conserve his tyres for the final laps. Not the conclusion to his time with Suzuki that Aleix wanted.

9 BRADLEY SMITH
Another more than respectable result given his injuries, although he was hoping to compete with his team-mate as they both prepare to leave Tech 3 and join KTM's new MotoGP effort.

10 ALVARO BAUTISTA
Signed off his two years with Aprilia

with his tenth top-ten finish of the year. Impressive after qualifying badly on a track not suited to the bike.

11 HECTOR BARBERA
Just failed to make the top ten after a good fight with Bautista, but sealed tenth overall in the championship – the objective the team set at the start of the year.

12 DANILO PETRUCCI
Mistakes early on meant Danilo had to push hard in the middle of the race and didn't have the resources left to fight with Bautista and Barbera for a top-ten finish.

LAP CHART

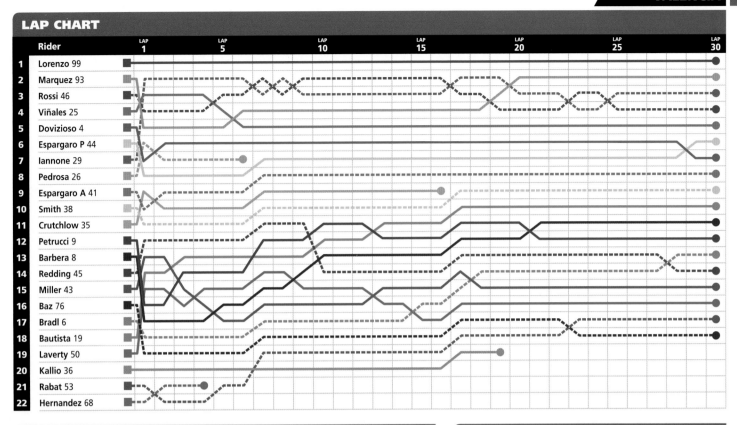

	Rider	LAP 1	LAP 5	LAP 10	LAP 15	LAP 20	LAP 25	LAP 30
1	Lorenzo 99							
2	Marquez 93							
3	Rossi 46							
4	Viñales 25							
5	Dovizioso 4							
6	Espargaro P 44							
7	Iannone 29							
8	Pedrosa 26							
9	Espargaro A 41							
10	Smith 38							
11	Crutchlow 35							
12	Petrucci 9							
13	Barbera 8							
14	Redding 45							
15	Miller 43							
16	Baz 76							
17	Bradl 6							
18	Bautista 19							
19	Laverty 50							
20	Kallio 36							
21	Rabat 53							
22	Hernandez 68							

RACE

	Rider	Motorcycle	Race time	Time +	Fastest lap	Avg. speed	Tyres
1	Lorenzo	Yamaha	45m 54.228s		1m 31.171s	97.6mph	NM/S
2	Marquez	Honda	45m 55.413s	1.185s	1m 31.299s	97.5mph	NH/S
3	Iannone	Ducati	46m 00.831s	6.603s	1m 31.196s	97.3mph	NM/S
4	Rossi	Yamaha	46m 01.896s	7.668s	1m 31.276s	97.3mph	NM/S
5	Viñales	Suzuki	46m 04.838s	10.610s	1m 31.313s	97.2mph	NM/S
6	Espargaro P	Yamaha	46m 12.606s	18.378s	1m 31.744s	96.9mph	M/S
7	Dovizioso	Ducati	46m 12.645s	18.417s	1m 31.317s	96.9mph	NM/S
8	Espargaro A	Suzuki	46m 12.906s	18.678s	1m 31.867s	96.9mph	NM/S
9	Smith	Yamaha	46m 20.221s	25.993s	1m 32.050s	96.6mph	M/S
10	Bautista	Aprilia	46m 29.293s	35.065s	1m 32.387s	96.3mph	NM/S
11	Barbera	Ducati	46m 30.653s	36.425s	1m 32.334s	96.3mph	NM/S
12	Petrucci	Ducati	46m 36.643s	42.415s	1m 32.452s	96.1mph	NM/S
13	Bradl	Aprilia	46m 44.051s	49.823s	1m 32.875s	95.8mph	M/S
14	Redding	Ducati	46m 46.263s	52.035s	1m 32.577s	95.8mph	NM/S
15	Miller	Honda	46m 49.853s	55.625s	1m 32.811s	95.6mph	NH/S
16	Laverty	Ducati	46m 52.482s	58.254s	1m 32.649s	95.5mph	H/S
17	Rabat	Honda	46m 52.783s	58.555s	1m 33.030s	95.5mph	NM/S
18	Baz	Ducati	47m 00.392s	1m 06.164s	1m 32.938s	95.3mph	NM/S
NC	Kallio	KTM	29m 57.584s	11 laps	1m 33.208s	94.6mph	NM/S
NC	Crutchlow	Honda	24m 42.868s	14 laps	1m 31.912s	96.6mph	NH/S
NC	Pedrosa	Honda	9m 18.522s	24 laps	1m 31.811s	96.2mph	M/S
NC	Hernandez	Ducati	6m 22.656s	26 laps	1m 33.188s	93.6mph	M/S

CHAMPIONSHIP

	Rider	Nation	Team	Points
1	Marquez	SPA	Repsol Honda Team	298
2	Rossi	ITA	Movistar Yamaha MotoGP	249
3	Lorenzo	SPA	Movistar Yamaha MotoGP	233
4	Viñales	SPA	Team Suzuki ECSTAR	202
5	Dovizioso	ITA	Ducati Team	171
6	Pedrosa	SPA	Repsol Honda Team	155
7	Crutchlow	GBR	LCR Honda	141
8	Espargaro P	SPA	Monster Yamaha Tech 3	134
9	Iannone	ITA	Ducati Team	112
10	Barbera	SPA	Avintia Racing	102
11	Espargaro A	SPA	Team Suzuki ECSTAR	93
12	Bautista	SPA	Aprilia Racing Team Gresini	82
13	Laverty	IRL	Pull & Bear Aspar Team	77
14	Petrucci	ITA	OCTO Pramac Yakhnich	75
15	Redding	GBR	OCTO Pramac Yakhnich	74
16	Bradl	GER	Aprilia Racing Team Gresini	63
17	Smith	GBR	Monster Yamaha Tech 3	62
18	Miller	AUS	Estrella Galicia 0,0 Marc VDS	57
19	Pirro	ITA	OCTO Pramac Yakhnich	36
20	Baz	FRA	Avintia Racing	35
21	Rabat	SPA	Estrella Galicia 0,0 Marc VDS	29
22	Hernandez	COL	Pull & Bear Aspar Team	20
23	Nakasuga	JPN	Yamalube Yamaha Factory	5
24	Lowes	GBR	Monster Yamaha Tech 3	3
25	Aoyama	JPN	Repsol Honda Team	1
	Hayden	USA	Estrella Galicia 0,0 Marc VDS	1
	Jones	AUS	Avintia Racing	1

13 STEFAN BRADL
Had the clutch replaced after warm-up and used the soft front for the first time in an afternoon session. Not surprisingly, took a while to adapt on a track not suited to the Aprilia, so happy to score points.

14 SCOTT REDDING
Another difficult weekend, mainly due to lack of feel from the front. Started the race well but the rear tyre went off and a mistake cost Scott three places; also mugged by Bradl at the finish.

15 JACK MILLER
Not comfortable with a full tank so lost ground on the Petrucci group fighting for 12th. Then hit some rear-tyre degradation and problems with downshifting into Turn 1, all of which meant that Jack finished in the same position he qualified.

16 EUGENE LAVERTY
Finished the season an impressive 12th overall, in front of a couple of GP15 Ducatis. Couldn't quite catch Miller on the last lap for a final point.

17 TITO RABAT
Distinct signs that Tito was getting to grips with a MotoGP bike. Lapped at a similar pace to his team-mate and had a good fight with Laverty in the final laps after dicing earlier with Baz and Kallio.

18 LORIS BAZ
Front-tyre problems at the start, rear-tyre problems in the middle, and exhausted at the end of the race. Will have surgery over winter after an injury-blighted season.

DID NOT FINISH

MIKA KALLIO
Débuted the KTM RC16. Started cautiously and got faster through the weekend, finishing with a race lap time only around two seconds slower than Lorenzo's best. Stopped by a sensor fault that first appeared around quarter distance.

CAL CRUTCHLOW
Not comfortable at any point in the weekend. Once he'd found his rhythm and started to push the front tyre pressure went up. Once it had gone back down, Cal crashed because of, he said, going over the limits of the package he had available.

DANI PEDROSA
Back from his Japan injury but got no further than Turn 2 on lap seven where he crashed despite not pushing hard.

YONNY HERNANDEZ
Lost the front as he let the brake off, a crash he's had more than once this season. Yonny returns to Moto2 for 2017.

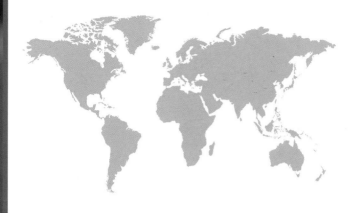

TAKE TWO

Johann Zarco became the first winner of back-to-back Moto2 titles and the first Frenchman to win two world titles

At the start of the year, Johann Zarco explained his decision to stay in Moto2 and defend his title. He wanted, he said, to go to MotoGP as a double champion in the middleweight class just as Dani Pedrosa and Jorge Lorenzo had done: 'Why not me?'

Why not indeed? Well, a jump-start penalty didn't help and neither did crashing at his home round, leaving Johann with only a single win from the first five races plus just one more rostrum finish, a third place in Texas. That left him fourth in the championship with Alex Rins looking like the favourite and Sam Lowes his main challenger. Rins looked calm, collected and unflappable with two wins, a third, a pole and two fastest laps in those opening five races. Lowes was his usual mercurial self with four rostrums in those races including a win, two seconds, two poles and two fastest laps. The other man in contention was Thomas Lüthi with a win, a pole and a third place.

It was easy to assume that the pattern of the season was set, but it wasn't. Zarco immediately put in back-to-back wins and took the championship lead with second place at Assen, where Rins finished eighth. Lowes was off the boil and Lüthi about to run into an uncharacteristic bout of crashing. Instead, some of the nearly men came through to take single wins. Takaaki Nakagami won at Assen and Lorenzo Baldassarri at Misano, both their first victories, although it should be said that after a slow start Nakagami

ABOVE As the rest faded, Thomas Lüthi secured second in the championship with a great late charge

ABOVE RIGHT Two riders whose challenges slipped away: Alex Rins leads Sam Lowes

RIGHT Simone Corsi kept the Speed Up flag flying with two rostrums; this is Le Mans and he's with Lüthi and Rins

was a threat for most of the year and 'Iron Balda' showed after the summer break that he would be a championship contender in 2017. The other winner was the enigmatic Jonas Folger, who always popped up with a strong race just when you'd forgotten about him.

Zarco strengthened his grip with a run of four wins in five races (the other one was second place) in the middle of the season, then stopped winning. Rins was chipping away at the points lead while Lowes's form slipped away. After a coming-together with Zarco at Silverstone that was entirely the Frenchman's fault, Sam's season went downhill. With the exception of the most dominant win of the year, at Aragón, he reverted to his crash-happy former self, including three in a row at the flyaway races. That ended his championship chances.

1 – QATARI GP	2 – ARGENTINIAN GP	3 – AMERICAS GP	4 – SPANISH GP	5 – FRENCH GP
It would be hard to imagine a more chaotic race than this Moto2 encounter, which got underway with almost a third of the grid jumping the start. Race Direction immediately handed out ride-through penalties to six of the offenders, among them reigning champion Johann Zarco.	Through pre-season testing and round one Johann Zarco had rarely shown the form that took him to a dominant world title in 2015. Had he been struggling to get the maximum feel from the 2016 Kalex frame or was it that rivals Sam Lowes and Alex Rins had taken another step?	Alex Rins would have had several more MotoGP teams chasing his signature for a 2017 contract after a perfect victory that had him taking the lead at the second corner and then resisting huge pressure from 2015 Austin winner Sam Lowes.	Sam Lowes rode an inch-perfect but mostly sideways race to Moto2 victory, defeating a dogged pursuit from 2015 Jerez winner Jonas Folger, who also had his hands full shaking off Austin winner Alex Rins.	With three of his title rivals having either secured a MotoGP deal for 2017 or in the process of doing so, Alex Rins seemed intent on using this GP to convince team bosses of his suitability for a full factory seat in racing's premier class.
Meanwhile pole-sitter and early leader Jonas Folger crashed out and the race turned into a duel between Thomas Lüthi and Franco Morbidelli, even though Morbidelli had made the biggest jump start of them all.	Argentina was the venue where he stepped up. Starting the race on a damp track with a drying line, Zarco was involved in early exchanges with Jonas Folger, pole-sitter Lowes and the impressive Franco Morbidelli, the group of four soon breaking clear of the tentative Rins from lap one.	Rins started from pole and didn't put a wheel wrong. Lowes gave it everything but he over-used his front tyre and was unable to counter-attack. At least the Briton's second consecutive runner-up finish moved him into the championship lead.	Folger led from the start but ran wide on lap two. The Briton swept into the lead and although his German rival kept up a relentless pursuit, Lowes had it all under control, backing his Kalex into pretty much every turn.	For the second time in 2016, Rins never wavered in a tense encounter that saw Simone Corsi produce his most accomplished performance in close to two years. Italian Corsi gave chase to Rins after the latter had dispensed with pole-sitter Thomas Lüthi on lap seven.
The battle moved towards a thrilling climax until Race Direction announced that Morbidelli had jumped the start, but it was too late to give him a ride-through, so when the young Italian chased Lüthi over the line he hadn't really finished second. A 20-second penalty relegated him to seventh.	Lowes's mistake five laps from the end ultimately handed the initiative to Zarco, whose stunning end-of-race pace ensured his first win of his title defence. Morbidelli's fall on lap 22 handed third to Folger.	The battle for final spot on the podium was typical Moto2 madness between reigning champion Johann Zarco, Dominique Aegerter, Jonas Folger, Simone Corsi, Thomas Lüthi and Takaaki Nakagami. Zarco's bike got better as the race went on and he won the contest.	'That way, I'm wider to pass!' he grinned.	'I know Corsi was pushing from behind,' said Rins, winner by 1.8 seconds, and whose pace never faltered all the way to the flag. 'I'm happy because I win but it was difficult. My lap marker on the screen went out so I just tried to push every lap.' With Corsi second, Lüthi completed the podium.
Sandro Cortese also received a 20-second penalty. The German crossed the line fifth behind Luis Salom, who had made an inspired charge from 18th on the grid, and Simone Corsi, but he was credited with 15th.	'I had the opportunity to lead the race. I felt more comfortable using my lines, taking advantage of the gap to push harder and get everything under control,' said Zarco.		Lowes finished 2.4 seconds ahead for his first win since Austin 2015. His second Moto2 win increased his championship over Rins, who eventually gave up pursuit of Folger.	American Danny Eslick was 25th aboard the JP Moto Suter. 'We were hoping to mix it up with some of the guys but they left me for dry. I was consistent, didn't drop off but we've got a long way to go to be up there.'
			VR46 rider Franco Morbidelli was fourth ahead of reigning champ Johann Zarco, who recovered well from 16th on the first lap. His last victim was Qatar GP winner Thomas Lüthi, who beat Takaaki Nakagami by less than four tenths of a second. First non-Kalex rider was Xavier Simeon in tenth.	

LEFT Lorenzo Baldassarri was another first-time winner, his victory coming at Misano

BELOW Takaaki Nakagami was yet another of a raft of first-time winners; his breakthrough came at Assen, where he's seen with Johann Zarco and Franco Morbidelli

Rins, meanwhile, closed in on Zarco before also appearing to lose focus at the flyaway races, scoring just two points from the three of them.

The two men who emerged later in the season, one as a title challenger, the other as the fastest man out there, were Thomas Lüthi and Franco Morbidelli. As the rest dithered, Lüthi won at Silverstone then took back-to-back wins for the first time in his career in Japan and Australia to go second in the table and for a moment look as if he could pull off a last-minute coup. At the same time Morbidelli was racking up rostrums and an impressive run of three fastest laps from Aragón to Australia. If there were a prize for combativity, as in the Tour de France, then it would have undoubtedly gone to the young Italian. He was fast, tough to pass and even more difficult to

6 – ITALIAN GP

World champion Johann Zarco bounced back from a disastrous home GP at Le Mans to score a hard-fought victory in a shortened Moto2 race, reduced to ten laps following an earlier crash that punctured a section of air-fence.

The ten-lap sprint was a thriller, with 19-year-old Italian Lorenzo Baldassarri and Qatar GP winner Thomas Lüthi disputing the lead, until Zarco fought his way through to the front with a few brave moves.

At the start of the final lap Baldassarri drafted past Zarco, but the Frenchman wouldn't be denied and retook the lead to cross the line three hundredths ahead.

The battle for the final podium place was similarly tough, with Sam Lowes passing Lüthi and Hafizh Syahrin in the last two laps.

Axel Pons, son of twice 250cc world champ Sito Pons, finished a best-ever sixth.

7 – CATALAN GP

Two races earlier, Zarco's title defence appeared to be thinning by the week, but wins at Mugello and Barcelona put the Frenchman back into the mix. His Catalan triumph over Alex Rins embodied the Frenchman's greatest strengths; shadowing his opponent until timing a relentless final push, when grip has all but disappeared, to perfection.

Here, both Zarco and Rins had ebbed clear of early leader Thomas Lüthi by lap six. From there it was a case of guessing when Zarco's attack would arrive. It came six laps from the flag, with Rins acknowledging defeat soon after. As Zarco's pace didn't relent, Lüthi faded into the grasps of Takaaki Nakagami and Hafizh Syahrin, with the Japanese securing a first podium finish since Misano 2015.

'We all knew this race was for Luis, to honour him,' said an emotional Zarco after the race, referring to the tragic death of Luis Salom during practice. 'The race win was the best way to end the weekend.'

8 – DUTCH TT

Takaaki Nakagami scored a richly deserved first GP win in a race that was red-flagged when the rain arrived with a few laps to go. The 24-year-old was the first Japanese rider to win a GP since Yuki Takahashi won the Catalan Moto2 race in 2010.

Nakagami, whose team is run by former Repsol Honda factory rider and 500cc GP winner Tadayuki Okada, grabbed the lead from Franco Morbidelli shortly before half distance and quickly escaped from the pack.

Reigning champ Johann Zarco worked hard to get Nakagami in his sights, but the rain ended his chance of a third consecutive win. However, his third podium in a row moved him into the championship lead, ahead of sixth-placed Alex Rins. Morbidelli was delighted to take third, his first podium result of the season, three seconds behind Zarco.

9 – GERMAN GP

World champion Johann Zarco scored a brilliant victory in the rain-soaked Moto2 race, fighting off an all-or-nothing attack from local hero Jonas Folger at the final corner. Zarco's winning advantage was just six hundredths of a seconds but the 25 points the championship leader took for his fourth win of 2016 were a huge bonus for him.

The race was most notable for the number of riders who fell victim to the treacherously slippery track, several of them sliding off and remounting, only to slide off again. Just 15 of the original 27 starters finished.

The most significant fallers were Alex Rins, who had been equal on points with Zarco, and Sam Lowes, who had been just five points behind Zarco and Rins, and fell twice. Third finisher was Julian Simon, scoring his first podium since 2012.

10 – AUSTRIAN GP

Johann Zarco is quickly making a mockery of early-season claims that the 2016 intermediate class struggle would be the tightest of them all. Never one to become flustered, the Frenchman expertly recovered from a poor start to reel in early leaders Franco Morbidelli, Marcel Schrotter and Thomas Lüthi.

By lap 17 Zarco assumed total control over Morbidelli and didn't relent until the flag, maintaining times in the middle of the 1m 29s bracket until the final lap. A slow-starting Alex Rins took advantage of Morbidelli's late move on Lüthi to take third, just behind the Italian.

With Sam Lowes crashing out twice, the title fight now appeared to be a two-way struggle between Zarco and Rins.

'I felt better as the race went on and other riders suffered a little more,' said Zarco, whose championship lead now stood at 24 points. 'When I passed Morbidelli I knew I could break away.'

11 – CZECH REPUBLIC GP

Just as Johann Zarco was building up an unshakeable head of steam, down came the rain. The Frenchman nabbed his second straight pole position from Sam Lowes at the death on Saturday. Yet on race day he was nowhere, leaving Jonas Folger to break free from the off.

If anyone was handed an early-morning reprieve, it was Alex Rins. Off the pace for most of the weekend, the Spaniard challenged Folger early on, before the German pulled clear in worsening conditions to win by a comfortable five seconds. Lowes gave chase, but he, too, had no answer for the man in front, leaving the podium positions set in place in the final laps.

'It was a fairly relaxed race to be honest, except for the last few laps, when I risked a lot to gain the four-second advantage. It was

12 – BRITISH GP

Home hero Sam Lowes was firm favourite for a British GP win after dominating practice and qualifying. But it wasn't to be: the young Briton was chasing leader Thomas Lüthi when he was wiped out by series leader Johann Zarco.

The pair were just behind Lüthi – who had missed the previous race due to a head injury – when Zarco dived across the inside kerb to collide with Lowes. Zarco stayed on but was given a ten-second penalty, which dropped him to 22nd.

The incident was a nightmare for Lowes, who was going all out for a home win, but it also looked as if it could play a major part in the outcome of the world championship. After the Austrian GP Zarco had led closest rival Alex Rins by 34 points; after this race his advantage was reduced to just

13 – SAN MARINO GP

At the close of this shoot-out it was the turn of Johann Zarco to look bewildered. The pole man had just come home a frustrating fourth after voicing his plans to break clear of the field on Saturday evening.

The Frenchman had no answer for the runaway leaders, Alex Rins, still riding with a painful, healing left collarbone, and Lorenzo Baldassarri, who ensured the 26-lap encounter went to the wire.

First Rins broke clear of a frantic scrap to build up a lead of 1.7s. But soon Baldassarri was on the chase, closing in for a famous win. The Italian moved by at Quercia two laps from home and resisted a brave last-lap attack from Rins to claim a famous home win, his first in GP racing. Takaaki Nakagami was third.

'I only realised I had beaten

14 – ARAGÓN GP

Sam Lowes totally dominated this Moto2 race, snatching the lead halfway through the first lap from Alex Marquez. The Briton was never headed, winning his first race since Jerez.

Former Moto3 world champion Marquez took his first Moto2 podium by resisting a last-corner attack by team-mate Franco Morbidelli.

But much of the attention during the race was focused on the battle for sixth place involving world championship contenders Alex Rins and Johann Zarco, with Misano winner Lorenzo Baldassarri between them. Rins won the three-way contest ahead of Baldassarri, with Zarco just behind in eighth place.

That result reduced Zarco's championship advantage to just one point with four races to go and brought Lowes to within 40

15 – JAPANESE GP

Thomas Lüthi led from the first corner to the flag, despite immense pressure from reigning champion and points leader Johann Zarco.

Zarco's hard-charging second place transformed the championship situation. Going into Motegi, Alex Rins had closed the gap to just one point, but a fall in practice aggravated a shoulder injury that left him 22nd in qualifying, which no doubt contributed to his lap-one tumble.

Although Lüthi dominated, Zarco was in no mood to settle for runner-up spot. After taking second place from Franco Morbidelli he closed to within four tenths of Lüthi at the flag.

The duel for the final podium place had Morbidelli and Assen winner Takaaki Nakagami swapping places on the final lap, the Italian winning by two tenths keep behind you if you did manage to get by. He and Baldassarri are the next wave of Italian talent heading for the top, and you could also include top rookie Luca Marini in that statement.

Old Italian talent, in the shape of Simone Corsi, ensured some technical diversity in what had now become rather too much like a Kalex cup. He put the Speed Up chassis on the rostrum twice in those first five races but then crashed too much to stay in contention. The arrival of KTM in 2017 plus the return of Suter will reintroduce some welcome variety. It would be easy to overlook the Mistral chassis but young Spanish rookie Xavi Vierge put in an amazing run of points-scoring rides in the second half of the year so technical variety isn't dead.

Zarco may have wobbled – in fact he did so more than once – but his seven race wins amounted to way more than anyone else, and he retained the crown in Malaysia with a superb win from a pole position that was over two seconds quicker than the rest – the biggest margin in the whole history of the middleweight class.

Zarco now goes up to MotoGP with the authority he wanted, as a double world champion.

FAR LEFT Double back flip from Johann Zarco and his brother Jerome to celebrate the second title

UPPER LEFT Sam Lowes won two races, including a dominating victory at Aragón, but then faded

LOWER LEFT At Brno Jonas Folger again proved he's a wet-weather ace

CHAMPIONSHIP STANDINGS

	Rider	Nat	Team	Motorcycle	Points
1	Johann Zarco	FRA	Ajo Motorsport	Kalex	276
2	Thomas Lüthi	SWI	Garage Plus Interwetten	Kalex	234
3	Alex Rins	SPA	Paginas Amarillas HP 40	Kalex	214
4	Franco Morbidelli	ITA	Estrella Galicia 0,0 Marc VDS	Kalex	213
5	Sam Lowes	GBR	Federal Oil Gresini Moto2	Kalex	175
6	Takaaki Nakagami	JPN	IDEMITSU Honda Team Asia	Kalex	169
7	Jonas Folger	GER	Dynavolt Intact GP	Kalex	167
8	Lorenzo Baldassarri	ITA	Forward Team	Kalex	127
9	Hafizh Syahrin	MAL	Petronas Raceline Malaysia	Kalex	118
10	Simone Corsi	ITA	Speed Up Racing	Speed Up	103
11	Mattia Pasini	ITA	Italtrans Racing Team	Kalex	72
12	Dominique Aegerter	SWI	CarXpert Interwetten	Kalex	71
13	Alex Marquez	SPA	Estrella Galicia 0,0 Marc VDS	Kalex	69
14	Marcel Schrotter	GER	AGR Team	Kalex	64
15	Sandro Cortese	GER	Dynavolt Intact GP	Kalex	61
16	Axel Pons	SPA	AGR Team	Kalex	55
17	Xavier Simeon	BEL	QMMF Racing Team	Speed Up	46
18	Julian Simon	SPA	QMMF Racing Team	Speed Up	40
19	Luis Salom	SPA	SAG Team	Kalex	37
20	Xavi Vierge	SPA	Tech 3 Racing	Tech 3	37
21	Miguel Oliveira	POR	Leopard Racing	Kalex	36
22	Danny Kent	GBR	Leopard Racing	Kalex	35
23	Luca Marini	ITA	Forward Team	Kalex	34
24	Isaac Viñales	SPA	Tech 3 Racing	Tech 3	19
25	Jesko Raffin	SWI	Sports-Millions-EMWE-SAG	Kalex	14
26	Remy Gardner	AUS	Tasca Racing Scuderia Moto2	Kalex	8
27	Anthony West	AUS	Montaze Broz Racing Team	Suter	6
28	Ratthapark Wilairot	THA	IDEMITSU Honda Team Asia	Kalex	6
29	Ramdan Rosli	MAL	Petronas AHM Malaysia	Kalex	4
30	Robin Mulhauser	SWI	CarXpert Interwetten	Kalex	4
31	Edgar Pons	SPA	Paginas Amarillas HP 40	Kalex	4
32	Tetsuta Nagashima	JPN	Ajo Motorsport Academy	Kalex	2

16 – AUSTRALIAN GP

Not for the first time this year, at the close of a puzzling Moto2 race we were left wondering whether any of the contenders actually wanted to win the championship. Contenders Alex Rins and Sam Lowes crashed out early on, while title leader Johann Zarco finished a below-par 12th.

Of the leading quartet, it was Thomas Lüthi who maintained a semblance of calm, winning out in a mad, three-way fight at the front. Not that it was easy. The Swiss rider was embroiled in a race-long scrap with Franco Morbidelli. Trailing the Italian out of the final corner, Lüthi expertly drafted past at the line to win by 0.01s, his first back-to-back triumph in 14 years of GP racing. Sandro Cortese ghosted through the pack for a fine third, 0.5s back.

'It feels brilliant,' Lüthi said. 'We really had to fight. I could go at a good pace but I could never make the break. I saw there was a chance to get Franco out of the last corner and I did it.'

With two races left, Lüthi was now second in the title chase, 22 points behind Zarco.

17 – MALAYSIAN GP

A hopeless 12th one week, a dominant victor and two-time world champion the next. Such is the unpredictable nature of Johann Zarco.

Zarco was keen to reassert his grip on the series after a perplexing showing in Australia. His two-second pole margin made him the pre-race favourite, and despite the efforts of Franco Morbidelli and Jonas Folger, his win rarely looked in doubt.

For 13 laps the Frenchman stalked Morbidelli in the rain while title adversary Thomas Lüthi struggled for rear grip midfield. Knowing the title was his if he maintained position, Zarco came into his own as the track dried, breaking clear on lap 14, and coming home three seconds to the good. Morbidelli and Folger had no answer, and were left to contest runner-up spot, with Italian Morbidelli getting the nod.

'A dry line began to emerge and I saw my time had come,' said Zarco. 'I didn't want to cry but it was impossible. To finish my time in the class in this way is magnificent.'

18 – VALENCIAN GP

Johann Zarco completed a remarkable two seasons of Moto2 domination with a hard-fought final victory. The Frenchman fought back and forth with up-and-coming Italian Franco Morbidelli for the first half of the race, with the pair overtaking each other several times each lap.

Finally, Zarco's experience told as Morbidelli asked too much of his rear tyre. Zarco retook the lead on lap 16, upped his pace and broke away from his pursuers to win his seventh victory of 2016 by more than three seconds.

'Franco is a young guy – he's very aggressive and never gives up, but after 15 laps I felt better than ever,' said Zarco.

Meanwhile Morbidelli fell back into the clutches of class veteran Thomas Lüthi, who took second place on the final lap. Moments later Sam Lowes pounced at the final corner to snatch fourth place from Alex Rins, with less than one second separating the men in third and fifth places.

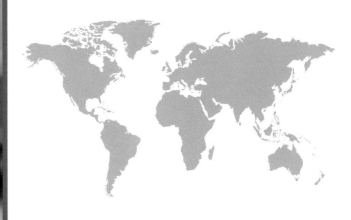

BINDER'S BLINDER

Brad Binder put together a near-perfect season that included seven race wins and a record points score in the lightweight class

A mid what seemed like a random-number generator, only one rider put together a season that could be called consistent. Brad Binder hadn't won a race before the start of 2016 but he began at the fourth round, Jerez, and just kept on going.

That first win, it should be noted, came after Binder was sent to the back of the grid for a technical infringement by the team. When you break your duck with a back-to-front effort like that, it's no wonder you make it a run of three in a row and open up the sort of points lead that means you're champion with four races still to go. He made just two significant mistakes all year. The first sent him off-track on the fastest part of the Assen circuit, but he recovered and finished 12th. Then he crashed out of the lead at Brno having set the fastest lap of the race. Other than that, Binder exhibited race craft of the highest order to emerge from the usual Moto3 brawl to win or to settle for good points. When he finished a race he was only off the rostrum three times: at Assen, at a soaking wet Sachsenring, and at Sepang after crashing on oil. Here was an object lesson in the truism that it's consistency that wins titles.

No-one else in a strong field put together anything like a consistent challenge. Niccolò Antonelli won the first race of the year and promptly disappeared off the radar. Romano Fenati won a race and was third in the table when he got himself fired by the VR46 team for persistent misbehaviour. Jorge Navarro was the only man

ABOVE Niccolò Antonelli won the first race of the year but never saw the rostrum again

ABOVE RIGHT Malaysian rookie Khairul Idham Pawi won two races in the wet but only scored points twice in the dry

who looked capable of challenging Binder, especially after he took his first win at Catalunya. Unfortunately, he then broke his leg in a training accident and faded. Enea Bastianini was invisible until he put together a string of rostrum finishes after the summer break, but he didn't win a race until after Binder had been confirmed as champion.

KTM and Honda continued to be the main players as Mahindra's challenge was blunted by a fragile transmission that wasn't fixed until the Sachsenring. Despite this handicap, Francesco Bagnaia won at Assen, one of the races of the year, and his and Mahindra's first GP win. Bagnaia had three more rostrum finishes before the new gearbox arrived in what must be counted one of the riding performances of the year. After the transmission remedy, it wasn't uncommon to see a front row or a rostrum with all three makes of

motorcycle – Honda, KTM, Mahindra – represented.

Mahindra got a 1–2 when John McPhee won in the rain at Brno with Jorge Martin second, and the Indian machine only looked at a disadvantage on tracks with lots of acceleration, such as Motegi. By contrast, the Mahindra appeared to have an advantage on the brakes and entering corners. By common consent the KTM had a little more power than the opposition while Honda was the best all-rounder. And in the wet there was no difference between the three.

Binder excepted, this was the year of the rookie: Khairul Idham Pawi ran away from the field to win two wet races by astonishing distances but lost his confidence in the dry. A fearsome trio – Joan Mir, Aron Canet and Nicolò Bulega – came up from the Junior World Championship and were rostrum contenders from the off. The biggest surprise came

1 – QATARI GP

The 68th season of Grand Prix racing got underway shortly after dusk with a typically madcap Moto3 race. Up to seven riders spent the entire race inches apart, hunting each other down the start/finish straight.

In the final dash it all came down to the slipstream: Niccolò Antonelli exited the last corner right behind Brad Binder, then drafted past the South African to win by half a metre.

The top seven were covered by less than seven tenths. Third went to Francesco Bagnaia, with Enea Bastianini fourth, after fighting through from tenth. Sixteen-year-old Italian rookie Nicolò Bulega, riding for Valentino Rossi's Sky VR46 KTM team, was arguably the hero, coming through from 12th to lead the race before slipping to fifth.

2 – ARGENTINIAN GP

If 2016 taught us anything about the junior category, it was that the year's crop of rookies could well be playing key roles in results sooner than anticipated. Nicolò Bulega lit up round one and in Argentina it was the turn of Malaysian teenager Khairul Idham Pawi to do so.

For the opening seven laps spectators watched in amazement as Pawi – riding on slick tyres on a damp but drying track – gapped his tentative pursuers to the tune of three seconds a lap. Understanding exactly where the grip lay was key to his advance, the 16-year-old stretching a 20-second lead by lap eight. Livio Loi, the only rider to choose wets, soon fell away from second, with Jorge Navarro and Adam Norrodin contesting second, until Norrodin high-sided at the penultimate corner. Brad Binder took third.

'During the race, I made my best to keep consistent lap times and pull away other riders,' said Pawi, the first ever Malaysian to win a GP. 'The race was not so difficult for me and I'd like to share this victory with everyone who supported me.'

3 – AMERICAS GP

Valentino Rossi's top VR46 rider, Romano Fenati, hunted down early leader Jorge Navarro to win his first race of the year. Navarro wanted to go with the Italian but set-up issues made it too risky, so he decided 20 points were better than none.

Navarro crossed the finish line six seconds down on Fenati and four seconds ahead of Brad Binder, who grabbed third on the final lap from pole-sitter Philipp Oettl to take over the championship lead.

Andrea Locatelli beat Enea Bastianini by less than three tenths of a second for fifth.

4 – SPANISH GP

Although Valentino Rossi was incomparable in the tricky MotoGP race, the rider of the day was surely Brad Binder. The South African came from the back of the grid to win, replicating the achievement of Marc Marquez in winning the 2012 Valencia Moto2 race from the back.

Binder had to start from the back after officials discovered his team had used non-homologated ECU software in qualifying. His maiden win was astonishing to watch as he carved his way through the entire 35-rider pack.

He took the lead from Jorge Navarro on lap 18 of 23, leaving Navarro to dispute second place with another VR46 rider, Nicolò Bulega, and Francesco Bagnaia. The trio took the final turn three abreast and finished in the order Bulega, Bagnaia and Navarro, covered by less than two tenths.

5 – FRENCH GP

Anyone doubting the value of a first race win to a rider's confidence need only look in Brad Binder's direction at Le Mans. Two weeks on from securing his first GP triumph, the South African stayed cool on the final lap in an absorbing four-way scrap involving championship rivals Romano Fenati and Jorge Navarro as well as Aron Canet, this rookie showing exuberance in abundance to repeatedly keep the other three occupied.

Fenati led for the most part but then Binder, knowing that his weakness lay in sector one, moved to the lead on the penultimate lap. Not even Fenati's late-braking prowess could stop the South African as he collected his second win in as many races.

'This weekend was so tough because three times my bike cut out and I don't know why. It happened again in warm-up,' said Binder. 'My team practically built me a brand-new bike from the warm-up to the race.'

ABOVE LEFT Romano Fenati talked himself out of a job; he was sacked by the VR46 squad on the Saturday of the Austrian GP

ABOVE Brad Binder's first win came from the very back of the grid at Jerez after he incurred a penalty for a technical infringement by the team

LEFT Jorge Navarro on the way to his first win, at Catalunya; he also won the Aragón race

6 – ITALIAN GP

This was another close encounter, with 19 riders in the lead pack! The first three finishers were separated by 0.069 second, while the top ten were covered by just 1.7 seconds.

South African Brad Binder was once again the star of the show. The winner of the two previous GPs rode a canny race, but the racing was so close that he was sixth at the start of the final lap.

He grabbed the lead at Turn One for the last time and only just held his advantage over 17-year-old rookie Fabio Di Giannantonio, with Francesco Bagnaia just behind.

Niccolò Antonelli fought his way through from 21st on the grid to finish fourth, 0.006 second off the podium.

7 – CATALAN GP

Here another Moto3 contender tasted inaugural success after a prolonged period of trying. Jorge Navarro became the 39th Spaniard to win a GP, and, fittingly, '39' was the racing number sported by Moto2 rider Luis Salom, who was tragically killed during practice.

There was so nearly a last-lap brawl between Navarro and Brad Binder. As it was the Spaniard went to the front of an eight-rider train when it mattered, while Binder narrowly avoided falling after colliding with Gabriel Rodrigo three laps from the flag. The incident left Binder eighth, but a resolute response saw him climb to second by the end. Navarro's advantage was half a second, enough for that first win, while Enea Bastianini was third.

'From Friday we thought today's race could have turned out as it did as we focused on finding a good pace when riding alone,' said Navarro. 'I had to win today to dedicate the victory to Luis.'

Would this maiden triumph, like Binder's, have a similarly transformative effect?

8 – DUTCH TT

This was a typically scary battle, with the top ten never separated by more than a second. There was plenty of bumping and barging and plenty of crashes – a third of the 33 starters fell even though this was the only fully dry race of the day.

Francesco Bagnaia made history by scoring the first GP victory for Indian factory Mahindra (albeit on a bike built in Switzerland and Italy) and he did it by inching past Andrea Migno on the rush to the line. But Migno was docked a place for exceeding track limits on the final lap, promoting Fabio Di Giannantonio to second. The top three were separated by two hundredths of a second!

Runaway points leader Brad Binder was in the thick of it until he ran off track. He finished 12th but still increased his title lead because closest challenger Jorge Navarro missed the race after breaking a leg in a training accident.

9 – GERMAN GP

The first race of the day got underway in torrential rain, with Honda Asia team-mates Khairul Idham Pawi and Hiroki Ono disputing the lead until Ono ran off the track. That left 19-year-old Malaysian rookie Pawi way ahead.

This was Pawi's second runaway win in wet conditions, following his Argentine GP success. By the end he had a huge advantage over Italian teenagers Andrea Locatelli and Enea Bastianini, who were 11 and 13 seconds back respectively.

World championship leader Brad Binder rode a conservative race to eighth, one place behind title rival Jorge Navarro, who made a heroic comeback just six weeks after breaking a leg.

10 – AUSTRIAN GP

What a crop of class rookies 2016 had on offer. Joan Mir was the latest young head to show off speed and intelligence to match the best in Moto3, achieving the first pole/win combination in the class in 15 races.

Engaged in a five-way scrap for victory, championship leader Brad Binder watched over his four challengers, who included Fabio Quartararo, Enea Bastianini and Philipp Oettl, with the grace of a man biding his time. That was until two mistakes at turn four pushed him back to fifth.

By the final lap, Mir had enough in hand to coolly take his début win from a recovering Binder, with Bastianini third. Not for the first time this year we write 'remember the name'.

'I managed my race perfectly, and was always in the leading group without letting anyone run away,' said Mir, who dedicated his triumph to fellow Majorcan Luis Salom.

11 – CZECH REPUBLIC GP

Just as Brad Binder had one hand on the Moto3 world championship, his rear Dunlop tyre gave way. Even in this year of dizzying consistency, the South African proved to be human after all.

Binder was leading in almost underwater conditions with only John McPhee able to give chase. That was until Binder fell foul of the wet track at turn one with three laps to go, leaving McPhee with an insurmountable eight-second lead.

Jorge Martin took advantage of wet-weather specialist Khairul Idham Pawi's mid-race mistake to collect a maiden podium place, after holding off promising rookie Fabio Di Giannantonio, who finished third.

'We had a good rhythm after warm up and I just had to keep calm. I'm absolutely delighted to bring it home,' said McPhee, the first Scottish winner of a solo GP since 1962.

12 – BRITISH GP

Brad Binder scored his fourth win of the year to move 86 points clear in the Moto3 title chase, but this was possibly the South African's toughest win so far. For much of the race the leading group comprised a dozen or more riders, positions changing every corner, with plenty of bumping and barging along the way.

The only potential winner who ended up on the floor was Jorge Navarro, who charged through from 18th on the grid only to be wiped out by another rider with two laps to go.

That incident split the huge lead pack, leaving Binder to fight for the win with team-mate Bo Bendsneyder and Francesco Bagnaia. Binder crossed the line 0.183 second ahead of Bagnaia, with first-time podium finisher Bendsneyder a further 0.336 second back. The top eight were separated by just one second.

13 – SAN MARINO GP

Enea Bastianini seemed to be enjoying his best ride of an underwhelming year, taking the fight to runaway title leader Brad Binder. But in reality pole-sitter Binder was toying with his younger rival, who remained in his shadows until lap 18.

Allowing the Italian by and seeing that Bastianini couldn't match his own pace, Binder knew where he would attack. With flawless precision, he made his move on the final lap at the frightening Curvone, which is taken flat in sixth gear.

Austria winner Joan Mir showed guile to beat another home hero, Nicolò Bulega, to the final podium spot after qualifying a lowly 16th.

'I tried to manage the gap to the fight for third before dropping into second to see what Bastianini could do,' explained Binder. 'On the last lap I made my move. Everything worked perfectly.'

Another crash for Jorge Navarro ensured that Binder's title lead to grow to a near insurmountable 106 points.

14 – ARAGÓN GP

Brad Binder became the first South African world champion since Jon Ekerold won the 1980 350cc world title with a superbly determined ride to second in a four-man dogfight for victory.

Jorge Navarro won the race, but only just, with Binder three hundredths back, and Enea Bastianini and Fabio Di Giannantonio were right behind. The top four finishers were covered by less than 0.2 second!

Until the last few laps the lead pack consisted of ten riders, but then Binder and the rest forced the pace. Binder moved ahead on the penultimate lap only to have all three Hondas go past him in one go, relegating him to fourth. That would have delayed his world title success but the 21-year-old fought back in fearsome style to get back into second and become the first world champion of motorcycle racing's 67th GP season.

15 – JAPANESE GP

Italian teenager Enea Bastianini took a perfectly judged Moto3 victory, diving past recently crowned world champion Brad Binder three corners before the flag. Binder complained of a lack of rear grip in the closing stages that left him unable to resist.

Hiroki Ono scored his first GP podium after a breathtaking battle with Sky VR46 KTM team-mates Andrea Migno and Nicolò Bulega. Ono made his move stick on the penultimate lap, then Migno collided with him and slid off, leaving Ono to take third. However, his day was ruined when his bike was found to be half a kilo under the minimum weight, so he was disqualified.

from 2015 Red Bull Rookies runner-up Fabio Di Giannantonio, who became a regular front runner once he'd emerged from the pack for a surprise second at Mugello.

Moto3 races were, without exception, glorious brawls from which Brad Binder usually emerged to claim the maximum number of points. He knew this was the season he had to stamp his authority on the class. Before the start of the season he had competed in 74 GPs without a win and now needed to guarantee his future in the sport. Binder, an intelligent young man, had to move from South Africa to Europe with his family and come up through the Red Bull Rookies. He completely understood his situation and the crucial nature of this year. That's pressure. He dealt with it and has, in the words of South Africa's first champion, Kork Ballington, 'all the tools' to do it again. For 2017, Binder moves to Moto2 to ride KTM's new challenger but still under the management of Aki Ajo. There's no reason why he shouldn't progress even further.

TOP LEFT Francesco Bagnaia gave Mahindra their historic first win, at Assen, and backed it up at Sepang

TOP RIGHT Joan Mir won in Austria and became Rookie of the Year

BOTTOM LEFT Enea Bastianini finished second overall after a very strong second half of the year that included victory in Japan

BOTTOM RIGHT John McPhee won in the Czech Republic despite this epic moment

CHAMPIONSHIP STANDINGS

	Rider	Nat	Team	Motorcycle	Points
1	Brad Binder	RSA	Red Bull KTM Ajo	KTM	319
2	Enea Bastianini	ITA	Gresini Racing Moto3	Honda	177
3	Jorge Navarro	SPA	Estrella Galicia 0,0	Honda	150
4	Francesco Bagnaia	ITA	Pull & Bear Aspar Mahindra Team	Mahindra	145
5	Joan Mir	SPA	Leopard Racing	KTM	144
6	Fabio Di Giannantonio	ITA	Gresini Racing Moto3	Honda	134
7	Nicolò Bulega	ITA	SKY Racing Team VR46	KTM	129
8	Jakub Kornfeil	CZE	Drive M7 SIC Racing Team	Honda	112
9	Andrea Locatelli	ITA	Leopard Racing	KTM	96
10	Romano Fenati	ITA	SKY Racing Team VR46	KTM	93
11	Niccolò Antonelli	ITA	Ongetta-Rivacold	Honda	91
12	Philipp Oettl	GER	Schedl GP Racing	KTM	85
13	Fabio Quartararo	FRA	Leopard Racing	KTM	83
14	Bo Bendsneyder	NED	Red Bull KTM Ajo	KTM	78
15	Aron Canet	SPA	Estrella Galicia 0,0	Honda	76
16	Jorge Martin	SPA	Pull & Bear Aspar Mahindra Team	Mahindra	72
17	Andrea Migno	ITA	SKY Racing Team VR46	KTM	63
18	Livio Loi	BEL	RW Racing GP BV	Honda	63
19	Khairul Idham Pawi	MAL	Honda Team Asia	Honda	62
20	Jules Danilo	FRA	Ongetta-Rivacold	Honda	58
21	Juanfran Guevara	SPA	RBA Racing Team	KTM	50
22	John McPhee	GBR	Peugeot MC Saxoprint	Peugeot	48
23	Hiroki Ono	JPN	Honda Team Asia	Honda	36
24	Gabriel Rodrigo	ARG	RBA Racing Team	KTM	31
25	Darryn Binder	RSA	Platinum Bay Real Estate	Mahindra	27
26	Marcos Ramirez	SPA	Platinum Bay Real Estate	Mahindra	19
27	Tatsuki Suzuki	JPN	CIP-Unicom Starker	Mahindra	16
28	Adam Norrodin	MAL	Drive M7 SIC Racing Team	Honda	14
29	Stefano Manzi	ITA	Mahindra Racing	Mahindra	13
30	Lorenzo Dalla Porta	ITA	SKY Racing Team VR46	KTM	12
31	María Herrera	SPA	MH6 Laglisse	KTM	7
32	Raul Fernandez	SPA	MH6 Team	KTM	5
33	Hafiq Azmi	MAL	Peugeot MC Saxoprint	Peugeot	5
34	Stefano Valtulini	ITA	3570 Team Italia	Mahindra	3
35	Albert Arenas	SPA	Peugeot MC Saxoprint	Peugeot	2
36	Lorenzo Petrarca	ITA	3570 Team Italia	Mahindra	2

16 – AUSTRALIAN GP

What happens when you put 34 Moto3 riders on a fast, sweeping, slipstream-friendly circuit with only a very limited amount of dry-weather testing? The answer is that you get 13 crashers in five laps, with some incidents causing more than a wince. An ugly fall at Lukey Heights for John McPhee, who was collected by Andrea Migno, warranted a red flag, bringing the chaos to a halt.

But it was only temporary. A ten-lap restart followed, with world champion Brad Binder storming clear from the off, keen to distance himself from the mêlée behind. Only Andrea Locatelli could get near in the opening five laps but he was 5.9 seconds behind at the flag. A 16-rider brawl ensued for third and eventually rookie Aron Canet pipped Brad's younger brother Darryn for the final podium place.

'I felt I could break away in the first part,' said Brad after his sixth win of the year. 'I knew everyone would fight a lot after the red flag. I pushed so hard in the first four laps and tried to keep a good rhythm. It was perfect.'

17 – MALAYSIAN GP

The Moto3 encounter was all but decided by lap three. By then 12 of the 31 riders had fallen – five in an ugly first-lap incident when Jorge Martin highsided at turn six, then four more at the same corner a lap later.

That second wave of fallers included race leader Joan Mir and title leader Brad Binder, leaving Francesco Bagnaia with some real breathing space. The question of why the second batch fell was puzzling, and suggested that the first-lap spill had left oil or water on the surface. More than one rider felt a red flag would have been appropriate.

Bagnaia coasted through the subsequent laps to record his second GP victory, while a red flag after female rider María Herrera fell ended the contest four laps early. That decided a tight scrap for second in Jakub Kornfeil's favour, with Bo Bendsneyder third.

'It was the hardest race of my life,' said Bagnaia. 'I was alone at the front and keeping concentration wasn't easy. It's a great result for us.'

18 – VALENCIAN GP

Brad Binder rode the classiest Moto3 swansong. He dropped to 22nd on lap two after a machine glitch ran him off track and then recovered to win at a circuit where it's notoriously difficult to overtake.

'Something happened with the bike,' explained Binder after his seventh win from 18 races. 'It cut out a couple of times and the second time it nearly had me off. I ran off the track, checked it over and got going again, but I thought the win was over.'

For much of the distance Joan Mir, Andrea Migno and Enea Bastianini swapped places for the lead, but all the while Binder was after them. He relentlessly moved forward, finally using his bike's superior straight-line speed to take the lead from Mir with four laps to go. But the South African wasn't safe until he got to the flag: Mir was just 0.05 second behind and Migno a further 0.3 second back.

RED BULL ROOKIES CUP

As Peter Clifford describes, Ayumu Sasaki of Japan won a close-fought year and will go to Moto3 for 2017

ABOVE Ayumu Sasaki (foreground) battles with Spain's Marc Garcia at the German round

Ayumu Sasaki's 2016 record was unbeatable: 2nd, 1st, 4th, 2nd, 1st, 3rd, 3rd, 2nd, 3rd, 3rd, 1st, 4th, 1st. Over 13 races you can't really overcome that blend of success and consistency, especially in the Red Bull MotoGP Rookies Cup when so many riders can win any race.

It was a season when the top five in the Cup chase all scored two or more wins each and the 15-year-old Japanese was the most prolific with four victories helping him to a 49-point winning margin after the final round at Aragón.

The teen who should have pushed Sasaki hardest was 15-year-old Spaniard Aleix Viu. Equally at home on the KTM RC 250 R and also in his second Cup season, Viu shared the lead with Sasaki leaving the first round at Jerez, where both took a win and a second from the two-race weekend.

Viu still had a chance to win the Cup starting the final race of the season, but his hopes rested on Sasaki not finishing. Misfortune befell Viu instead as he was knocked off by another rider on the first lap.

So Sasaki knew he had the Cup after a pit signal from his father and it changed his attitude to the race, with caution no longer required. He was locked in a three-way contest for the lead with fellow second-year Rookies, Spaniards Raúl Fernández and Rufino Florido.

Fernández already had two wins to his name and came to Aragón with an outside chance of taking the Cup but the 15-year-old lost that possibility when Sasaki took fourth in Race 1 while Fernández finished seventh. Still looking for his first Rookies Cup win, 16-year-old Florido had often run at the front but never crossed the line first.

Sasaki had done plenty of following through the season, kept himself out of trouble, and was always well placed at the right time. At Aragón he knew he needed something special to beat the locals on the final lap as it would be a slipstreaming and out-braking battle at the end of the back straight. The man who led down the back straight for the final time was setting himself up to be mugged.

In third place and out of sight of his rivals, Sasaki made a plan. He tested it out by running down the extreme left of the back straight a couple of times, the opposite side to the normal racing line. The plan involved taking the lead going into the final lap and when Sasaki did that Florido and Fernández thought they were in luck.

Heading down the back straight for the final time, Sasaki pulled to the left, the others followed and picked up a good slipstream. At the end of the straight Sasaki swung back right, and Florido and Fernández ducked out of the slipstream and out-braked him. They hadn't practised the move from there, however, and were in a bit to deep, just enough for Sasaki to have the better line through and out of the corner – and he stole victory on the run to the line.

It perfectly summed up Sasaki's season: he only ever did as much as he had to and he did it brilliantly. Others looked faster and flashier. Viu is also a genuine star and led many more laps than Sasaki; he even crossed the line first just as many times but was only credited with two wins because he was twice demoted for exceeding track limits.

Besides missing those two wins, Viu's Cup chances were also harmed by a disastrous Assen in the wet and being knocked off on that last lap at Aragón. Unlucky? Perhaps, certainly at Aragón, but in Race 1 at Assen, while desperately tricky with only half the 24 Rookies finishing, he made an error and it wasn't just down to misfortune. That also cost him in Race 2 when he rode to a damp and cautious tenth.

Perhaps Viu was unlucky in Race 1 at the Red Bull Ring when he bettered Garcia in a private duel only to be demoted for exceeding track limits. There was a warning, with plenty of riders losing lap times in qualifying for the same transgression, but it was the first time it had affected the result.

It happened again at Misano as the chase for the Cup intensified, with only the two Aragón contests to follow. The Misano battle – a single race as always in Italy – was a Rookies classic with six in the hunt for the win. Viu, Kaito Toba and Florido crossed the line first, second and third, but all three were judged to have exceeded track limits multiple times. Sasaki was fourth across the stripe but hadn't transgressed and so jumped to the win as the trio were demoted one place as a group.

It was a miserable-looking group on the podium, and Sasaki wasn't happy to have won in that way. He also felt that 16-year-old Toba had pushed too hard to be top Japanese, something he had shrugged off with a degree of amusement after Race 1 at the Red Bull Ring but the pressure had built by Misano and it was no longer amusing.

Kaito Toba should have been in the hunt for the Cup but didn't always have the best relationship with his bike. In the first three races he crashed out, which was especially galling at Jerez as he had started from pole there. He won twice, Race 2 at Sachsenring and Race 1 at Aragón, before being thrown off in Race 2 at Aragón. Toba's tumultuous two-season affair with his KTM ended and he won't forget the extremes or the lessons learned.

Fernández was in the hunt for the Cup. He was third in the first race of the season at Jerez, then slid out of the lead battle at the last corner in Race 2 before remounting for 13th place. A brilliant double victory in treacherous conditions at Assen made him look favourite but after that he only once finished in front of Sasaki and steadily lost ground.

Marc Garcia has the greatest claim as the unluckiest Rookie. The 16-year-old Spaniard was put off the track on the sighting lap by another rider in Race 1 at Jerez and missed the race. He clawed his way back and three wins in four races at the Red Bull Ring and Brno put him back in Cup contention. He missed Misano with a badly broken finger following a multi-bike crash on an oil slick at a non-championship race and was still not 100 per cent for Aragón, scoring two sixth places for fourth position in the title standings.

In ten years of the Rookies Cup there have been 119 thrilling races with 41 different winners. These are great numbers but the wider legacy is the alumni who have gone on to success around the globe, including so far winning four World Championships and 54 Grands Prix.

BELOW Typical Rookies action, this time at the Czech round: Aleix Viu and Marc Garcia of Spain sandwich Ayumu Sasaki

BOTTOM Not surprisingly, Honda are taking an interest in Sasaki's future

TWO WHEELS FOR LIFE

In 2016 something weird happened at MotoGP's charity, as co-founder Barry Coleman explains

TWO WHEELS FOR LIFE

ABOVE Day of Champions and the events that go with it, like the Ride-In, remain an essential part of Two Wheels for Life

On 30 November 2015, Riders for Health, the hugely successful charity started by the motorcycle community in the now-distant 1980s, ran life-saving programmes in seven countries in Africa. It worked with ministries of health, international non-governmental agencies and vital global-health bodies such as the World Health Organization (WHO) and the Centers for Disease Control (CDC) out of Atlanta, Georgia. It was credited by reliable experts with having regularly reached 24 million people with health care that otherwise they would have had to manage without. That is to say they reached people with care for HIV, AIDS, TB, you name it, and that eye-catching newcomer, Ebola.

Spot the difference. On 1 January 2016, Riders for Health, the hugely successful charity started by the motorcycle community in the now-distant 1980s, ran life-saving programmes in seven countries in Africa. It worked with ministries of health, etc, etc – you get the picture.

If you have been following the growth of Riders since, say, 1988, you will know that this unique organisation within the motorcycle community (a fancy word for those of us around the world who love bikes and love motorcycle racing) has successfully addressed a problem that had totally defeated the rest of the human species, namely the problem of how to reach remote communities in Africa (it would work anywhere) with health care. Not just once in a while but all the time, predictably and reliably. Which is the way we all want our health care to be.

But in the meantime, especially during December 2015, a number of people with agendas of various kinds threatened the closure of Riders. Dizzy? So were we. But because, after a terrible and (literally) life-threatening fight, we were able – thanks to persistence, loyalty and determination from our amazing African colleagues – to save all the programmes in Africa. Furthermore, the programmes are emerging stronger and more forceful than ever and the Africa teams are now renamed Riders International.

Every year I point out that NO OTHER SPORT in human history has produced a sustained humanitarian movement and I usually give an example of how the programme teams have become so good at what they do.

This year I draw your attention to none other than the next global horror – Ebola. You will be interested to learn that the WHO and US government (through the CDC) fund the role of Riders in the fight against Ebola in Liberia because they know that the constant, nationwide Riders' surveillance system – the motorcycle couriers

– is what stands between the present calm and another outbreak. And they got all this, after more than 25 years of development, from the motorcycle community. No-one else. Just us. And you will be relieved to hear that the work goes on – more strongly than ever. Because of us. Because of you.

There were certainly some people who threatened Riders and of that there's more to be said, but that's for another day, even another book. But those who wanted to take over Riders for Health tried, among other things, to stop Day of Champions, and therefore to deprive the Riders International programmes in Africa of what turned out to be £218,000 (thank you everyone) – and, of course, to threaten a completely unique event in world sport that Riders has been running since 1989.

The idea of Day of Champions is to bring the fans close to their heroes as well as to raise money for the work of using motorcycles to save lives in Africa. The first Day of Champions was at Brands Hatch and the whole Kenny Roberts team came for it. Kenny, Eddie, Randy, Wayne and Little John as well as Kevin and team Suzuki. Then we moved on to Donington in 1991 before Grand Prix became MotoGP! When Dorna arrived they wondered what mad thing was happening in their paddock. Dennis Noyce (great and much missed journalist) and Carmelo Ezpeleta (boss of Dorna) got behind it and, well, made it the official charity.

During the dramatic circumstances this year, when Day of Champions was under threat, Dorna and IRTA (the International Racing Teams Association headed by hero Mike Trimby) were,

once more, solidly behind us and our work. Fluent Spanish speakers report that it was quite easy to detect that Carmelo Ezpeleta wasn't happy about this turn of events when he heard the news. And that commitment from them meant that 'Two Wheels for Life' was born.

The heroes insisted that Day of Champions would go ahead. And the MotoGP riders, teams and commentators were out in force on the day. Everyone who came and everyone who wanted to come were heroes too. We were months late in confirming that it would happen, but Day of Champions sold out in hours. And somehow, on the day, it seemed better than ever.

The Riders Africa teams explained to the people who wanted to take over the organisation that they could probably run their own affairs quite handily after their 25 years or so of work in Africa. They're motorcyclists, after all. The new fund-raising body, Two Wheels for Life, includes representatives from Dorna and the FIM on the board. The programmes are organised locally, with oversight from Riders International led by Ngwarati Mashonga, whom many of you will have met at Day of Champions. This is real development and another first for the motorcycle community.

So, we start a new chapter. I noticed that Andrea got a special big kiss and hug from Valentino on the stage at Day of Champions. I suppose that says it all.

What always really mattered was the work in Africa. That goes ahead because of the MotoGP paddock and all of you.

Thank you.

BELOW LEFT Scott Redding, like all the rest of the MotoGP grid, was at the Day of Champions auction

BELOW The important news is that, despite the new name, all the charity's projects in Africa continue their work uninterrupted

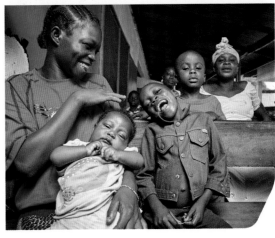

WORLD CHAMPIONSHIP CLASSIFICATION

MotoGP

	Rider	Nation	Motorcycle	QAT	ARG	AME	SPA	FRA	ITA	CAT	NED	GER	AUT	CZE	GBR	RSM	ARA	JPN	AUS	MAL	VAL	Points
1	Marc Marquez	SPA	Honda	16	25	25	16	3	20	20	20	25	11	16	13	13	25	25	–	5	20	298
2	Valentino Rossi	ITA	Yamaha	13	20	–	25	20	–	25	–	8	13	20	16	20	16	–	20	20	13	249
3	Jorge Lorenzo	SPA	Yamaha	25	–	20	20	25	25	–	6	1	16	–	8	16	20	–	10	16	25	233
4	Maverick Viñales	SPA	Suzuki	10	–	13	10	16	10	13	7	4	10	7	25	11	13	16	16	10	11	202
5	Andrea Dovizioso	ITA	Ducati	20	3	–	–	–	11	9	–	16	20	–	10	10	5	20	13	25	9	171
6	Dani Pedrosa	SPA	Honda	11	16	–	13	13	13	16	4	10	9	4	11	25	10	–	–	–	–	155
7	Cal Crutchlow	GBR	Honda	–	–	–	5	–	5	10	–	20	1	25	20	8	11	11	25	–	–	141
8	Pol Espargaro	SPA	Yamaha	9	10	9	8	11	1	11	13	–	6	3	–	7	8	10	11	7	10	134
9	Andrea Iannone	ITA	Ducati	–	–	16	9	–	16	–	11	11	25	8	–	–	–	–	–	–	16	112
10	Hector Barbera	SPA	Ducati	7	11	7	6	8	4	5	10	7	–	11	2	3	3	–	–	13	5	102
11	Aleix Espargaro	SPA	Suzuki	5	5	11	11	10	7	–	–	2	–	–	9	–	9	13	–	3	8	93
12	Alvaro Bautista	SPA	Aprilia	3	6	5	–	7	–	8	–	6	–	–	6	6	7	9	4	9	6	82
13	Eugene Laverty	IRL	Ducati	4	13	4	7	5	3	3	9	5	–	10	4	2	2	–	2	4	–	77
14	Danilo Petrucci	ITA	Ducati	–	–	–	–	9	8	7	–	–	5	9	7	5	–	8	7	6	4	75
15	Scott Redding	GBR	Ducati	6	–	10	–	–	–	–	16	13	8	1	–	1	–	7	9	1	2	74
16	Stefan Bradl	GER	Aprilia	–	9	6	2	6	2	4	8	–	–	2	–	4	6	6	5	–	3	63
17	Bradley Smith	GBR	Yamaha	8	8	–	4	–	9	–	3	3	7	–	–	–	–	3	8	2	7	62
18	Jack Miller	AUS	Honda	2	–	–	–	–	–	6	25	9	–	–	–	–	–	–	6	8	1	57
19	Michele Pirro	ITA	Ducati	–	4	8	–	–	6	1	–	–	4	–	–	9	4	–	–	–	–	36
20	Loris Baz	FRA	Ducati	–	–	1	3	4	–	–	–	–	3	13	–	–	–	–	11	–	–	35
21	Tito Rabat	SPA	Honda	1	7	3	–	–	–	2	5	–	2	6	1	–	–	2	–	–	–	29
22	Yonny Hernandez	COL	Ducati	–	–	2	1	–	–	–	–	–	–	5	5	–	–	4	3	–	–	20
23	Katsuyuki Nakasuga	JPN	Yamaha	–	–	–	–	–	–	–	–	–	–	–	–	–	–	5	–	–	–	5
24	Alex Lowes	GBR	Yamaha	–	–	–	–	–	–	–	–	–	–	–	3	–	–	–	–	–	–	3
25	Hiroshi Aoyama	JPN	Honda	–	–	–	–	–	–	–	–	–	–	–	–	–	–	1	–	–	–	1
	Nicky Hayden	USA	Honda	–	–	–	–	–	–	–	–	–	–	–	–	–	1	–	–	–	–	1
	Mike Jones	AUS	Ducati	–	–	–	–	–	–	–	–	–	–	–	–	–	–	–	1	–	–	1

CONSTRUCTOR

	Motorcycle	QAT	ARG	AME	SPA	FRA	ITA	CAT	NED	GER	AUT	CZE	GBR	RSM	ARA	JPN	AUS	MAL	VAL	Points
1	Honda	16	25	25	16	13	20	20	25	25	11	25	20	25	25	25	25	8	20	369
2	Yamaha	25	20	20	25	25	25	25	13	8	16	20	16	20	20	10	20	20	25	353
3	Ducati	20	13	16	9	9	16	9	16	16	25	13	10	10	5	20	13	25	16	261
4	Suzuki	10	5	13	11	16	10	13	7	4	10	7	25	11	13	16	16	10	11	208
5	Aprilia	3	9	6	2	7	2	8	8	6	–	2	6	6	7	9	5	9	6	101

TEAM

	Team name	QAT	ARG	AME	SPA	FRA	ITA	CAT	NED	GER	AUT	CZE	GBR	RSM	ARA	JPN	AUS	MAL	VAL	Points
1	Movistar Yamaha MotoGP	38	20	20	45	45	25	25	6	9	29	20	24	36	36	–	30	36	38	482
2	Repsol Honda Team	27	41	25	29	16	33	36	24	35	20	20	24	38	35	26	–	5	20	454
3	Ducati Team	20	3	16	9	–	27	9	11	27	45	8	10	19	9	20	13	25	25	296
4	Team Suzuki ECSTAR	15	5	24	21	26	17	13	7	6	10	7	34	11	22	29	16	13	19	295
5	Monster Yamaha Tech 3	17	18	9	12	11	10	11	16	3	13	3	3	7	8	13	19	9	17	199
6	OCTO Pramac Yakhnich	6	4	18	–	9	8	7	16	13	13	10	7	6	–	15	16	7	6	161
7	Aprilia Racing Team Gresini	3	15	11	2	13	2	12	8	6	–	2	6	10	13	15	9	9	9	145
8	LCR Honda	–	–	–	5	–	5	10	–	20	1	25	20	8	11	11	25	–	–	141
9	Avintia Racing	7	11	8	9	12	4	6	10	7	3	24	2	3	3	–	1	24	5	139
10	Pull & Bear Aspar Team	4	13	6	8	5	3	3	9	5	–	15	9	2	2	4	5	4	–	97
11	Estrella Galicia 0,0 Marc VDS	3	7	3	–	–	–	8	30	9	2	6	1	–	1	2	6	8	1	87